The Question of
HENRY JAMES

The Question of
HENRY JAMES

A COLLECTION

OF CRITICAL ESSAYS

EDITED BY

F. W. DUPEE

OCTAGON BOOKS

A DIVISION OF FARRAR, STRAUS AND GIROUX

New York   1973

Copyright 1945 by Holt, Rinehart and Winston, Inc.

Reprinted 1973
by arrangement with Holt, Rinehart and Winston, Inc.

OCTAGON BOOKS
A Division of Farrar, Straus & Giroux, Inc.
19 Union Square West
New York, N. Y. 10003

Library of Congress Catalog Card Number: 77-159243
ISBN 0-374-92417-1

Contents

[v]

Contents

[vi]

Contents

Introduction

ALTHOUGH Henry James died in 1916, the worth of his art is still in question, and the question can still cause high temperatures among his critics. On hearing that the present volume was being planned, a well-known American novelist wrote the editor: "Now more than ever I believe that the H. J. boom is the gravest thing that has happened to our U.S. culture in our time." On the other hand a respected periodical lately devoted an entire issue to appreciative studies of James's work—it was the fourth such symposium on him since his death. Obviously Henry James is not an author whom it is easy to take or leave.

So from the 1860's to the present, numerous writers—poets and novelists as well as professional critics—have needed to say their say about him. In trying to say it, moreover, they have felt obliged to explore a variety of critical approaches—textual, historical, psychological, metaphysical, etc.—and a variety of manners ranging from solemnity to parody. Even readers who will not allow much virtue to James himself will have to admit he was the cause it was abundantly present in his critics. Some of the essays in this volume illustrate various aspects of the Jamesian controversy; others simply aim at expounding his work from a position outside the battle. They are all, it is hoped, significant examples of modern criticism faced with a peculiarly intricate and engrossing subject.

The question of Henry James brings into play acute convictions on very lively subjects and is therefore of greater density and wider consequence than most readers may believe. This introduction will try to expose briefly some of the more frequent causes of disagreement; but since the causes are in James as well as in his critics, the introduction will have to approach

Introduction

James with certain assumptions of its own. And, although the question is really all one, it will have to be broken down into more or less distinct items. The danger is that James, whose genius is problematical largely for the very reason that it is such a living tissue of contradictions, will emerge from this treatment resembling an efficient department store.

First of all, then, there is an aesthetic question. An "advanced" writer, at any rate in his later work, James shares some of the attitudes behind that kind of writing and stirs up some of the familiar arguments as to its merits. Like Joyce, Yeats, Eliot, and others, he seems to have believed that the traditional rights of the creative imagination were infringed upon by the empirical spirit of our scientific culture. And like them, too, James appropriated to the imagination, conceived in its classical role as the organizer and intensifier of life, those features of empiricism which stress the importance of concrete experience and the value of method. He thoroughly respected the power of nineteenth-century fiction to register "the life of the times" in well-documented writing. To him, however, documentation meant not the assembling of masses of data but the intensive scrutiny and careful deployment of a few. A kind of visionary of the small fact, he compels a maximum of meaning from a minimum of evidence. And in proportion as he stylizes the materials of experience, he elaborates the form of his work. In a James novel the style, the dialogue, the imagery, the symbolism, the various narrative devices, all constitute high pressures under which, to the extent that he is successful, the minutiae of life and sensibility are transformed into great witnesses. Above all, perhaps, his work is a triumph of the word—to the extent, again, that it is a triumph at all. Although he brings us many of the regular delights of fiction, such as humor, notable characters, and keen psychological observations, it is probably just to remark that his imagination asserts itself primarily through a profound analytical sense of language and an exceptional power to employ it dramatically.

It is at this point that the disagreements begin. By some readers the novels are declared insubstantial, deficient in life, and therefore devoid of the usual satisfactions of novels. Some-

Introduction

times James is charged with sacrificing substance to an undue concern for the niceties of form; again it is said that he simply knew too little of the world to be able to invent anything but shadowy characters entangled in farfetched situations. The most famous attack on James from this point of view is probably the passage in H. G. Wells's *Boon, the Mind of the Race,* which compares the James novel to a church, brilliantly lighted but quite empty of people, every line of which leads to the high altar whereon "very reverently placed, intensely there, is a dead kitten, an egg-shell, a piece of string." Wells's epigram summed up the objections to James of a whole generation of realists, British and American. It continues to reverberate.

But among Wells's contemporaries were other writers—Conrad, Ford Madox Ford, Percy Lubbock—whose appreciation of James's art was profound. For them his researches in form were an integral feature of his genius; and they did not hesitate, if they were novelists, to take over certain of his innovations; or if they were critics, to adopt his theories as their own. The whole period in England was one of experiment in novel writing; and James's literary principles, as embodied in his novels and stories and explained in the prefaces to the New York Edition of his work, helped to stimulate some very good books on the poetics of the novel and inspired even in those who disagreed an attention which at that time they seldom received in America.

Until recently, and with some notable exceptions, American critics have been rather incurious as to James's art, preferring to investigate his relation to his native country. That relation makes up another large item in the Jamesian controversy, for reasons that have to do with the complexion of American thought on American writing. Usually a revolutionary country in its literary image of itself, the United States has been slow to embrace any multitradition system in literature to match the admirable multiparty arrangement that prevails in its political life. Those who accept, say, Mark Twain and Walt Whitman as types of the American writer are apt to disparage or even read out of the national literature writers whose sense of America is more complex—for example, T. S. Eliot and Henry James. In James's case the excommunication was actually attempted, and not by some insignificant fanatic but by Vernon Louis Parrington. And although Van Wyck Brooks allows James great importance, it is the symbolic importance of an American who left his country and so failed as an artist. In America, therefore, James criticism often veils a dispute between those who want to keep our literary image comparatively simple, comparatively faithful to our democratic professions, and those who believe it is improved by the sort of complication that comes from recognizing in our society as it exists deep contradictions and broad areas of faulty practice.

In the criticism of James considered as an American, one important strain is occupied with the causes and effects of his residence in Europe. The question here is whether his expatriation cut him off from certain vital influences and so deformed his mind and work; or whether, by placing him among circumstances more favorable to his temperament, it helped him to become a great international artist. But there are many critics for whom James's Americanism is a question not of the conditions of his life but of the character of his work as its stands. The serious critics who find the work completely foreign to American traditions are very few. For most of them, from his contemporary W. D. Howells on, the study of James is a family drama culminating in a recognition scene wherein the supposed stranger reveals himself as the lost Orestes or the prodigal son. In other words, the aristocratic and worldly James turns out to be a continuator of the severe ethics of New England. The temptations of Europe have only exaggerated his inherited passion for fine scruples and heroic renunciations. In the name of American righteousness, his candid heroines even think to conquer the world.

In *The American Scene* James spoke of "the great adventure of a society reaching out into the apparent void for the amenities, the consummations, after having earnestly gathered in so many of the preparations and necessities." The society was that of the United States at the time of what James believed to be its emergence from a relatively crude pioneering stage into a stage where leisure, enjoyment, and reflection might become more immediate realities. Philip Rahv, one of the most original of

Introduction

James's recent critics, has suggested that the whole Jamesian question can be better understood if we see him as the artist of that "great adventure," at once the exponent and the expression of America's cultural aspirations, with all the hope and doubt, the alternating arrogance and humility, that attended them. For James "culture" is certainly a complex and problematical value, as it is in those ancient myths where culture is experience, experience is knowledge, and knowledge is loss of innocence. In his novels the innocent people, who are usually Americans, are confronted with the possibilities for good and evil in a life of superior cultivation and worldly enjoyment; while the worldly people, who are usually Europeans or Europeanized Americans, are acted upon, changed, sometimes even destroyed, by the singular power of innocence. James's sense of the equivocal nature of culture, his tendency to identify it with something at once inviting and menacing, is illustrated by the divisions of *The Portrait of a Lady:* in the first half the American heroine's European visit is an agreeable experience full of lessons in taste and manners; in the second half she becomes so embroiled in the evils of Europe that her journey there has become a trip to Hell. And so thoroughly did the drama of conscience and culture, innocence and experience, possess James's imagination that it continued to be latent in certain of his novels where the settings and the characters were entirely non-American.

Compared with the epic subjects to which, it is sometimes assumed, James might have helped himself in the new and challenging America of his day, this theme has sometimes been declared trivial in itself. It has proved easy for some of James's readers to overlook the multiple implications culture had for him and so to assume he was simply a pedant and a snob. In the main, however, it was his management of the theme that proved most controversial. In his famous creation, the international novel, he involved Europe and America, Europeans and Americans, in an elaborate pattern of moral and cultural antinomies, a myth of his own making. No matter how delicately it was conceived or how conscientiously it was varied from novel to novel, the pattern could not but bring into play the national loyalties of readers, as well as their sense of historical fact. He

Introduction

often portrayed Americans as innocent in the unfavorable as well as the favorable sense, assuming on their part an ignorance of the world and a deprivation of essential experience which were counter to their prevailing assumptions about themselves. And from the European point of view James could be suspected of a certain ethical chauvinism which consisted in allowing Europe glamor but denying her the higher conscience.

Yet there have always been readers for whom James's international fables required no apology. If their treatment of history was sometimes arbitrary, that was altogether justified by their wealth of finely observed detail; by their essential insight into national characteristics; by the way they ministered to the excitement we feel, in an age of exasperated nationalism, at contemplating nuances in the texture of life from country to country; by the very transatlantic scope of their vision, unique in the history of the novel. And then, the more deeply the novels are studied the more they are seen to secrete ironies within ironies, in respect to nationalities as well as to everything else. For example, two recent students of *The Golden Bowl*, Louise Bogan and Ferner Nuhn, arrive at such different conclusions as to the relative merits of the Europeans and the Americans in this novel, that one wonders if they have consulted the same text. To Nuhn the book is proof of Van Wyck Brooks's old contention that for James Europe remained "a fairy tale to the end"; to Miss Bogan it is a work of "stern, prodigious human facts" concerning not only Europeans and Americans, but also personality in general. It is possible that we have still not come to the core of James's meaning; and that time, in addition to revealing much else about him, will show his international theme to have the same value—no more and no less—that Italian politics have in the total vision of Dante.

But what kind of prophet of experience does James make, finicking as he admittedly was about sex? Needless to say, this particular Jamesian question seems not to have troubled his older contemporaries, for whom he was daring enough for any good purpose. But owing to the changed sexual values of recent years, James's reticence is often declared to be at odds, not only with the easy naturalism of the average novel, but also with his own frequent commands to "Live, live." Stephen Spender and Edmund Wilson are among the critics who have written at length on this subject; and Spender, for all his admiration, even charges James with a peculiar sexual vulgarity. "In the early novels and stories, with the exception of *The Princess Casamassima*, wherever James approaches the physical side of life he seems to draw on his gloves, and his nouns draw on their inverted commas. When his subject is sex, he sheers away from it by reducing it to a formality, and if one tries to imagine his characters physically, one feels that one is lifting a veil which conceals something repulsive. Here the vulgarity lies in the tastelessness of what is artificial when a comparison is forced with what is natural." What Spender is deploring in James is not of course the absence of an ardent—Freudian naturalism like his own—for such an expectation would be counter to the whole ethical tendency of James's mind—but a failure to dramatize passion in such a way that when his characters renounce it they strike us as renouncing something real. But Spender goes on to say that in the later books the sexual inhibition works itself out in half-conscious fantasies and images of violence, which are very beautiful and meaningful if interpreted on the plane of symbolism. In all this Spender is following the lead of Edmund Wilson and Edna Kenton in their Freudian studies of the novels, particularly *The Turn of the Screw*.

In regard to social questions, insofar as these are distinct from what has already been discussed, James is again full of difficulties for his readers. From a democratic standpoint, what are we to think of novels in which, as it is generally agreed, the rich and the wellborn are the center of interest while the poor and declassed exist solely in relation to them—on the whole, a not very flattering relation of acute curiosity, conscientious dependency, or active yearning? For in James wealth seems to be a definite value, though shot through with possible evils, while poverty and labor (the labors of the artist excepted) are frankly limbos of dreariness. On this evidence many critics have deplored the novels as snobbishly false. But there has been another strain in criticism—it is rather recent—which has found him worthy of

Introduction

highly sympathetic analysis in the light of modern political theory. And strangely enough, James the supposed aristocrat owes to socialist and near-socialist critics like Edmund Wilson, Robert Cantwell, Stephen Spender, Newton Arvin, and F. O. Matthiessen some of the most careful and appreciative comment he has ever received. Again it is a question of whether we take him literally or symbolically, as an exponent or as a witness. Like other modern critics, they discourage any reading of James that takes a part of his effect for the whole. Their interpretation allows for the presence in his work, at least intermittently, of a realistic social insight; an insight which, because it came to him by virtue not of theory but of patient and anxious observation, is never simply assumed or stated in his work but is revealed through the most reticent suggestions and involved ironies. According to this view, then, James's fascination with a baronial state of society was a very condition of his literary existence. To it he owed whatever was tiresome or objectionable in his limited range and occasional heavy fumbling after social truths which are obvious to others; but it also contributed to that characteristic irony, that effect of a world of confused splendor and terror, of a bright jungle concealing a dim beast, which those who admire him find so exciting and prophetic in his work. In other words, he could so warmly reject the principle of acquisition because he had so passionately suffered its temptations; and indeed he is simply a special instance of that Machiavellian strain without which the novel of modern society would lack experiential power and so be a mere sermon.

F. W. Dupee

Acknowledgments

from *Short Studies of American Authors* by Thomas Wentworth Higginson, published in 1880 by Ticknor and Fields.

"Henry James in the World" by Edna Kenton appeared in the April-May 1934 issue of *Hound & Horn,* and is reprinted by permission of the publishers. "Attitudes Toward Henry James" by Philip Rahv and "The Altar of Henry James" by William Troy are both reprinted by permission of The New Republic, Copyright 1943 by Harrison-Blaine of New Jersey, Inc. "Henry James and His Countrymen" by Herbert Croly appeared in the February 1904 issue of *Lamp,* and is reprinted by permission of Mrs. Louise Mary Croly. "Mr. Henry James's Later Work" by William Dean Howells appeared in the January 1903 issue of the *North American Review.* "Henry James, Melodramatist" by Jacques Barzun originally appeared in the Autumn 1943 issue of the *Kenyon Review,* was reprinted in *The Energies of Art,* 1956, Harper and Brothers, and is reprinted by permission of the author. "On Henry James" by T. S. Eliot is reprinted from two articles that appeared originally in the *Egoist,* London (January 1918) and the *Little Review,* Chicago (August 1918), by permission of Mrs. Valerie Eliot and Faber & Faber Ltd.

The editor wishes to thank the following authors who have given him permission to reprint their articles: R. P. Blackmur, for "In the Country of the Blue" which appeared in the March 1930 issue of the *Yale Review* and was reprinted in Richard P. Blackmur's *Primer of Ignorance* in 1967; Andre Gide, for "Henry James," which appeared in the March 1930 issue of the *Yale Review;* and Morton D. Zabel, for "The Poetics of Henry James," which was written not as an essay but as a book review for the February 1935 issue of *Poetry: A Magazine of Verse.*

The quotation from *The Art of the Novel* by R. P. Blackmur is reprinted by permission of the publishers, Charles Scribner's Sons. The quotations from *New England: Indian Summer* and *The Pilgrimage of Henry James* by Van Wyck Brooks are reprinted by permission of E. P. Dutton & Co., Inc.

Grateful acknowledgment is made to the following publishers for permission to use the quotations from the works of Henry James which appear within the articles in this collection: Harper and Brothers, for the quotations from *The Ambassadors, The*

Acknowledgments

American Scene, The Death of the Lion, and *An International Episode;* Houghton Mifflin Company, for the quotations from *The American, London Notes, The Portrait of a Lady, Roderick Hudson, The Spoils of Poynton,* and *The Tragic Muse;* The Macmillan Company, Inc., for the quotations from *The Lesson of the Master,* from "The Next Time" and "The Figure in the Carpet" in *Embarrassments,* and from "The Turn of the Screw" in *Two Magics;* Charles Scribner's Sons, for the quotations from *The Altar of the Dead, The Golden Bowl, Notes of a Son and Brother, The Sacred Fount, The Wings of the Dove,* from the essays on D'Annunzio and George Sand in *Notes on Novelists,* and from "The Jolly Corner" and "The Private Life" in *Novels and Tales.*

Biographical Note

HENRY JAMES was born April 15, 1843, at 2 Washington Place, New York City. He was the son of Henry James, religious philosopher, and the brother of William James, the psychologist and philosopher of pragmatism. Much of James's youth was spent in Europe, where he traveled with his family and attended various schools. After a brief residence in Newport, R. I., he attended Harvard Law School from 1862 to 1864. In the later sixties he began to publish reviews and stories. His first novel, *Watch and Ward*, appeared in the *Atlantic Monthly* in 1871. In 1875 he went to live in Europe, first in Paris, then in England, where, except for three trips to the United States and frequent tours on the continent, he remained all his life. *Roderick Hudson* appeared in 1876, *The American* in 1877, *Daisy Miller* in 1879, and *The Portrait of a Lady*, his most important novel so far, in 1881. In 1882 his father died and he returned briefly to the United States. *The Bostonians* and *The Princess Casamassima* were published in 1886, *The Tragic Muse* in 1890. For the next five years he tried, not very successfully, to write for the English theater. *Terminations*, containing important short stories, appeared in 1896. In 1897 he moved from London to Lamb House, Rye, Sussex. *The Spoils of Poynton* and *What Maisie Knew* were published in 1897, *The Turn of the Screw* in 1898, *The Awkward Age* in 1899, *The Sacred Fount* in 1901, *The Wings of the Dove* in 1902, *The Better Sort* (short stories), *The Ambassadors* in 1903, and *The Golden Bowl* in 1904. In 1904-05 he visited America and toured the country, gathering material for *The American Scene*, a book of impressions, which appeared in 1907. In the same year there appeared the first volumes of the New York Edition of his work, a selection of his novels and stories, together with prefaces explaining

Biographical Note

his principles as an artist. In 1910 his brother William died and he paid his last visit to the United States. That same year he published a book of short narratives, *The Finer Grain*. In 1913 he published *A Small Boy and Others*, and in the following year *Notes of a Son and Brother*, both volumes of memoirs. In 1915, during the World War, he became a naturalized British subject. On February 28, 1916, after repeated illnesses, he died in London. Two important posthumous novels, *The Ivory Tower* and *The Sense of the Past*, both fragments, appeared in 1917.

The Question of
HENRY JAMES

THOMAS WENTWORTH HIGGINSON

Henry James, Jr.

[1879]

WE are growing more cosmopolitan and varied, in these United States of America; and our authors are gaining much, if they are also losing a little, in respect to training. The early career of an American author used to be tolerably fixed and clear, if limited; a college education, a few months in Europe, a few years in some practical vocation, and then an entrance into literature by some side door. In later times, the printing office has sometimes been substituted for the college, and has given a new phase of literary character distinct from the other, but not less valuable. Mr. Henry James, Jr., belongs to neither of these classes; he may be said to have been trained in literature by literature itself, so early did he begin writing, and so incessantly has he written. We perhaps miss in his writings something of the method which the narrower classical nurture was supposed to give; we miss also the contact with the mass of mankind which comes through mere daily employment to the professional man, the businessman, the journalist. Mr. James has kept a little too good company; we do not find in his books that vigorous and breezy natural man whom Howells, with all his daintiness, can so easily depict in Colonel Ellison and the skipper of the *Aroostook*. Then Mr. James's life has been so far transatlantic that one hardly knows whether he would wish to be counted as an American writer, after all; so that his training, his point of view, his methods, all unite to place him in a class by himself.

It is pleasant to see a man write, as he has always done, with abundant energy and seemingly from the mere love of writing.

The Question of Henry James

Yet it is impossible to deny that he has suffered from this very profusion. Much of his early work affects one as being a sort of self-training, gained at the expense of his readers; each sheet, each story, has been hurried into print before the ink was dry, in order to test it on the public—a method singularly removed from the long and lonely self-criticism of Hawthorne. Even the later books of Mr. James, especially his travels and his essays, show something of this defect. What a quarry of admirable suggestions is, for instance, his essay on Balzac; but how prolix it is, what repetitions, what a want of condensation and method! The same is true, in a degree, of his papers on George Sand and Turgenev, while other chapters in the same volume are scarcely more than sketches; the paper on the Théâtre Français hardly mentions Sarah Bernhardt, and indeed that on Turgenev says nothing of his masterpiece, *Terres Vierges*. Through all these essays he shows delicacy, epigram, quickness of touch, penetration, but he lacks symmetry of structure and steadiness of hand.

We can trace in the same book, also, some of the author's limitations as an imaginative artist, since in criticizing others a man shows what is wanting in himself. When he says, for instance, that a monarchical society is "more available for the novelist than any other," he shows that he does not quite appreciate the strong point of republicanism, in that it develops real individuality in proportion as it diminishes conventional distinctions. The truth is that the modern novel has risen with the advance of democratic society, on the ruins of feudalism. Another defect is seen, from time to time, when in criticizing some well-known book, he misses its special points of excellence. Take, for instance, his remarks on that masterly and repulsive novel, *Madame Bovary*. To say of the author of that book that his "theory as a novelist, briefly expressed, is to begin at the outside," seems almost whimsically unjust; there is not a character in modern fiction developed more essentially from within than that of this heroine; all her sins and sorrows are virtually predicted in the first chapter; even Mr. James has to admit that it "could not have been otherwise" with her, thereby taking back his own general assertion. Then he says "everything in the book is ugly," whereas one of its salient points is the beauty of the

Thomas Wentworth Higginson

natural descriptions in which its most painful incidents are framed. Finally, and this is the most puzzling misconception of all, Mr. James utterly fails to see the bearing of one of the pivotal points of the narrative—an unfortunate surgical operation performed by the heroine's husband, a country doctor; he calls it an "artistic bravado," and treats it as a mere episode of doubtful value, when it is absolutely essential to the working out of the plot. The situation is this: Madame Bovary is being crushed to the earth by living in a social vacuum, with a stupid husband whom she despises and has already deceived—when suddenly this husband is presented to her eyes in a wholly new light, that of an unappreciated man of genius, who has by a single act won a place among the great surgeons of his time. All that is left undepraved in her nature is touched and roused by this; she will do anything, bear anything, for such a husband. The illusion lasts but a few days and is pitilessly torn away; the husband proves a mere vulgar, ignorant quack, even duller, emptier, more hopeless than she had dreamed. The reaction takes her instantly downward, and with that impulse she sinks to rise no more. The author himself tells us why he introduces the incident; and it seems as if there must be something wanting, some defect of artistic sensibility, in any critic who misses a meaning so plain. Or else—which is more probable—it is another instance of that haste in literary workmanship which is one of Mr. James's besetting sins.

It may be one result of this extreme rapidity of production that Mr. James uses certain catchwords so often as to furnish almost a shibboleth for his style; such words for instance as "brutal," "puerile," "immense." Another result is seen in his indifference to careful local coloring, especially where the scene is laid in the United States. When he draws Americans in Europe he is at home; when he brings Europeans across the Atlantic he never seems quite sure of his ground, except in Newport, which is indeed the least American spot on this continent. He opens his *The Europeans* by exhibiting horsecars in the streets of Boston nearly ten years before their introduction, and his whole sketch of the Wentworth family gives a sense of vagueness. It is not difficult to catch a few unmistakable points, and portray a re-

[3]

spectable elderly gentleman reading the *Daily Advertiser;* but all beyond this is indefinite, and when otherwise, sometimes gives an utterly incorrect impression of the place and period described. The family portrayed has access to "the best society in Boston"; yet the daughter, twenty-three years old, has "never seen an artist," though the picturesque figure of Allston had but lately disappeared from the streets, where Cheney, Staigg, and Eastman Johnson might be seen any day, with plenty of others less known. The household is perfectly amazed and overwhelmed at the sight of two foreigners, although there probably were more cultivated Europeans in Boston thirty years ago than now, having been drawn thither by the personal celebrity or popularity of Agassiz, Ticknor, Longfellow, Sumner, and Dr. Howe. The whole picture—though it is fair to remember that the author calls it a sketch only—seems more like a delineation of American society by Fortunio or Alexandre Dumas, *fils,* than like a portraiture by one to the manor born. The truth is that Mr. James's cosmopolitanism is after all limited; to be really cosmopolitan a man must be at home even in his own country.

There are no short stories in our recent literature, I think, which are so good as Mr. James's best—*Madame de Mauves,* for instance, and *The Madonna of the Future.* Even these sometimes lack condensation, but they have a thoroughly original grasp and fine delineations of character. It is a great step downward from these to the somewhat vulgar horrors contained in *The Romance of Certain Old Clothes.* The author sometimes puts on a cynicism, which does not go very deep, and the young lovers of his earlier tales had a disagreeable habit of swearing at young ladies and ordering them about. Yet he has kept himself very clear from the disagreeable qualities of the French fiction he loves; his books never actually leave a bad taste in one's mouth, as Charlotte Brontë said of the French, and indeed no one has touched with more delicate precision the vexed question of morality in art. He finely calls the longing after a moral ideal "this Southern slope of the mind," and says of the ethical element, "It is in reality simply a part of the richness of inspiration, it has nothing to do with the artistic process, and it has everything to do with the artistic effect." This is admirable;

Thomas Wentworth Higginson

and it is a vindication of this attribute when we find that Mr. James's most successful social stories, *An International Episode* and *Daisy Miller,* have been written with distinct purpose and convey lessons. He has achieved no greater triumph than when in the last book he succeeds in holding our sympathy and even affection, after all, for the essential innocence and rectitude of the poor wayward girl whose follies he has so mercilessly portrayed.

It cannot be said that Mr. James has yet succeeded in producing a satisfactory novel; as a clever woman has said, he should employ someone else to write the last few pages. However strong the characterizations, however skillful the plot, the reader is left discontented. If in this respect he seems behind Howells it must be remembered that James habitually deals with profounder emotions and is hence more liable to be overmastered. Longfellow says to himself in his *Hyperion,* "O thou poor authorling! Reach a little deeper into the human heart! Touch those strings, touch those deeper strings more boldly, or the notes shall die away like whispers, and no ear shall hear them save thine own." It is James rather than Howells who has heeded this counsel. The very disappointment which the world felt at the close of *The American* was in some sense a tribute to its power; the author had called up characters and situations which could not be cramped, at last, within the conventional limits of a stage ending. As a piece of character drawing the final irresolution of the hero was simply perfect; it seemed one of the cases where a romancer conjures up persons who are actually alive, and who insist on working out a destiny of their own, irrespective of his wishes. To be thus conquered by one's own creation might seem one of those defeats that are greater than victories; yet it is the business of the novelist, after all, to keep his visionary people well in hand, and contrive that they shall have their own way and yet not spoil his climax. In life, as in *The American,* the most complicated situations often settle themselves unseen, and the most promising tragedies are cheated of their crisis. But it is not enough that literary art should be a true transcript from nature; for the very fact that it is a work of art implies that it must have a beginning, a middle, and an end.

[5]

WILLIAM DEAN HOWELLS

Mr. Henry James's Later Work

[1903]

IT has been Mr. James's lot from the beginning to be matter
of unusually lively dispute among his readers. There are
people who frankly say they cannot bear him, and then either
honestly let him alone, or secretly hanker for him, and every
now and then return to him, and try if they cannot like him,
or cannot bear him a little better. These are his enemies, or may
be called so for convenience' sake; but they are hardly to be
considered his readers. Many of his readers, however, are also
his enemies: they read him in a condition of hot insurrection
against all that he says and is; they fiercely question his point
of view, they object to the world that he sees from it; they declare that there is no such world, or that, if there is, there ought
not to be, and that he does not paint it truly. They would like
to have the question out with him personally: such is their difference of opinion that, to hear them talk, you would think
they would like to have it out with him pugilistically. They
would, to every appearance, like to beat also those who accept
his point of view, believe in his world, and hold that he truly
portrays it. Nothing but the prevailing sex of his enemies saves
them, probably, from offering the readers who are not his enemies the violence to which their prevailing sex tempts them.
You cannot, at least, palliate his demerits with them without
becoming of the quality of his demerits, and identifying yourself with him in the whole measure of these. That is why, for
one reason, I am going to make my consideration of his later
work almost entirely a study of his merits, for I own that he has

[6]

his faults, and I would rather they remained his faults than became mine.

I

The enmity to Mr. James's fiction among his readers is mostly feminine because the men who do not like him are not his readers. The men who do like him and are his readers are of a more feminine fineness, probably, in their perceptions and intuitions, than those other men who do not read him, though of quite as unquestionable a manliness, I hope. I should like to distinguish a little farther, and say that they are the sort of men whose opinions women peculiarly respect, and in whom they are interested quite as much as they are vexed to find them differing so absolutely from themselves.

The feminine enmity to Mr. James is of as old a date as his discovery of the Daisy Miller type of American girl, which gave continental offense among her sisters. It would be hard to say why that type gave such continental offense, unless it was because it was held not honestly to have set down the traits which no one could but most potently and powerfully allow to be true. The strange thing was that these traits were the charming and honorable distinctions of American girlhood as it convinced Europe, in the early 1870's, of a civilization so spiritual that its innocent daughters could be not only without the knowledge but without the fear of evil. I am not going back, however, to that early feminine grievance, except to note that it seems to have been the first tangible grievance, though it was not the first grievance. I, with my gray hairs, can remember still earlier work of his whose repugnant fascination was such that women readers clung to it with the wild rejection which has in a measure followed all his work at their hands.

It has been the curious fortune of this novelist, so supremely gifted in divining women and portraying them, that beyond any other great novelist (or little, for that matter) he has imagined few heroines acceptable to women. Even those martyr women who have stood by him in the long course of his transgressions, and maintained through thick and thin that he is by all odds the novelist whom they could best trust with the cause

[7]

of woman in fiction, have liked his anti-heroines more—I mean, found them realer—than his heroines. I am not sure but I have liked them more myself, but that is because I always find larger play for my sympathies in the character which needs the reader's help than in that which is so perfect as to get on without it. If it were urged that women do not care for his heroines because there are none of them to care for, I should not blame them, still less should I blame him for giving them that ground for abhorrence. I find myself diffident of heroines in fiction because I have never known one in life, of the real faultless kind; and heaven forbid I should ever yet know one. In Mr. James's novels I always feel safe from that sort, and it may be for this reason, among others, that I like to read his novels when they are new, and read them over and over again when they are old, or when they are no longer recent.

II

At this point I hear from far within a voice bringing me to book about Milly Theale in *The Wings of the Dove*, asking me, if *there* is not a heroine of the ideal make, and demanding what fault there is in her that renders her lovable. Lovable, I allow she is, dearly, tenderly, reverently lovable, but she has enough to make her so, besides being too good, too pure, too generous, too magnificently unselfish. It is not imaginable that her author should have been conscious of offering in her anything like an atonement to the offended divinity of American womanhood for Daisy Miller. But if it were imaginable the offended divinity ought to be sumptuously appeased, appeased to tears of grateful pardon such as I have not yet seen in its eyes. Milly Theale is as entirely American in the qualities which you can and cannot touch as Daisy Miller herself; and (I find myself urged to the risk of noting it) she is largely American in the same things. There is the same self-regardlessness, the same beauteous insubordination, the same mortal solution of the problem. Of course, it is all in another region, and the social levels are immensely parted. Yet Milly Theale is the superior of Daisy Miller less in her nature than in her conditions.

[8]

William Dean Howells

There is, in both, the same sublime unconsciousness of the material environment, the same sovereign indifference to the fiscal means of their emancipation to a more than masculine independence. The sense of what money can do for an American girl without her knowing it, is a "blind sense" in the character of Daisy, but in the character of Milly it has its eyes wide open. In that wonderful way of Mr. James's by which he imparts a fact without stating it, approaching it again and again, without actually coming in contact with it, we are made aware of the vast background of wealth from which Milly is projected upon our acquaintance. She is shown in a kind of breathless impatience with it, except as it is the stuff of doing willfully magnificent things, and committing colossal expenses without more anxiety than a prince might feel with the revenues of a kingdom behind him. The ideal American rich girl has never really been done before, and it is safe to say that she will never again be done with such exquisite appreciation. She is not of the new rich; an extinct New York ancestry darkles in the retrospect: something vaguely bourgeois, and yet with presences and with lineaments of aristocratic distinction. They have made her masses of money for her, those intangible fathers, uncles, and grandfathers, and then, with her brothers and sisters, have all perished away from her, and left her alone in the world with nothing else. She is as convincingly imagined in her relation to them, as the daughter of an old New York family, as she is in her inherited riches. It is not the old New York family of the unfounded Knickerbocker tradition, but something as fully patrician, with a nimbus of social importance as unquestioned as its money. Milly is not so much the flower of this local root as something finer yet: the perfume of it, the distilled and wandering fragrance. It would be hard to say in what her New Yorkishness lies, and Mr. James himself by no means says; only if you know New York at all, you have the unmistakable sense of it. She is New Yorkish in the very essences that are least associable with the superficial notion of New York: the intellectual refinement that comes of being born and bred in conditions of illimitable ease, of having had everything that one could wish to have, and the cultivation that seems to come of the mere

ability to command it. If one will have an illustration of the
final effect in Milly Theale, it may be that it can be suggested
as a sort of a Bostonian quality, with the element of *conscious*
worth eliminated, and purified as essentially of pedantry as of
commerciality. The wonder is that Mr. James in his prolonged
expatriation has been able to seize this lovely impalpability, and
to impart the sense of it; and perhaps the true reading of the
riddle is that such a nature, such a character is most appreciable
in that relief from the background which Europe gives all
American character.

III

"But that is just what does not happen in the case of Mr.
James's people. They are merged in the background so that you
never can get behind them, and fairly feel and see them all
round. Europe *doesn't* detach them; *nothing* does. 'There they
are,' as he keeps making his people say in all his late books, when
they are not calling one another dear lady, and dear man, and
prodigious and magnificent, and of a vagueness or a richness,
or a sympathy, or an opacity. No, he is of a tremendosity, but
he worries me to death; he kills me; he really gives me a head-
ache. He fascinates me, but I have no patience with him."

"But, dear lady," for it was a weary woman who had inter-
rupted the flow of my censure in these unmeasured terms, and
whom her interlocutor—another of Mr. James's insistent words
—began trying to flatter to her disadvantage, "a person of your
insight must see that this is the conditional vice of all painting,
its vital fiction. You cannot get behind the figures in any picture. They are always merged in their background. And there
you are!"

"Yes, I know I am. But that is just where I don't want to be.
I want figures that I *can* get behind."

"Then you must go to some other shop—you must go to the
shop of a sculptor."

"Well, why isn't *he* a sculptor?"

"Because he is a painter."

"Oh, that's no reason. He ought to be a sculptor."

"Then he couldn't give you the color, the light and shade, the delicate *nuances*, the joy of the intimated fact, all that you delight in him for. What was that you were saying the other day? That he was like Monticelli in some of his pastorals or picnics: a turmoil of presences which you could make anything, everything, nothing of as you happened to feel; something going on that you had glimpses of, or were allowed to guess at, but which you were rapturously dissatisfied with, any way."

"Did I say that?" my interlocutress—terrible word!—demanded. "It was very good."

"It was wonderfully good. I should not have named Monticelli, exactly, because though he is of a vagueness that is painty, he is too much of a denseness. Mr. James does not trowel the colors on."

"I see what you mean. Whom should you have named?"

"I don't know. Monticelli will do in one way. He gives you a sense of people, of things undeniably, though not unmistakably, happening, and that is what Mr. James does."

"Yes, he certainly does," and she sighed richly, as if she had been one of his people herself. "He does give you a sense."

"He gives you a sense of a tremendous lot going on, for instance, in *The Wings of the Dove,* of things undeniably, though not unmistakably, happening. It is a great book."

"It is, it is," she sighed again. "It wore me to a thread."

"And the people were as unmistakable as they were undeniable: not Milly, alone, not Mrs. Stringham, as wonderfully of New England as Milly of New York; but all that terribly frank, terribly selfish, terribly shameless, terribly hard English gang."

"Ah, Densher wasn't really hard or really shameless, though he was willing—to please that unspeakable Kate Croy—to make love to Milly and marry her money so that when she died, they could live happy ever after—or at least comfortably. And you cannot say that Kate was frank. And Lord Mark really admired Milly. Or, anyway, he wanted to marry her. Do you think Kate took the money from Densher at last and married Lord Mark?"

"Why should you care?"

"Oh, one oughtn't to care, of course, in reading Mr. James. But with anyone else, you would like to know who married who. It is all too wretched. Why should he want to picture such life?"

"Perhaps because it exists."

"Oh, do you think the English are really so bad? I'm glad he made such a beautiful character as Milly, American."

"My notion is that he didn't 'make' any of the characters."

"Of course not. And I suppose some people in England are actually like that. We have not got so far here, yet. To be sure, society is not so all-important here, yet. If it ever is, I suppose we shall pay the price. But *do* you think he ought to picture such life because it exists?"

"Do you find yourself much the worse for *The Wings of the Dove?*" I asked. "Or for *The Sacred Fount?* Or for *The Awkward Age?* Or even for *What Maisie Knew?* They all picture much the same sort of life."

"Why, of course not. But it isn't so much what he says—he never *says* anything—but what he insinuates. I don't believe that is good for young girls."

"But if they don't know what it means? I'll allow that it isn't quite *jeune fille* in its implications, all of them; but maturity has its modest claims. Even its immodest claims are not wholly ungrounded in the interest of a knowledge of our mother civilization, which is what Mr. James's insinuations impart, as I understand them."

"Well, young people cannot read him aloud together. You can't deny that."

"No, but elderly people can, and they are not to be ignored by the novelist, always. I fancy the reader who brings some knowledge of good and evil, without being the worse for it, to his work is the sort of reader Mr. James writes for. I can imagine him addressing himself to a circle of such readers as this *Review's* with a satisfaction, and a sense of liberation, which he might not feel in the following of the family magazines, and still not incriminate himself. I have heard a good deal said in reproach of the sort of life he portrays in his later books; but I have not found his people of darker deeds or murkier motives than the average in fiction. I don't say, life."

"No, certainly, so far as he tells you. It is what he *doesn't*

William Dean Howells

tell that is so frightful. He leaves you to such awful conjectures.
For instance, when Kate Croy—"
  "When Kate Croy—?"
  "No. I *won't* discuss it. But you know what I mean; and I
don't believe there ever was such a girl."
  "And you believe there was ever such a girl as Milly Theale?"
  "Hundreds! She is true to the life. So perfectly American.
My husband and I read the story aloud together, and I wanted
to weep. We had such a strange experience with that book. We
read it half through together; then we got impatient, and tried
to finish it alone. But we could not make anything of it apart;
and we had to finish it together. We could not bear to lose a
word; every word—and there were a good many!—seemed to
tell. If you took one away you seemed to miss something important. It almost destroyed me, thinking it all out. I went round
days with my hand to my forehead; and I don't believe I understand it perfectly yet. Do you?"

IV

  I pretended that I did, but I do not mind being honester with
the reader than I was with my interlocutress. I have a theory
that it is not well to penetrate every recess of an author's meaning. It robs him of the charm of mystery, and the somewhat labyrinthine construction of Mr. James's later sentences lends itself
to the practice of the self-denial necessary to the preservation
of this charm. What I feel sure of is that he has a meaning in it
all, and that by and by, perhaps when I least expect it, I shall
surprise his meaning. In the meanwhile I rest content with what
I do know. In spite of all the Browning Clubs—even the club
which has put up a monument to the poet's butler ancestor—
all of Browning is not clear, but enough of Browning is clear
for any real lover of his poetry.
  I was sorry I had not thought of this in time to say it to my
interlocutress; and I was sorry I had not amplified what I did
say of his giving you a sense of things, so as to make it apply to
places as well as persons. Never, in my ignorance, have I had a
vivider sense of London, in my knowledge a stronger sense of

[13]

Venice, than in *The Wings of the Dove*. More miraculous still, as I have tried to express, was the sense he gave me of the anterior New York where the life flowered which breathed out the odor called Milly Theale—a heartbreaking fragrance as of funeral violets—and of the anterior New England subacidly fruiting in Mrs. Stringham. As for social conditions, predicaments, orders of things, where shall we find the like of the wonders wrought in *The Awkward Age*? I have been trying to get phrases which should convey the effect of that psychomancy from me to my reader, and I find none so apt as some phrase that should suggest the convincingly incredible. Here is something that the reason can as little refuse as it can accept. Into quite such particles as the various characters of this story would the disintegration of the old, rich, demoralized society of an ancient capital fall so probably that each of the kaleidoscopic fragments, dropping into irrelevant radiance around Mrs. Brookenham, would have its fatally appointed tone in the "scheme of color." Here is that inevitable, which Mr. Brander Matthews has noted as the right and infallible token of the real, It does not matter, after that, how the people talk—or in what labyrinthine parentheses they let their unarriving language wander. They strongly and vividly exist, and they construct not a drama, perhaps, but a world, floating indeed in an obscure where it seems to have its solitary orbit, but to be as solidly palpable as any of the planets of the more familiar systems, and wrapt in the aura of its peculiar corruption. How bad the bad people on it may be, one does not know, and is not intended to know, perhaps; that would be like being told the gross facts of some scandal which, so long as it was untouched, supported itself not unamusingly in air; but of the goodness of the good people one is not left in doubt; and it is a goodness which consoles and sustains the virtue apt to droop in the presence of neighborly remissness.

I might easily attribute to the goodness a higher office than this; but if I did I might be trenching upon that ethical delicacy of the author which seems to claim so little for itself. Mr. James is, above any other, the master of the difficult art of never doing more than to "hint a fault, or hesitate dislike," and I am not

going to try committing him to conclusions he would shrink
from. There is nothing of the clumsiness of the "satirist" in his
design, and if he notes the absolute commerciality of the modern London world, it is with a reserve clothing itself in frankness which is infinitely, as he would say, "detached." But somehow, he lets you know how horribly *business* fashionable English life is; he lets Lord Mark let Milly Theale know, at their
first meeting, when he tells her she is with people who never do
anything for nothing, and when, with all her money, and perhaps because of it, she is still so trammeled in the ideal that she
cannot take his meaning. Money, and money bluntly; gate
money of all kinds; money the means, is the tune to which that
old world turns in a way which we scarcely imagine in this
crude new world where it is still so largely less the means than
the end.

But the general is lost in the personal, as it should be in Mr.
James's books, earlier as well as later, and the allegory is so faint
that it cannot always be traced. He does not say that the limit-
less liberty allowed Nanda Brookenham by her mother in *The
Awkward Age* is better than the silken bondage in which the
Duchess keeps her niece Aggie, though Nanda is admirably lovable, and little Aggie is a little cat; that is no more his affair
than to insist upon the loyalty of old Mr. Longdon to an early
love, or the generosity of Mitchett, as contrasted with the rapac-
ity of Mrs. Brookenham, who, after all, wants nothing more
than the means of being what she has always been. What he does
is simply to show you those people mainly on the outside, as you
mainly see people in the world, and to let you divine them and
their ends from what they do and say. They are presented with
infinite pains; as far as their appearance (though they are very
little described) goes, you are not suffered to make a mistake.
But he does not analyze them for you; rather he synthesizes
them, and carefully hands them over to you in a sort of integrity very uncommon in the characters of fiction. One might
infer from this that his method was dramatic, something like
Turgenev's, say; but I do not know that his method is dramatic.
I do not recall from the book more than one passage of dramatic
intensity, but that was for me of very great intensity; I mean

the passage where old Mr. Longdon lets Vanderbank understand that he will provide for him if he will offer himself to
Nanda, whom he knows to be in love with Vanderbank, and
where Vanderbank will not promise. That is a great moment,
where everything is most openly said, most brutally said, to
American thinking; and yet said with a restraint of feeling that
somehow redeems it all.

Nothing could well be more perfected than the method of
the three books which I have been supposing myself to be talking about, however far anyone may think it from perfect. They
express mastery, finality, doing what one means, in a measure
not easily to be matched. I will leave out of the question the
question of obscurity; I will let those debate that whom it interests more than it interests me. For my own part I take it that
a master of Mr. James's quality does not set out with a design
whose significance is not clear to himself, and if others do not
make it clear to themselves, I suspect them rather than him of
the fault. All the same I allow that it is sometimes not easy to
make out; I allow that sometimes I do not make it out, I, who
delight to read him almost more than any other living author,
but then I leave myself in his hands. I do not believe he is going
finally to play me the shabby trick of abandoning me in the
dark; and meanwhile he perpetually interests me. If anything,
he interests me too much, and I come away fatigued, because
I cannot bear to lose the least pulse of the play of character;
whereas from most fiction I lapse into long, delicious absences of
mind, now and then comfortably recovering myself to find out
what is going on, and then sinking below the surface again.

The Awkward Age is mostly expressed in dialogue; *The
Wings of the Dove* is mostly in the narration and the synthesis
of emotions. Not the synthesis of the motives, please; these in
both books are left to the reader, almost as much as they are in
The Sacred Fount. That troubled source, I will own, "is of a
profundity," and in its depths darkles the solution which the
author makes it no part of his business to pull to the top; if the
reader wants it, let him dive. But why should not a novel be
written so like to life, in which most of the events remain the
meaningless, that we shall never quite know what the author

meant? Why, in fact, should not people come and go, and love and hate, and hurt and help one another as they do in reality, without rendering the reader a reason for their behavior, or offering an explanation at the end with which he can light himself back over the way he has come, and see what they meant? Who knows what anyone means here below, or what he means himself, that is, precisely stands for? Most people mean nothing, except from moment to moment, if they indeed mean anything so long as that, and life which is full of propensities is almost without motives. In the scribbles which we suppose to be imitations of life, we hold the unhappy author to a logical consistency which we find so rarely in the original; but ought not we rather to praise him where his work confesses itself, as life confesses itself, without a plan? Why should we demand more of the imitator than we get from the creator?

Of course, it can be answered that we are *in* creation like characters in fiction, while we are outside of the imitation and spectators instead of characters; but that does not wholly cover the point. Perhaps, however, I am asking more for Mr. James than he would have me. In that case I am willing to offer him the reparation of a little detraction. I wish he would leave his people more, not less, to me when I read him. I have tried following their speeches without taking in his comment, delightfully pictorial as that always is, and it seems to me that I make rather more of their meaning, that way. I reserve the pleasure and privilege of going back and reading his comment in the light of my conclusions. This is the method I have largely pursued with the people of *The Sacred Fount,* of which I do not hesitate to say that I have mastered the secret, though, for the present I am not going to divulge it. Those who cannot wait may try the key which I have given.

But do not, I should urge them, expect too much of it; I do not promise it will unlock everything. If you find yourself, at the end, with nothing in your hand but the postulate with which the supposed narrator fantastically started, namely, that people may involuntarily and unconsciously prey upon one another, and mentally and psychically enrich themselves at one another's expense, still you may console yourself, if you do not think this enough, with the fact that you have passed the time in the company of men and women freshly and truly seen, amusingly shown, and abidingly left with your imagination. For me, I am so little exacting, that this is enough.

The Sacred Fount is a most interesting book, and you are teased through it to the end with delightful skill, but I am not going to say that it is a great book like *The Awkward Age*, or *The Wings of the Dove*. These are really incomparable books, not so much because there is nothing in contemporary fiction to equal them as because there is nothing the least like them. They are of a kind that none but their author can do, and since he is alone master of their art, I am very well content to leave him to do that kind of book quite as he chooses. I will not so abandon my function as to say that I could not tell him how to do them better, but it sufficiently interests me to see how he gets on without my help. After all, the critic has to leave authors somewhat to themselves; he cannot always be writing their books for them; and when I find an author, like Mr. James, who makes me acquainted with people who instantly pique my curiosity by "something rich and strange," in an environment which is admirably imaginable, I gratefully make myself at home with them, and stay as long as he will let me.

V

"But"—here is that interlocutress, whom I flattered myself I had silenced, at me again—"do you like to keep puzzling things out, so? I don't. Of course, the books *are* intensely fascinating, but I do not like to keep guessing conundrums. Why shouldn't we have studies of life that are not a series of conundrums?"

"Dear lady," I make my answer, "what was I saying just now but that life itself is a series of conundrums, to which the answers are lost in the past, or are to be supplied us, after a long and purifying discipline of guessing, in the future? I do not admit your position, but if I did, still I should read the author who keeps you guessing, with a pleasure, an edification, in the suggestive, the instructive way he has of asking his conundrums beyond that I take in any of the authors who do not tax my

William Dean Howells

curiosity, who shove their answers at me before I have had a chance to try whether I cannot guess them. Here you have the work of a great psychologist, who has the imagination of a poet, the wit of a keen humorist, the conscience of an impeccable moralist, the temperament of a philosopher, and the wisdom of a rarely experienced witness of the world; and yet you come back at me with the fact, or rather the pretense, that you do not like to keep puzzling his things out. It is my high opinion of you that you precisely do like to keep puzzling his things out; that you are pleased with the sort of personal appeal made to you by the difficulties you pretend to resent, and that you enjoy the just sense of superiority which your continual or final divinations give you. Mr. James is one of those authors who pay the finest tribute an author can pay the intelligence of his reader by trusting it, fully and frankly. There you are; and if you were not puzzling out those recondite conundrums which you complain of, what better things, in the perusal of the whole range of contemporary fiction, could you be doing? For my part I can think for you of none. There is no book like *The Awkward Age,* as I said, for it is sole of its kind, and no book that at all equals it, since Mr. Hardy's *Jude,* for the intensity of its naturalness. I don't name them to compare them; again I renounce all comparisons for Mr. James's work; but I will say that in the deeply penetrating anguish of *Jude,* I felt nothing profounder than the pathos which aches and pierces through those closing scenes of *The Awkward Age,* in Nanda's last talk with Vanderbank, whom she must and does leave for her mother's amusement, and her yet later talk with old Mr. Longdon, to whom she must and does own her love for Vanderbank so heartbreaking. What beautiful and gentle souls the new-fashioned young girl and the old-fashioned old man are, and how beautifully and gently they are revealed to us by the perfected art of the book in which they continue to live after we part with them! How—"

"Ah, there," my interlocutress broke in, as if fearful of not having the last word, "I certainly agree with you. I wish you were as candid about everything else."

FRANK MOORE COLBY

In Darkest James

[1904]

SOME time ago, when Henry James wrote an essay on women
that brought to my cheek the hot, rebellious blush, I said
nothing about it, thinking that perhaps, after all, the man's
style was his sufficient fig leaf, and that few would see how
shocking he really was. And, indeed, it had been a long time
since the public knew what Henry James was up to behind that
verbal hedge of his, though half-suspecting that he meant no
good, because a style like that seemed just the place for guilty
secrets. But those of us who had formed the habit of him early
could make him out even then, our eyes having grown so used
to the deepening shadows of his later language that they could
see in the dark, as you might say. I say this not to brag of it,
but merely to show that there were people who partly understood him even in *The Sacred Fount,* and he was clearer in his
essays, especially in that wicked one on *George Sand: The New
Life,* published in an American magazine.

Here he was as bold as brass, telling women to go ahead and
do and dare, and praising the fine old hearty goings on at the
court of Augustus the Strong, and showing how they could be
brought back again if women would only try. His impunity was
due to the sheer laziness of the expurgators. They would not
read him, and they did not believe anybody else could. They
justified themselves, perhaps, by recalling passages like these in
The Awkward Age:

What did this feeling wonderfully appear unless strangely irrelevant. . . .

Frank Moore Colby

But she fixed him with her weary penetration. . . .

He jumped up at this, as if he couldn't bear it, presenting as he walked across the room a large, foolish, fugitive back, on which her eyes rested as on a proof of her penetration. . . .

"My poor child, you're of a profundity. . . ."

He spoke almost uneasily, but she was not too much alarmed to continue lucid.

"You're of a limpidity, dear man!"

"Don't you think that's rather a back seat for one's best?"

"A back seat?" she wondered, with a purity.

"Your aunt didn't leave me with you to teach you the slang of the day."

"The slang?" she spotlessly speculated.

Arguing from this that he was bent more on eluding pursuit than on making converts, they let things pass that in other writers would have been immediately rebuked. He had, in fact, written furiously against the proprieties for several years. "There is only one propriety," he said, "that the painter of life can ask of a subject: Does it or does it not belong to life?" He charged our Anglo-Saxon writers with "a conspiracy of silence," and taunted them with the fact that the women were more improper than the men. "Emancipations are in the air," said he, "but it is to women writers that we owe them." The men were cowards, rarely venturing a single coarse expression, but already in England there were pages upon pages of women's work so strong and rich and horrifying and free that a man could hardly read them. Halcyon days, they seemed to him, and woman the harbinger of a powerful Babylonish time when the improprieties should sing together like the morning stars. Not an enthusiastic person generally, he always warmed to this particular theme with generous emotion.

His essay on George Sand discussing what he calls the "new life," cited the heart history of that author as "having given her sex for its new evolution and transformation the real standard and measure of change." It was all recorded in Madame Karénine's biography, and Madame Karénine, being a Russian with an "admirable Slav superiority to prejudice," was able to treat the matter in a "large, free way." A life so amorously

The Question of Henry James

profuse was sure to set an encouraging example, he thought. Her heart was like an hotel, occupied, he said, by "many more or less greasy males" in quick succession. He hoped the time would come when other women's hearts would be as miscellaneous:

> In this direction their aim has been, as yet, comparatively modest and their emulation low; the challenge they have hitherto picked up is but the challenge of the average male. The approximation of the extraordinary woman has been, practically, in other words, to the ordinary man. Madame Sand's service is that she planted the flag much higher; her own approximation, at least, was to the extraordinary. She reached him, she surpassed him, and she showed how, with native dispositions, the thing could be done. These new records will live as the precious text-book, so far as we have got, of the business.

This was plain enough. Any other man would have been suppressed. In a literature so well policed as ours, the position of Henry James was anomalous. He was the only writer of the day whose unconventional notions did not matter. His dissolute and complicated Muse might say just what she chose. Perhaps this was because it would have been so difficult to expose him. Never did so much "vice" go with such sheltering vagueness. Whatever else may be said of James at this time, he was no tempter, and though the novels of this period deal only with unlawful passions, they make but chilly reading on the whole. It is a land where the vices have no bodies and the passions no blood, where nobody sins because nobody has anything to sin with. Why should we worry when a spook goes wrong? For years James did not create one shadow-casting character. His love affairs, illicit though they be, are so stripped to their motives that they seem no more enticing than a diagram. A wraith proves faithless to her marriage vow, elopes with a bogie in a cloud of words. Six phantoms meet and dine, three male, three female, with two thoughts apiece, and, after elaborate geometry of the heart, adultery follows like a Q.E.D. Shocking it ought to be, but yet it is not. Ghastly, tantalizing, queer, but never near enough human to be either good or bad. To be a sinner, even in the books you need some carnal attributes—lungs, liver, tastes, at least a pair of legs. Even the fiends have palpable tails; wise men have so depicted them. No flesh, no frailty; that may be why our sternest moralists licensed Henry James to write his wickedest. They saw that whatever the moral purport of these books, they might be left wide open in the nursery.

To those who never liked him he is the same in these writings as in those before and since. They complain that even at his best he is too apt to think that when he has made a motive he has made a man. Nevertheless, though the world of his better novels is small, it is always credible—humanity run through a sieve, but still humanity. During this dark period his interests seemed to drop off one by one, leaving him shut in with his single theme—the rag, the bone, and the hank of hair, the complicated amours of skeletons. They called it his later manner, but the truth is, it was a change in the man himself. He saw fewer things in this spacious world than he used to see, and the people were growing more meager and queer and monotonous, and it was harder and harder to break away from the stump his fancy was tied to.

In *The Wings of the Dove* there were signs of a partial recovery. There were people who saw no difference between it and *The Sacred Fount* or *The Awkward Age*, but they were no friends of his. By what vice of introspection he got himself lashed to that fixed idea it is impossible to say, but it was clear that neither of those books was the work of a mind entirely free. In one aspect it was ridiculous; but if one laughed, it was with compunctions, for in another aspect it was exceedingly painful. This only from the point of view of his admirers. It is not forgotten that there is the larger class (for whom this world in the main was made) to whom he is merely ridiculous. They do not see why thoughts so unwilling to come out need be extracted.

To be sure in *The Wings of the Dove* there is the same absorption in the machinery of motive and in mental processes the most minute. Through page after page he surveys a mind as a sick man looks at his counterpane, busy with little ridges and grooves and undulations. There are chapters like wonderful games of solitaire, broken by no human sound save his own chuckle when he takes some mysterious trick or makes a move that he says is "beautiful." He has a way of saying "There you are" that is most exasperating, for it is always at the precise moment at which you know you have utterly lost yourself. There is no doubt that James's style is often too puffed up with its secrets. Despite its air of immense significance, the dark, unfathomed caves of his ocean contain sometimes only the same sort of gravel you could have picked up on the shore. I have that from deep-sea thinkers who have been down him. But though this unsociable way of writing continued through *The Wings of the Dove*, it came nearer than any other novel that he had published for some years to the quality of his earlier work. It deals with conditions as well as with people. Instead of merely souls anywhere, we have men and women living in describable homes. It would be hard to find in those other novels anything in the spirit of the following passage, which is fairly typical of much in this:

> It was after the children's dinner . . . and the two young women were still in the presence of the crumpled tablecloth, the dispersed pinafores, the scraped dishes, the lingering odour of boiled food. Kate had asked, with ceremony, if she might put up a window a little, and Mrs. Condrip had replied, without it, that she might do as she liked. She often received such inquiries as if they reflected in a manner on the pure essence of her little ones. . . . Their mother had become for Kate —who took it just for the effect of being their mother—quite a different thing from the mild Marian of the past; Mr. Condrip's widow expansively obscured that image. She was little more than a ragged relic, a plain prosaic result of him, as if she had somehow been pulled through him as through an obstinate funnel, only to be left crumpled and useless and with nothing in her but what he accounted for.

Not that the passage shows him at his best, but it shows him as at least concerned with the setting of his characters.

It is not worth while to attempt an outline of the story. Those who have done so have disagreed in essentials. It is impossible to hit off in a few words characters that James has picked out for their very complexity; and the story counts for little with him as against the business of recording the play of mind. One

Frank Moore Colby

does not take a watch to pieces merely to tell the time of day; and with James analysis is the end in itself.

If the obscurity of the language were due to the idea itself, and if while he tugs at an obstinate thought you could be sure it was worth the trouble, there would be no fault to find, but to him one thing seems as good as another when he is mousing around in a mind. It is a form of self-indulgence. He is as pleased with the motives that lead nowhere as with anything else. It is his even emphasis that most misleads. He writes a staccato chronicle of things both great and small, like a constitutional history half made up of the measures that never passed. And in one respect he does not play fairly. He makes his characters read each other's minds from clues that he keeps to himself. To invent an irreverant instance, suppose I were a distinguished author with a psychological bent and wished to represent two young people as preternaturally acute. I might place them alone together and make them talk like this:

> "If—" she sparkled.
> "If!" he asked. He had lurched from the meaning for a moment.
> "I might"—she replied abundantly.
> His eye had eaten the meaning—"Me!" he gloriously burst.
> "Precisely," she thrilled. "How splendidly you *do* understand."

I, the distinguished author, versed in my own psychology— the springs of my own marionettes—I understand it perfectly. For me there are words aplenty. But is it fair to you, the reader?

Nevertheless—and this is the main point about Henry James —by indefinable means and in spite of wearisome prolixity he often succeeds in his darkest books in producing very strange and powerful effects. It is a lucky man who can find a word for them. Things you had supposed incommunicable certainly come your way. These are the times when we are grateful to him for pottering away in his nebulous workshop among the things that are hard to express. Even when he fails we like him for making the attempt. We like him for going his own gait, though he leaves us straggling miles behind. We cannot afford at this time to blame any writer who is a little reckless of the average mind. Consider the case of Browning and all that his lusty independ-

[2 5]

The Question of Henry James

ence has done for us. Browning was quite careless of the average mind; he would as lief wreck it. He was careless of anybody else's mind, so bent was he on indulging his own. His question was not, What will you have? but What do I feel like doing? and readers had to take their chances, some to give him up as too deep, and others to beat their brains for inner meanings where there were none. He liked life so well that he prized its most vapid moments and expressed his mind at its best and at its worst, wrote sometimes as other men drum on windowpanes, catalogued a lot of objects he liked the look of, relaxed in verse, ate in it, sometimes slept in it, used it, in short, for so many strange little personal purposes that reading it sometimes seems an intrusion. Hence, he is quite as much a puzzle to the too thoughtful as he is to those who prefer not to think, for a great man's nonsense is sure to drive his commentators mad looking for a message. Browning differed from others not so much in the greatness of his mind as in the fact that he showed more of it. He seems obscure sometimes because people are unprepared for that degree of confidence. Then, there are certain preconceived notions as to the limits of literature, an expectation of large, plain things, of truth with a doorknob, of smooth, symmetrical thoughts, not at all in the shape they come to the mind, but neatly trimmed for others to see when they leave it. No living man understands Browning; but for that matter, few men understand their wives. It is not fatal to enjoyment. People who are perfectly clear to each other are simply keeping things back. Any man would be a mystery if you could see him from the inside, and Browning puzzles us chiefly because we are not accustomed to seeing a mind exposed to view. It is the man's presence, not his message, that we care for in Browning's books; his zest for everything, his best foot and his worst foot, his deepest feelings and his foolishness, and the tag ends of his dreams. They are not the greatest poems in the world, but there was the greatest pleasure in the making of them. It is just the place for a writer to go and forget his minor literary duties, the sense of his demanding public, the obligation of the shining phrase, the need of making editorial cats jump, the standing orders for a *jeu d'esprit*.

Frank Moore Colby

It is also the place for a reader to go who is a little weary of the books which are written with such patient regard for the spiritual limitations of the public. And part of the obscurity of Henry James springs from the same pleasing and honorable egotism.

HERBERT CROLY

Henry James and His Countrymen

[1904]

MR. HENRY JAMES, so it is stated on excellent authority, is on the point of returning to the United States for a number of months, in order to renew his impressions of this country; and to anyone who is familiar in a general way with the course of Mr. James's work and the length of his expatriation, the announcement is one of altogether extraordinary interest. It provokes the question, indeed, whether during all the years of his absence, his native country has grown away from Mr. James or towards him. Would it or would it not fulfill any more completely at the present time the demands which he made upon it in the seventies, and which apparently at that time it failed to satisfy? What, on the other hand, has been the effect of his expatriation upon Mr. James himself? What has he gained thereby? And what has he lost? These questions cannot be answered without some discussion of the motive which induced one of the foremost American novelists and the first American stylist of his generation to persist in living abroad, and of the relation which he and his work occupy to the new American life, letters, and literary ideals.

Here is an American man of letters, who started abroad when he was a very young fellow, and, like many of his literate countrymen before and since, straightway succumbed to the fascination of Europe. In most of the other "cases," the pilgrimage cast a spell, the effect of which persisted in one way or another throughout the rest of their lives. In the case of Henry James it did more; it wrought a revolution; it transformed or reformed his whole intellectual and spiritual outlook. Deeply

Herbert Croly

rooted in his disposition, there was an instance, of which it is sufficient to say at present, that it demanded for its satisfaction the utmost refinement and completeness of form. That instinct was starved in America. Europe aroused it into happy and vigorous activity, the sense of which overflowed immediately in his work. He began to write stories about passionate pilgrims. His earlier books are peopled with young Americans who are famished by the artistic and intellectual dearth and disorder of their native land, and who do not reach their full growth until they have fed upon the ripe fruit of European art and history. All this was, of course, the reflex of his own experience, the benefit of which he did not and could not forego. It determined the form, the purpose, and the circumstances of his subsequent life and work.

Other American men of letters returned home after their European pilgrimage and took up their pre-established tasks. Europe became to them a sentimental association, a pensive memory, the subject matter for essays and histories, and even, as in the case of Cooper, the standard whereby they in some measure estimated and criticized American society. A robust and austere mind like that of Emerson was strengthened by the experience, without being perturbed by the contrast; to the weak and impressionable spirit of N. P. Willis the memory of his pilgrimage and the sense of his loss were merely enervating; James Russell Lowell had a way that was all his own of keeping his feet planted on both sides of the water. It was the strength and the weakness of Henry James, however, that in his case both the experience and the dilemma which issued from it were more critical. He could not be content with writing about his pilgrimages merely as travelers' gossip, or of translating it into art criticism or history; neither could he unconcernedly resume his profession as novelist in this country, but with his subject matter and standards partly derived from Europe. As a novelist, he must deal with the vision and values of life as they appeared to him; and according to his moral outlook European life was life itself raised to a higher power, because more richly charged, more significantly composed, and more completely informed. He could not renounce this vision without intellectual mutilation;

yet he could not give it free and sufficient expression in his native country.

The dilemma was one of the most momentous which can occur in the life of an artist; and it is no wonder that Mr. James hesitated for some time before making a final choice. During the ten years following his trip to Europe in 1872, he spent part of his time on one side of the water and part on the other, and the people in his stories followed in his footsteps. It was the period chiefly of his studies in comparative national psychology and manners. He not only shifted extremely American Americans, such as Christopher Newman, to Europe, so as to see how they might look and behave in Paris; but he also tested the behavior of some Europeanized Americans, when returned to the self-conscious simplicities of native American society. While most of his stories were concerned with these international comparisons, he did attempt some elaborate searching of undiluted American life; but such books as *Washington Square* and *The Bostonians* do not rank among his successes. If one may judge from the result, Mr. James, during these years, was convincing himself by conscientious experimentation that his method and point of view demanded European surroundings and chiefly a European material. At any rate, he finally took up his permanent residence abroad, and for twenty-two years he has not returned to his native country. He decided that in his own case the penalties of expatriation were less to be feared than the divided allegiance inseparable from a residence in the United States.

Whatever we may think of the choice, it obviously was not made without a clear consciousness that he was running a risk and incurring a penalty. Intellectual work of any kind derives much of its momentum and effect from the extent to which it embodies and fulfills a national purpose and tradition; and the artist, whether literary or plastic, who forsakes his country is necessarily thrown back to a much greater extent upon his personal resources. The loss of this national impulse does not make so much difference to a painter or a sculptor, because the United States, at any rate of a generation ago, was without any local tradition proper to the arts of design, but even James, Whistler, and William Story, while they can hardly be imagined in any surroundings but those of their own selection, did not make the selection with impunity. As Henry James says in his *William Wetmore Story and His Friends,* "He (William Story), therefore, never failed of any plenitude in feeling—in the fullness of time and on due occasion—that a man always pays, in one way or another for expatriation, for detachment from his plain primary heritage, and that this tax is levied in an amusing diversity of ways." In his second volume (page 222) Mr. James takes up the parable on his own account and explains what manner of payment Story managed to make. "This moral seems to be," he says, "that somehow in the long run, Story *paid*—paid for having sought his development even among the circumstances that at the time of his choice appeared not alone the only propitious, but the only possible." He classes Story among "those existences, numerous enough, that in alien air, far from their native soil, have found themselves the prey of more beguilement"; so that he figures Story's career as "a sort of beautiful sacrifice to a noble mistake."

So far as I know, Mr. James has not told us how he himself has paid for his detachment from his "plain primary heritage"; but manifestly the payment exacted from a man of letters must both be different from and in its way heavier than that exacted from a sculptor. He himself suggests that Story might have been more of a poet in Cambridge than he was a sculptor in Rome, which could scarcely be true unless the "plain primary heritage" of an American man of letters contained what the heritage of an American sculptor did not contain—a local tradition, proper to literary art, of some power and consequence. It follows that an American man of letters in forsaking his own country, both sacrifices something of greater value to his work, and under ordinary circumstances, acquires something of decidedly smaller value, in suchwise that while a great many artists have felt impelled to live permanently abroad, very few men of letters have submitted to a similar compulsion. Mr. James's "case," however, was, it must be admitted, in every way exceptional; and its peculiarity consisted in the fact that his work was more closely allied in method and purpose with the structural and plastic arts

The Question of Henry James

than it was with previous or subsequent American literature. He could afford to forego the impulse of the national habit and tradition, because his method and purpose were peculiar to himself and derived their power from an intense and exclusive personal faith. As an American man of letters, permanently resident abroad, he was very conscious of his situation and very resolute to justify his choice. Whatever penalty he had to pay, the very last mistake he was like to make was that of Story—that of permitting himself to be diverted by his surroundings. No one knew better than he that he was thrown back on his individual—as compared to the national—intellectual outlook, that he must "live with his conception"; and the way in which he has paid his penalty issues as directly from this personal concentration as Story's did from his easier beguilement.

In any attempt to estimate the rewards and penalties of Mr. James's expatriation, the fact must be constantly kept in mind that it was in London he took up his residence. His earlier stories were as much, if not more, concerned with France and Italy as with England. Christopher Newman, like all good Americans in the seventies, went to Paris to live. Roderick Hudson, at the bidding of the prevalent preference for inspiration to technique, followed one of the roads that led to Rome. Daisy Miller had the Forum and St. Peter's as the scenery for her colloquial exploits. In the beginning, Mr. James himself seems to have passed as much time on the continent as in England. Finally, however, the neighborhood of London became definitely his home; and the study of English society, with an occasional American interpolated by way of relief or contrast, more persistently his task. Even when the scene shifts to the continent, as it frequently does, English people, however modified by the scenery, remain his subject matter; and though in his last novel, *The Ambassadors,* he returns to his earlier study of the effect which Paris and a Parisian woman may have upon susceptible Americans, the liveliness of the effect is partly due to its novelty.

The expatriated American of the present day, even when he lives on the continent, takes on English characteristics; and the fact that Mr. James lives in England and writes chiefly about its inhabitants, helps both to qualify and define his expatriation.

Herbert Croly

He is, after all, no more than half divided from his native country. He is writing of a people whose language we use in our own way, whose literary traditions we have in some measure inherited, and of whom he may write and we may read without any violent intellectual transposition. Of course, these very facts have in some cases only helped to Anglicize an American resident of London much more thoroughly than he could possibly have been Italianized in Rome; but no such disaster, at least so far as his work is concerned, has befallen Mr. James. He has taken what England had to give him. He has found the maturity of English life, its treasures of fully formed types, of fixed traditions and of domestic scenery, the incomparable social spectacle that it offers—he has found this all very much to his purpose. Yet this purpose is as alien to English as it is to American literature. It is nothing but his own purpose, his own conception; and Mr. James, in writing of Story, classes London with Boston or New York as a city in which an artist must "live with his conception." So, while it cannot be said that he has remained much of an American in London, at least he has not become, artistically speaking, much of an Englishman, and we may at least surmise that he has been more of an American in London than he would have been in New York.

The great fact about Mr. James is that wherever he lives, he is, above all, deliberately and decisively the individual artist. In England the American literary artist was allowed free personal expression, whereas in this country he was not. English life he could approach more sympathetically from his point of view, and he could handle it more saliently with his equipment and methods. The artist, as Mr. James sees him, is the man who seeks fullness of insight and perfection of form at any cost. Art is second only to religion in the sacrifices which it demands from its followers. What all artists need and what American artists can obtain only by some violence of behavior, is moral and mental detachment—the freedom from practical obligations which will compromise his work, the freedom from intellectual and social ties which will obscure his vision. In *The Lesson of the Master,* for instance, Mr. James makes it out that the artist, in this case a novelist, should not

The Question of Henry James

marry, because after marriage his work, if he be conscientious and successful, will be subject to a jointure in his wife's interest; it becomes tied to a fixed income and the whole social establishment. So far as I know, he nowhere advises the artist to deny himself a country as well as a wife, but patriotism, either enthusiastic or official, obviously has its dangers for a man to whom intellectual integrity is of the first importance. In a remarkable passage in the second volume of Story's life (pages 53 and following) he complains of Mrs. Browning that her "beautiful mind and high gift were discredited by their engrossment" with the Italian cause, not, of course, because her Italian patriotism was passionate, but because her passion destroyed that "saving and sacred sense of proportion," which we demand from great genius. The patriotic American, particularly the patriotic American artist, whether genius or not, is not much troubled by any saving sense of proportion, for there seems to be something about American patriotism which levies a heavy tax in the way of intellectual and moral credulity. The momentum of our practical life certainly tends to convert the novelist who attempts to formulate its issues, into something of a stump speaker; and one can easily understand that an artist who places such a high value upon a large and disinterested intellectual outlook may find it desirable to exalt his art at the expense of his patriotism.

American life is in the making. Its social forms are confused and indefinite; its social types either local, or evasive, or impermanent. Its ideal of a democratic society in a democratic state is constantly present as an ideal, but mostly absent as a reality, offering a problem to be worked out rather than an achievement to be generalized and portrayed. Its intellectual interests are for the present subordinated to its moral, practical, and business interests. The atmosphere of its life is charged with activity and endeavor rather than with observation and reflection. The novelist who attempts to represent this life finds himself in a difficult situation. It is hard to reach or to maintain any sufficient intellectual concentration or detachment. He is himself generally caught up and whirled along by these powerful illusions, which strenuous Americans are trying to convert into

Herbert Croly

realities. He becomes either a patriotic orator, masked as a novelist, or he confines himself to the description of the social eddies which the flood of American life occasionally casts off to one side. In such a society the permanent aspects which a novelist may fix, tend to be, as the work of Mr. Howells shows, somewhat unimportant; and if the better American novelists are particularly deficient in the power of coherent, salient, and edifying thought, if they seem unable to compose large, powerful, and vivid social pictures, the difficulty lies both with the material itself, and with the effect of their surroundings in diluting the blood of their intellectual purpose.

In abandoning his own country, Mr. James seems to have been driven by the logic of his choice to fasten his attention more exclusively than ever upon those social traits in which his countrymen, when at home, are most completely lacking. He instinctively, he consciously, preferred the study of definite and mature social types. Although coming from the country of little leisure, Mr. James almost always portrays leisured people, or people in their leisured moments—men and women who have for one cause or another abandoned the day's work. They may not be rich; but if so they have either consented to their poverty, or are seeking wealth, as did Kate Croy, by devious and daring social diplomacy. They are not interested in trade, in politics, nor as a rule in ideas; but they are "wonderfully" interested in each other; and the only active working people who are admitted to this set of economic parasites are the artists—the people whose active work illuminates the play of social contrast, diplomacy, and adventure. Mr. James likes to arrange people of this kind in effective and significant combinations, heightened by an effective and significant background. It is a subtle, exciting, and finished social situation, which he isolates, analyzes, interprets, and composes, with his eyes fastened exclusively upon the psychological aesthetics of the people and the social aesthetics of their attitudes toward one another.

London is obviously much more in the shadow of this kind of social foliage than is New York or Boston. It contains a very large number of people, in good "society" and out, who would rather pursue interesting inquiries in human nature, or assume and watch interesting social attitudes than play the strenuous part. That there should be so many of these people in good "society," is in itself perhaps a sign of deterioration. This society has abandoned the solid distinction of aspect and behavior which it possessed in 1850, and Mr. James regretfully notes and even chronicles its loss of form; but the very contrast between its high memories and survivals and its present pursuit of the socially curious and remunerative person provides him with many an amusing situation. From his point of view, also, the value of these situations is enormously enhanced by the background of domestic scenery, partly historic and partly personal, which he can arrange around them. No writer of historical or romantic stories has been more careful to give his fables an appropriate historic or emotional setting than has Henry James to place his characters in houses and rooms which illuminate and intensify their personalities. He has given, indeed, a new value in the art of novel writing to domestic properties and scenery—to such an extent that a woman like Madame de Vionnet is as absolutely identified with her house and is as inconceivable apart from it as Meg Merrilies would be apart from Scottish moorland. Undoubtedly one of Mr. James's strongest reasons for preferring England to his own country is that, abroad, these finer proprieties of domestic life have had time to become authentic and definite. They are the creation of social position, of personal leisure, of historic accumulation, and in our own country the historic accumulation is meager, social position vague and doubtful, and personal leisure almost a minus quality.

We are now, perhaps, better prepared to understand how wide the gulf is which divides Mr. James from the life and literature of his contemporary fellow countrymen. While he has renounced any attempt to deal with action, achievement, it is just such action and achievement by which they are fascinated and engrossed. The social and psychological spectacle which Mr. James presents makes little of the common general appeal of the great traditional plot; and it is a literary rendering, adapted to American life, of the great traditional plot which Americans demand and which dominates our contemporary novel. Whatever else this novel possesses, it must possess energy, excitement, mo-

Herbert Croly

mentum, and purpose. Even the ordinary historical novel, which has, of course, always tried to be exciting, is often becoming infused with a patriotic purpose, which gives something more than a personal and romantic significance to its issues. As to the novel of contemporary life, while it is still circumscribed to a large extent by localities and the romantic convention of a pair of lovers, it is making an ambitious attempt to be both dramatic and important—to give a thrilling version of some of the salient activities of American industry, politics, and society. In short, it is character which fulfills itself in vigorous performance, which is swept along, almost always to success, by the living, conspicuous, national forces that the younger writers are trying to represent; and this material, as well as the literary methods whereby it is handled and the artistic point of view wherefrom it is approached, is as different as possible from the material, the methods, and the point of view of Mr. James.

One cannot keep sympathizing strongly with the strenuous innocence of the contemporary American novel and literary purpose. As yet, it has not been dignified by the appearance of any man who can write well or think deep. Its work is impressive only in the mass, and for what it promises. Earnest as it is, it is lacking in artistic and intellectual integrity; it is the issue of a curious moral and mental superficiality which is the result partly of inexperience, partly of want of imagination, partly of a naïve faith in good intentions. It tries harder to be contemporary, representative, popular, and vital than it does to be well-fashioned, well-observed, or well-considered. In short, the younger American novelist, like the American politician, has his ear to the ground and fails to be representative and formative in a large way, because he tries so hard to be immediately influential and "efficient." Yet, in spite of the superficiality of this work, its lack of manners, of reserve, of weight, and of dignity, it is the product of a genuine impulse; it is in line with the great storytelling tradition. The desire to give a vigorous and thrilling version of American life, to portray its typical actions, its momentous achievements, contains at least the chance of a great national literature and drama. The penalty which Mr. James pays for his expatriation, for his exclusive and consistent

The Question of Henry James

loyalty to his personal faith and vision, is just the penalty of being wholly separated from this main stream of American literary fulfillment. He will appeal profoundly only to an intellectual interest as restricted and as special as the point of view which has characterized his work, and I mean by this something more than the familiar comment that he is not and will not be a popular novelist. Not only will his public be small, but it does not and will not include—not to any effective extent—his American fellow craftsmen—the men who will carry on the work, and, perhaps, have their share in the consummation.

It should be added, however, that if the consummation is reached, it will be reached only by the acquisition on the part of his literary fellow countrymen of an artistic and intellectual integrity analogous to that of Henry James. What they need above all is some infusion of his incorruptible artistic purpose, of his devotion to good workmanship, of his freedom from stupefying moral and social illusions, of his ability, limited by his outlook though it be, really to simplify his material and really to construct his effect. Their need of an infusion of this kind can scarcely be exaggerated. Without it their work will remain at best a kind of literary journalism and will be as certainly ephemeral, as are all slovenly and superficial works of art. Much as his literate fellow countrymen need Mr. James, however, it is the misfortune of his position that they do not and cannot derive this artistic leaven directly from his books. In individual cases, of course, the ferment has been transmitted, but on the whole they cannot obtain any conspicuous benefit from him without a dangerous imaginative transposition. They cannot submit to his influence without risking what is best in their own point of view. He who is in some ways so great and admirable a master will be shunned or ignored as a teacher and model by his American fellow craftsmen; and if they acquire any of his merits, it must necessarily be from a source which has some of Henry James's intellectual incorruptibility and disinterestedness, but which also has the quality of being momentous, contagious, and popular.

To possess much of the style and intellectual vision which one's countrymen need, and yet to be so divided from them that you cannot help them in their poverty, seems to me a high price to pay for the advantages of Mr. James's expatriation. Yet I am not bold enough to say that the price is too high. An achievement so extraordinary and so individual as that of Henry James is absolutely its own justification, and American critics should recognize this plain condition by considering it chiefly upon its own merits, rather than upon its defects or effects.

These merits will in any case exact their due recognition in American literary history; and, provided American criticism plays its proper part, they may even have their due influence on American literature. An influence which cannot be exercised directly may be exercised indirectly—provided the men, who should understand the height of the achievement on the one hand and the greatness of the need on the other, have the sense to read the lesson and the voice to proclaim it.

MAX BEERBOHM

The Mote in the Middle Distance

[1912]

IT was with the sense of a, for him, very memorable something that he peered now into the immediate future, and
tried, not without compunction, to take that period up where
he had, prospectively, left it. But just where the deuce *had* he
left it? The consciousness of dubiety was, for our friend, not,
this morning, quite yet clean-cut enough to outline the figures
on what she had called his "horizon," between which and himself the twilight was indeed of a quality somewhat intimidating.
He had run up, in the course of time, against a good number of
"teasers"; and the function of teasing them back—of, as it
were, giving them, every now and then, "what for"—was in
him so much a habit that he would have been at a loss had there
been, on the face of it, nothing to lose. Oh, he always had offered rewards, of course—had ever so liberally pasted the win-
dows of his soul with staring appeals, minute descriptions,
promises that knew no bounds. But the actual recovery of the
article—the business of drawing and crossing the check,
blotched though this were with tears of joy—had blankly appeared to him rather in the light of a sacrilege, casting, he sometimes felt, a palpable chill on the fervor of the next quest. It
was just this fervor that was threatened as, raising himself on
his elbow, he stared at the foot of his bed. That his eyes refused
to rest there for more than the fraction of an instant, may be
taken—*was*, even then, taken by Keith Tantalus—as a hint of
his recollection that after all the phenomenon wasn't to be singular. Thus the exact repetition, at the foot of Eva's bed, of
the shape pendulous at the foot of *his* was hardly enough to ac-

count for the fixity with which he envisaged it, and for which
he was to find, some years later, a motive in the (as it turned
out) hardly generous fear that Eva had already made the great
investigation "on her own." Her very regular breathing presently reassured him that, if she *had* peeped into "her" stocking,
she must have done so in sleep. Whether he should wake her
now, or wait for their nurse to wake them both in due course,
was a problem presently solved by a new development. It was
plain that his sister was now watching him between her eye-
lashes. He had half expected that. She really was—he had often
told her that she really was—magnificent; and her magnificence
was never more obvious than in the pause that elapsed before
she all of a sudden remarked, "They so very indubitably *are*,
you know!"

It occurred to him as befitting Eva's remoteness, which was a
part of Eva's magnificence, that her voice emerged somewhat
muffled by the bedclothes. She was ever, indeed, the most tele-
phonic of her sex. In talking to Eva you always had, as it were,
your lips to the receiver. If you didn't try to meet her fine
eyes, it was that you simply couldn't hope to: there were too
many dark, too many buzzing and bewildering and all frankly
not negotiable leagues in between. Snatches of other voices
seemed often to intertrude themselves in the parley; and your
loyal effort not to overhear these was complicated by your fear
of missing what Eva might be twittering. "Oh, you certainly
haven't, my dear, the trick of propinquity!" was a thrust she
had once parried by saying that, in that case, *he* hadn't—to
which his unspoken rejoinder that she had caught her tone from
the peevish young women at the Central seemed to him (if not
perhaps in the last, certainly in the last but one, analysis) to
lack finality. With Eva, he had found, it was always safest to
"ring off." It was with a certain sense of his rashness in the
matter, therefore, that he now, with an air of feverishly "holding the line," said, "Oh, as to that!"

Had *she*, he presently asked himself, "rung off"? It was characteristic of our friend—was indeed "him all over"—that his
fear of what she was going to say was as nothing to his fear of
what she might be going to leave unsaid. He had, in his con-

[41]

verse with her, been never so conscious as now of the intervening leagues; they had never so insistently beaten the drum of his ear; and he caught himself in the act of awfully computing, with a certain statistical passion, the distance between Rome and Boston. He has never been able to decide which of these points he was psychically the nearer to at the moment when Eva, replying, "Well, one does, anyhow, leave a margin for the pretext, you know!" made him, for the first time in his life, wonder whether she were not more magnificent than even he had ever given her credit for being. Perhaps it was to test this theory, or perhaps merely to gain time, that he now raised himself to his knees, and, leaning with outstretched arm towards the foot of his bed, made as though to touch the stocking which Santa Claus had, overnight, left dangling there. His posture, as he stared obliquely at Eva, with a sort of beaming defiance, recalled to him something seen in an "illustration." This reminiscence, however—if such it was, save in the scarred, the poor dear old woebegone and so very beguilingly *not* refractive mirror of the moment—took a peculiar twist from Eva's behavior. She had, with startling suddenness, sat bolt upright, and looked to him as if she were overhearing some tragedy at the other end of the wire, where, in the nature of things, she was unable to arrest it. The gaze she fixed on her extravagant kinsman was of a kind to make him wonder how he contrived to remain, as he beautifully did, rigid. His prop was possibly the reflection that flashed on him that, if *she* abounded in attenuations, well, hang it all, so did *he!* It was simply a difference of plane. Readjust the "values," as painters say, and there you were! He was to feel that he was only too crudely "there" when, leaning further forward, he laid a chubby forefinger on the stocking, causing that receptacle to rock ponderously to and fro. This effect was more expected than the tears which started to Eva's eyes, and the intensity with which "Don't you," she exclaimed, "see?"

"The mote in the middle distance?" he asked. "Did you ever, my dear, know me to see anything else? I tell you it blocks out everything. It's a cathedral, it's a herd of elephants, it's the whole habitable globe. Oh, it's, believe me, of an obsessiveness!"

Max Beerbohm

But his sense of the one thing it *didn't* block out from his purview enabled him to launch at Eva a speculation as to just how far Santa Claus had, for the particular occasion, gone. The gauge, for both of them, of this seasonable distance seemed almost blatantly suspended in the silhouettes of the two stockings. Over and above the basis of (presumably) sweetmeats in the toes and heels, certain extrusions stood for a very plenary fulfillment of desire. And, since Eva *had* set her heart on a doll of ample proportions and practicable eyelids—*had* asked that most admirable of her sex, their mother, for it with not less directness than he himself had put into his demand for a sword and helmet—her coyness now struck Keith as lying near to, at indeed a hardly measurable distance from, the border line of his patience. If she didn't *want* the doll, why the deuce had she made such a point of getting it? He was perhaps on the verge of putting this question to her, when, waving her hand to include both stockings, she said, "Of course, my dear, you *do* see. There they are, and you know I know you know we wouldn't, either of us, dip a finger into them." With a vibrancy of tone that seemed to bring her voice quite close to him, "One doesn't," she added, "violate the shrine—pick the pearl from the shell!"

Even had the answering question "Doesn't one just?" which for an instant hovered on the tip of his tongue, been uttered, it could not have obscured for Keith the change which her magnificence had wrought in him. Something, perhaps, of the bigotry of the convert was already discernible in the way that, averting his eyes, he said, "One doesn't even peer." As to whether, in the years that have elapsed since he said this either of our friends (now adult) has, in fact, "peered," is a question which, whenever I call at the house, I am tempted to put to one or other of them. But any regret I may feel in my invariable failure to "come up to the scratch" of yielding to this temptation is balanced, for me, by my impression—my sometimes all but throned and anointed certainty—that the answer, if vouchsafed, would be in the negative.

JOSEPH CONRAD

The Historian of Fine Consciences

[1905]

IN one of his critical studies, published some fifteen years ago, Mr. Henry James claims for the novelist the standing of the historian as the only adequate one, as for himself and before his audience. I think that this claim cannot be contested, and that the position is unassailable. Fiction is history, human history, or it is nothing. But it is also more than that; it stands on firmer ground, being based on the reality of forms and the observation of social phenomena, whereas history is based on documents, and the reading of print and handwriting—on secondhand impression. Thus, fiction is nearer truth. But let that pass. A historian may be an artist, too, and a novelist is a historian, the preserver, the keeper, the expounder, of human experience. As is meet for a man of his descent and tradition, Mr. Henry James is the historian of fine consciences.

Of course, this is a general statement; but I don't think its truth will be, or can be, questioned. Its fault is that it leaves so much out; and, besides, Mr. Henry James is much too considerable to be put into the nutshell of a phrase. The fact remains that he has made his choice, and that his choice is justified up to the hilt by the success of his art. He has taken for himself the greater part. The range of a fine conscience covers more good and evil than the range of conscience which may be called, roughly, not fine; a conscience, less troubled by the nice discrimination of shades of conduct. A fine conscience is more concerned with essentials; its triumphs are more perfect, if less profitable, in a worldly sense. There is, in short, more truth in its working for a historian to detect and to show. It is a thing of infinite complication and suggestion. None of these escapes the art of Mr. Henry James. He has mastered the country, his domain, not wild indeed, but full of romantic glimpses, of deep shadows and sunny places. There are no secrets left within his range. He has disclosed them as they should be disclosed—that is, beautifully. And, indeed, ugliness has but little place in this world of his creation. Yet it is always felt in the truthfulness of his art; it is there, it surrounds the scene, it presses close upon it. It is made visible, tangible, in the struggles, in the contacts of the fine consciences, in their perplexities, in the sophism of their mistakes. For a fine conscience is naturally a virtuous one. What is natural about it is just its fineness, and abiding sense of the intangible, ever-present right. It is most visible in their ultimate triumph, in their emergence from miracle, through an energetic act of renunciation. Energetic, not violent; the distinction is wide, enormous, like that between substance and shadow.

Through it all Mr. Henry James keeps a firm hold of the substance, of what is worth having, of what is worth holding. The contrary opinion has been, if not absolutely affirmed, then at least implied, with some frequency. To most of us, living willingly in a sort of intellectual moonlight, in the faintly reflected light of truth, the shadows so firmly renounced by Mr. Henry James's men and women, stand out endowed with extraordinary value, with a value so extraordinary that their rejection offends, by its uncalled-for scrupulousness, those businesslike instincts which a careful Providence has implanted in our breasts. And, apart from that just cause of discontent, it is obvious that a solution by rejection must always present a certain lack of finality, especially startling when contrasted with the usual methods of solution by rewards and punishments, by crowned love, by fortune, by a broken leg or a sudden death. Why the reading public which, as a body, has never laid upon a storyteller the command to be an artist, should demand from him this sham of divine omnipotence, is utterly incomprehensible. But so it is; and these solutions are legitimate inasmuch as they satisfy the desire for finality, for which our hearts yearn, with a longing greater than the longing for the loaves and fishes of this earth. Perhaps the only true desire of mankind, coming thus to light in its hours of leisure, is to be set at rest. One is never set at rest by Mr. Henry James's novels. His books end as an episode in life ends. You remain with the sense of the life still going on; and even the subtle presence of the dead is felt in that silence that comes upon the artist-creation when the last word has been read. It is eminently satisfying, but it is not final. Mr. Henry James, great artist and faithful historian, never attempts the impossible.

FORD MADOX FORD

The Old Man

[1932]

THIRTY years ago the novel was still the newest, as it remains the Cinderella, of art forms. (That of the "movies"
had not yet appeared.) The practice of novel writing had existed for a bare two hundred and fifty years; the novelist was
still regarded as a rogue and vagabond, and the novel as a "waste
of time"—or worse. And the idea of the novel as a work of art,
capable of possessing a form, even as sonnets or sonatas possess
forms—that idea had only existed since 1850, and in the France
of Flaubert alone, at that. Writers had certainly aimed at "pro-
gressions of effect" in short efforts since the days of Margaret
of Navarre; and obviously what the typical English novelist
had always aimed at—if he had aimed at any form at all—and
what the typical English critic looked for—if ever he conde-
scended to look at a novel—was a series of short stories with
linked characters and possibly a culmination. Indeed, that conception of the novel has been forced upon the English novelist
by the commercial exigencies of hundreds of years. The ro-
mances of Shakespeare, novels written for ranted recitation, and
admirable in the technique of that form, were molded by the
necessity for concurrent action in varying places; the curtain
had to be used. So you had the "strong situation," in order that
the psychological stages of Othello should be firm in the hearer's
mind whilst Desdemona was alone before the audience. The
novels of Fielding, of Dickens, and of Thackeray were written
for publication in parts; at the end of every part must come
the "strong situation," to keep the plot in the reader's head until
the first of next month. So with the eminent contemporaries of

[47]

ours in the nineties of the last century; if the writer was to make a living wage he must aim at serialization; for that once again you must have a strong scene before you write "To be Continued," or the reader would not hanker for the next number of the magazine you served. But you do not need to go to commercial fiction to find the origin of the tendency; if the reader has ever lain awake in a long school dormitory or a well-peopled children's bedroom, listening to or telling long, long tales that went on from day to day or from week to week, he will have known, or will have observed, the necessity of retaining the story in the hearer's mind, and to introduce, just before each listener's head sank on the pillow—the "strong situation." Indeed, Scheherazade knew that pressing need.

It was against the tyranny of this convention that Conrad was revolting, when he sought so passionately for the "new form." How often, in those distant days, lamenting the unlikelihood of our making even modest livings by our pens, have we not sighingly acknowledged that serialization was not for us! For I think we both started out with at least this much of a new form in our heads: we considered a novel to be a rendering of an affair. We used to say, I will admit, that a subject must be seized by the throat until the last drop of dramatic possibility was squeezed out of it. I suppose we had to concede that much to the cult of the strong situation. Nevertheless, a novel was the rendering of an affair: of one embroilment, one set of embarrassments, one human coil, one psychological progression. From this the novel got its unity. No doubt it might have its caesura —or even several; but these must be brought about by temperamental pauses, markings of time when the treatment called for them. But the whole novel was to be an exhaustion of aspects, was to proceed to one culmination, to reveal once and for all, in the last sentence—or the penultimate—in the last phrase, or the one before it, the psychological significance of the whole. (Of course, you might have what is called in music the coda.) But it is perfectly obvious that such a treatment of an affair could not cut itself up into strong situations at the end of every four or every seven thousand words. *That* market at least was closed to us.

Ford Madox Ford

I have suggested that we were more alone in our search for the new form than, very likely, we actually were. Mr. Bennett, at least at that date, was engaged in acquiring the immense knowledge of French tricks and devices that his work afterward displayed. And there was always Mr. George Moore.

In the meantime, magisterially and at leisure, in Rye, Henry James was performing the miracles after whose secrets we were merely groping. I don't know why—but we rather ignored that fact. For, in the end, Conrad and I found salvation not in any machined form, but in the sheer attempt to reproduce life as it presents itself to the intelligent observer. I daresay, if we could only perceive it, life has a pattern. I don't mean that of birth, apogee, and death, but a woven symbolism of its own. "The Figure in the Carpet," Henry James called it—and that he saw something of the sort was no doubt the secret of his magic. But, though I walked with and listened to the Master day after day, I remember only one occasion on which he made a remark that was a revelation of his own aims and methods. That I will reserve until it falls in place in the pattern of my own immediate carpet. For the rest, our intercourse resolved itself into my listening silently, and wondering unceasingly at his observation of the littlest things of life.

He would, if he never talked of books, frequently talk of the personalities of their writers—not infrequently in terms of shuddering at their social excess, much as he shuddered at contact with Crane. He expressed intense dislike for Flaubert who "opened his own door in his dressing-gown" and he related, not infrequently, unrepeatable stories of the menages of Maupassant—but he much preferred Maupassant to "poor dear old Flaubert." Of Turgenev's appearance, personality, and habits, he would talk with great tenderness of expression; he called him nearly always "the beautiful Russian genius," and would tell stories of Turgenev's charming attentions to his peasant mistresses. He liked, in fact, persons who were suave when you met them—and I daresay that his preference of that sort colored his literary tastes. He preferred Maupassant to Flaubert because Maupassant was *homme du monde*—or at any rate had *femmes du monde* for his mistresses; and he preferred Turgenev to

The Question of Henry James

either because Turgenev was a quiet aristocrat and an invalid of the German bathing towns to the finger tips. And he liked—he used to say so—people who treated him with proper respect.

Flaubert he hated with a lasting, deep rancor. Flaubert had once abused him unmercifully—over a point in the style of Prosper Mérimée, of all people in the world. You may read about it in the *Correspondence* of Flaubert, and James himself referred to the occasion several times. It seemed to make it all the worse that, just before the outbreak, Flaubert should have opened the front door of his flat to Turgenev and James, in his dressing-gown.

Myself, I suppose he must have liked, because I treated him with deep respect, had a low voice—appeared, in short, a *jeune homme modeste*. Occasionally he would burst out at me with furious irritation, as if I had been a stupid nephew. This would be particularly the case if I ventured to have any opinions about the United States, which, at that date, I had visited much more lately than he had. I remember one occasion very vividly—the place, beside one of the patches of thorn on the Rye road, and his aspect, the brown face with the dark eyes rolling in the whites, the compact, strong figure, the stick raised so as to be dug violently into the road. He had been talking two days before of the provincialism of Washington in the sixties. He said that when one descended the steps of the Capitol in those days *on trébuchait sur des vaches*—one stumbled over cows, as if on a village green. Two days later, I don't know why—I happened to return to the subject of the provincialism of Washington of the sixties. He stopped as if I had hit him, and, with the coldly infuriated tone of a country squire whose patriotism had been outraged, exclaimed:

"Don't talk such *damnable* nonsense!" He really shouted these words with a male fury. And when, slightly outraged myself, I returned to the charge with his own *on trébuchait sur des vaches*, he exclaimed: "I should not have thought you would have wanted to display such ignorance," and hurried off along the road.

I do not suppose that this was as unreasonable a manifestation of patriotism as it appears. No doubt he imagined me in-

capable of distinguishing between material and cultural poverties and I am fairly sure that, at the bottom of his mind lay
the idea that in Washington of the sixties there had been some
singularly good cosmopolitan and diplomatic conversation and
society, whatever the cows might have done outside the Capitol.
Indeed, I know that towards the end of his life, he came to
think that the society of early, self-conscious New England,
with its circumscribed horizon and want of exterior decoration
or furnishings, was a spiritually finer thing than the mannered
Europeanism that had so taken him to its bosom. As these years
went on, more and more, with a sort of trepidation, he hovered
round the idea of a return to the American scene. When I first
knew him you could have imagined no oak more firmly planted
in European soil. But, little by little, when he talked about
America there would come into his tones a slight tremulousness
that grew with the months. I remember once he went to see
some friends—Mrs. and Miss Lafarge, I think—off to New
York from Tilbury Dock. He came back singularly excited,
bringing out a great many unusually complicated sentences.
He had gone over the liner: "And once aboard the lugger . . .
And if . . . Say a toothbrush . . . And circular notes . . .
And something for the night . . ." All this with a sort of dif-
fident shamefacedness.

I fancy that his mannerisms, his involution, whether in speech
or in writing, were due to a settled conviction that, neither in
his public nor in his acquaintance, would he ever find anyone
who would not need talking down to. The desire of the artist,
of the creative writer, is that his words and his "scenes" shall
suggest—of course with precision—far more than they actually
express or project. But, having found that his limpidities, from
Daisy Miller to *The Real Thing*, not only suggested less than he
desired, but carried suggestions entirely unmeant, he gave up
the attempt at impressionism of that type—as if his audiences
had tired him out. So he talked down to us, explaining and explaining, the ramifications of his mind. He was aiming at ex-
plicitness, never at obscurities—as if he were talking to children.

At any rate, then, he had none of that provincialism of the
literary mind which must forever be dragging in allusions to

some book or local custom. If he had found it necessary to allude to one or the other, he explained them and their provenance. In that you saw that he had learned in the same school as Conrad and Stephen Crane. And indeed he had.

It has always seemed to me inscrutable that he should have been so frequently damned for his depicting only one phase of life; as if it were his fault that he was not also Conrad, to write of the sea, or Crane, to project the life of the New York slums. The Old Man knew consummately one form of life; to that he restricted himself. I have heard him talk with extreme exactness and insight of the life of the poor—at any rate of the agricultural poor, for I do not remember ever to have heard him discuss industrialism. But he knew that he did not know enough to treat of farm laborers in his writing. So that, mostly, when he discoursed of these matters he put his observations in the form of question: "Didn't I agree to this?" "Hadn't I found that?"

But indeed, although I have lived amongst agricultural laborers a good deal at one time or another, I would cheerfully acknowledge that his knowledge—at any rate of their psychologies—had a great deal more insight than my own. He had such an extraordinary gift for observing minutiae—and a gift still more extraordinary for making people talk. I have heard the secretary of a golf club, a dour, silent man who never addressed five words to myself though I was one of his members, talk for twenty minutes to the Master about a new bunker that he was thinking of making at the fourteenth hole. And James had never touched a niblick in his life. It was the same with market women, tram conductors, shipbuilders' laborers, auctioneers. I have stood by and heard them talk to him for hours. Indeed, I am fairly certain that he once had a murder confessed to him. But he needed to stand on extraordinarily firm ground before he would think that he knew a world. And what he knew he rendered, along with its amenities, its gentlefolkishness, its pettinesses, its hypocrisies, its make-believes. He gives you an immense—and an increasingly tragic—picture of a leisured society that is fairly unavailing, materialist, emasculated—and doomed. No one was more aware of all that than he.

Ford Madox Ford

Stevie [1] used to rail at English literature, as being one immense, petty, parlor game. Our books he used to say were written by men who never wanted to go out of drawing rooms for people who wanted to live at perpetual tea parties. Even our adventure stories, colonial fictions, and tales of the boundless prairie were conducted in that spirit. The criticism was just enough. It was possible that James never wanted to live outside tea parties—but the tea parties that he wanted were debating circles of a splendid aloofness, of an immense human sympathy, and of a beauty that you do not find in Putney—or in Passy!

It was his tragedy that no such five o'clock ever sounded for him on the timepiece of this world. And that is no doubt the real tragedy of all of us—of all societies—that we never find in our Spanish Castle our ideal friends living in an assured and permanent Republic. Crane's utopia, but not his literary method, was different. He gave you the pattern in—and the reverse of—the carpet in physical life, in wars, in slums, in western saloons, in a world where the "gun" was the final argument. The life that Conrad gives you is somewhere halfway between the two; it is dominated—but less dominated—by the revolver than that of Stephen Crane, and dominated, but less dominated, by the moral scruple than that of James. But the approach to life is the same with all these three; they show you that disillusionment is to be found alike at the tea table, in the slum, and on the tented field. That is of great service to our Republic.

[1] Stephen Crane. *Ed.*

PERCY LUBBOCK

The Mind of an Artist [1]

[1920]

WHEN Henry James wrote the reminiscences of his youth he showed conclusively, what indeed could be doubtful to none who knew him, that it would be impossible for anyone else to write his life. His life was no mere succession of facts, such as could be compiled and recorded by another hand; it was a densely knit cluster of emotions and memories, each one steeped in lights and colors thrown out by the rest, the whole making up a picture that no one but himself could dream of undertaking to paint. Strictly speaking this may be true of every human being; but in most lives experience is taken as it comes and left to rest in the memory where it happens to fall. Henry James never took anything as it came; the thing that happened to him was merely the point of departure for a deliberate, and as time went on a more and more masterly, creative energy, which could never leave a sight or sound of any kind until it had been looked at and listened to with absorbed attention, pondered in thought, linked with its associations, and which did not spend itself until the remembrance had been crystallized in expression, so that it could then be appropriated like a tangible object. To recall his habit of talk is to become aware that he never ceased creating his life in this way as it was lived; he was always engaged in the poetic fashioning of experience, turning his share of impressions into rounded and lasting images. From the beginning this had been his only method of dealing with existence, and in later years it even meant a tax upon his strength with which he had consciously to reckon. Not long

[1] Written as the Introduction to *The Letters of Henry James*.

before his death he confessed that at last he found himself too much exhausted for the "wear and tear of discrimination"; and the phrase indicates the strain upon him of the mere act of living. Looked at from without his life was uneventful enough, the even career of a man of letters, singularly fortunate in all his circumstances. Within, it was a cycle of vivid and incessant adventure, known only to himself except in so far as he himself put it into words. So much of it as he left unexpressed is lost, therefore, like a novel that he might have written, but of which there can now be no question, since its only possible writer is gone.

Fortunately a great part of it survives in his letters, and it is of these that his biography must be composed. The material is plentiful, for he was at all times a copious letter writer, overflowing into swift and easy improvisation to his family and to the many friends with whom he corresponded regularly. His letters have been widely preserved, and several thousands of them have passed through my hands, ranging from his twenty-fifth year until within a few days of his last illness. They give as complete a portrait of him as we can now hope to possess. His was a nature in which simplicity and complexity were very curiously contrasted, and it would need all his own power of fusing innumerable details into coherency to create a picture that would seem sufficient to those who knew him. Yet even his letters, varied as they are, give full expression to one side of his life only, the side that he showed to the world he lived in and loved. After all the prodigal display of mind that is given in these volumes, the free outpouring of curiosity and sympathy and power, a close reader must still be left with the sense that something, the most essential and revealing strain, is little more than suggested here and there. The daily drama of his work, with all the comfort and joy it brought him, does not very often appear as more than an undertone to the conversation of the letters. It was like a mystery to which he was dedicated, but of which he shrank from speaking quite openly. Much as he always delighted in sociable communion, citizen of the world, child of urbanity as he was, all his friends must have felt that at heart he lived in solitude and that few were ever admitted into the inner shrine of his labor. There it was, nevertheless, that he lived most intensely and most serenely. In outward matters he was constantly haunted by anxiety and never looked forward with confidence; he was of those to whom the future is always ominous, who dread the treachery of apparent calm even more than actual ill weather. It was very different in the presence of his work. There he never knew the least failure of assurance; he threw his full weight on the belief that supported him and it was never shaken.

That belief was in the sanctity and sufficiency of the life of art. It was a conviction that needed no reasoning and he accepted it without question. It was absolute for him that the work of the imagination was the highest and most honorable calling conceivable, being indeed nothing less than the actual creation of life out of the void. He did not scruple to claim that except through art there is no life that can be known or appraised. It is the artist who takes over the deed, so called, from the doer, to give it back again in the form in which it can be seen and measured for the first time; without the brain that is able to close round the loose unappropriated fact and render all its aspects, the fact itself does not exist for us. This was the standard below which Henry James would never allow the conception of his office to drop, and he had the reward of complete exemption from any chill of misgiving. His life as a creator of art, alone with his work, was one of unclouded happiness. It might be hampered and hindered by external accidents, but none of them could touch the real core of his security, which was his faith in his vocation and his knowledge of his genius. These certainties remained with him always, and he would never trifle with them in any mood. His impatience with argument on the whole aesthetic claim was equally great, whether it was argument in defense of the sanctuary or in profanation of it. Silence, seclusion, concentration, he held to be the only fitting answer for an artist. He disliked the idea that the service of art should be questioned and debated in the open, still more to see it organized and paraded and publicly celebrated, as though the world could do it any acceptable honor. He had as little in common with those who would use the artistic profession to persuade and proselytize as with those who would brandish it defiantly in the face of the vulgar.

Thus it is that he is seldom to be heard giving voice to the matters which most deeply occupied him. He preferred to dwell with them apart and to leave them behind when he emerged. Sometimes he would drop a word that showed what was passing beneath; sometimes, on a particular challenge, or to one in whom he felt an understanding sympathy, he would speak out with impressive authority. But generally he liked to enter into other people's thought and to meet them on their own ground. There his natural kindliness and his keen dramatic interest were both satisfied at once. He enjoyed friendship, his letters show how freely and expansively; and with his steady and vigilant eye he watched the play of character. He was insatiable for anything that others could give him from their personal lives. Whatever he could seize in this way was food for his own ruminating fancy; he welcomed any grain of reality, any speck of significance round which his imagination could pile its rings. It was very noticeable how promptly and eagerly he would reach out to such things, as they floated by in talk; it was as though he feared to leave them to inexpert hands and felt that other people could hardly be trusted with their own experience. He remembered how much of his time he had spent in exploring their consciousness when he spoke of himself as a confirmed spectator, one who looked on from the brink instead of plunging on his own account; but if this seemed a pale substitute for direct contact he knew very well that it was a much richer and more adventurous life, really, than it is given to most people to lead. There is no life to the man who does not feel it, no adventure to the man who cannot see the whole of it; the greatest share goes to the man who can taste it most fully, however it reaches him. Henry James might sometimes look back, as he certainly did, with a touch of ruefulness in reflecting on all the experience he had only enjoyed at second hand; but he could never doubt that what he had he possessed much more truly than any of those from whom he had taken it. There was no hour in which he was not alive with the whole of his sensibility; he could scarcely persuade himself that he might have had time for more. And indeed at other moments he would admit that he had lived in the way that was at any rate the right way for him. Even his very twinges of regret were not wasted; like everything else they helped to swell the sum of life, as they did to such purpose for Strether, the "poor sensitive gentleman" of *The Ambassadors,* whose manner of living was very near his creator's.

These letters, then, while they show at every point the abundant life he led in his surroundings, have to be read with the remembrance that the central fact of all, the fact that gave everything else its meaning to himself, is that of which least is told. The gap, moreover, cannot be filled from other sources; he seems to have taken pains to leave nothing behind him that should reveal this privacy. He put forth his finished work to speak for itself and swept away all the traces of its origin. There was a high pride in his complete lack of tenderness towards the evidence of past labor—the notes, manuscripts, memoranda that a man of letters usually accumulates and that show him in the company of his work. It is only to the stroke of chance which left two of his novels unfinished that we owe the outspoken colloquies with himself, since published, over the germination of those stories—a door of entry into the presence of his imagination that would have been summarily closed if he had lived to carry out his plan. And though in the prefaces to the collected edition of his works we have what is perhaps the most comprehensive statement ever made of the life of art, a *biographia literaria* without parallel for fullness and elaboration, he was there dealing with his books in retrospect, as a critic from without, analyzing and reconstructing his own creations; or if he went further than this, and touched on the actual circumstances of their production, it was because these had for him the charm of an old romance, remote enough to be recalled without indiscretion. So it is that while in a sense he was the most personal of writers—for he could not put three words together without marking them as his own and giving them the very ring of his voice—yet, compared with other such deliberate craftsmen as Stevenson or Gustave Flaubert, he baffles and evades curiosity about the private affairs of his work. If curiosity were merely

futile it would be fitting to suppress the chance relic I shall offer
in a moment—for it so happens that a single glimpse of unique
clarity is open to us, revealing him as no one saw him in his life.
But the attempt to picture the mind of an artist is only an intrusion if it is carried into trivial and inessential things; it can
never be pushed too far, as Henry James would have been the
first to maintain, into a real sharing of his aesthetic life.

The relic in question consists of certain penciled pages, found
among his papers, in which he speaks with only himself for
listener. They belong to the same order as the notes for the
unfinished novels, but they are even more informal and confi-
dential. Nothing else of the kind seems to have survived; the
schemes and motives that must have swarmed in his brain, far
too numerously for notation, have all vanished but this one. At
Rye, some years before the end, he began one night to feel his
way toward a novel which he had in mind—a subject afterward
abandoned in the form projected at first. The rough notes in
which he casts about to clear the ground are mostly filled with
the mere details of his plan—the division of the action, the characters required, a tentative scenario. These I pass over in order
to quote some passages where he suddenly breaks away, leaves
his imaginary scene, and surrenders to the awe and wonder of
finding himself again, where he has so often stood before, on the
threshold and brink of creation. It is as though for once, at an
hour of midnight silence and solitude, he opened the innermost
chamber of his mind and stood face to face with his genius.
There is no moment of all his days in which it is now possible to
approach him more closely. Such a moment represented to himself the pith of life—the first tremor of inspiration, in which he
might be almost afraid to stir or breathe, for fear of breaking
the spell, if it were not that he goes to meet it with a peculiar
confidence.

"I take this up again after an interruption—I in fact throw
myself upon it under the *secousse* of its being brought home to
me even more than I expected that my urgent material reasons
for getting settled at productive work again are of the very
most imperative. Je m'entends—I have had a discomfiture

The Question of Henry James

(through a stupid misapprehension of my own indeed;) and I must now take up projected tasks—this long time *entrevus* and brooded over, with the firmest possible hand. I needn't expatiate on this—on the sharp consciousness of this hour of the dimly dawning New Year, I mean; I simply make an appeal to all the powers and forces and divinities to whom I've ever been loyal and who haven't failed me yet—after all: never, never yet! Infinitely interesting—and yet somehow with a beautiful sharp poignancy in it that makes it strange and rather exquisitely formidable, as with an unspeakable deep agitation, the whole artistic question that comes up for me in the train of this idea . . . of the *donnée* for a situation that I began here the other day to fumble out. I mean I come back, I come back yet again and again, to my only seeing it in the dramatic way—as I can only see everything and anything now; the way that filled my mind and floated and uplifted me when a fortnight ago I gave my few indications to X. Momentary side-winds—things of no real authority—break in every now and then to put their inferior little questions to me; but I come back, I come back, as I say, I all throbbingly and yearningly and passionately, oh mon bon, come back to this way that is clearly the only one in which I can do anything now, and that will open out to me more and more, and that has overwhelming reasons pleading all beautifully in its breast. What really happens is that the closer I get to the problem of the application of it in any particular case, the more I get *into* that application, so that the more doubts and torments fall away from me, the more I know where I am, the more everything spreads and shines and draws me on and I'm justified of my logic and my passion. . . . Causons, causons, mon bon—oh celestial, soothing, sanctifying process, with all the high sane forces of the sacred time fighting, through it, on my side! Let me fumble it gently and patiently out—with fever and fidget laid to rest—as in all the old enchanted months! It only looms, it only shines and shimmers, *too* beautiful and too interesting; it only hangs there too rich and too full and with too much to give and to pay; it only presents itself too admirably and too vividly, too straight and square and vivid, as a little organic and effective Action. . . .

Percy Lubbock

"Thus just these first little wavings of the oh so tremulously passionate little old wand (now!) make for me, I feel, a sort of promise of richness and beauty and variety; a sort of portent of the happy presence of the elements. The good days of last August and even my broken September and my better October come back to me with their gauge of divine possibilities, and I welcome these to my arms, I press them with unutterable tenderness. I seem to emerge from these recent bad days—the fruit of blind accident—and the prospect clears and flushes, and my poor blest old Genius pats me so admirably and lovingly on the back that I turn, I screw round, and bend my lips to passionately, in my gratitude, kiss its hands."

To the exaltation of this wonderful unbosoming he had been brought by fifty years of devout and untiring service. Where so little is heard of it all, the amount of patience and energy that he had consecrated to it might easily be mistaken. His immense industry all through his crowded London years passes almost unnoticed, so little it seems to conflict with this life in the world, his share in which, with the close friendships he formed and the innumerable relations he cultivated, could have been no fuller if he had had nothing to do but to amuse himself with the spectacle. In one way, however, it is possible to divine how heavily the weight of his work pressed on him. The change that divides the general tone and accent of his younger and middle age from that of his later years is too striking to be overlooked. The impression is unmistakable that for a long while, indeed until he was almost an old man, he felt the constant need of husbanding and economizing his resources; so that except to those who knew him intimately he was apt to seem a little cold and cautious, hesitating to commit himself freely or to allow promiscuous claims. Later on all this was very different. There were certain habits of reserve, perhaps, that he never threw off; all his friends remember, for example, how carefully he distinguished the different angles of his affection, so to call them— adjusting his various relations as though in fear lest they should cross each other and form an embarrassing complexity. Yet any scruples or precautions of this sort that still hung about him only enhanced the large and genial authority of his presence. There seemed to have come a time when after long preparation and cogitation he was able to relax and to enjoy the fruit of his labor. Not indeed that his labor was over; it never was that, while strength lasted; but he gave the effect of feeling himself to be at length completely the master of his situation, at ease and at home in his world. The new note is very perceptible in the letters, which broaden out with opulent vigor as time goes on, reaching their best comparatively late.

That at last he felt at home was doubtless indeed the literal truth, and it was enough to account for this ample liberation of spirit. His decision to settle in Europe, the great step of his life, was inevitable, though it was not taken without long reflection; but it was none the less a decision for which he had to pay heavily, as he was himself very well aware. If he regarded his own part as that of an onlooker, the sense in which he understood observation was to the highest degree exacting. He watched indeed, but he watched with every faculty, and he intended that every thread of intelligence he could throw out to seize the truth of the old historic world should be as strong as instruction, study, general indoctrination could make it. It would be useless for him to live where the human drama most attracted him unless he could grasp it with an assured hand; and he could never do this if he was to remain a stranger and a sojourner, merely feeding on the picturesque surface of appearances. To justify his expatriation he must work his own life completely into the texture of his new surroundings, and the story of his middle years is to be read as the most patient and laborious of attempts to do so. Its extraordinary success need hardly be insisted on; its failure, necessary and foredoomed, from certain points of view, is perhaps not less obvious. But the great fact of interest is the sight of him taking up the task with eyes, it is needless to say, fully open to all its demands, and never resting until he could be certain of having achieved all that was possible. So long as he was in the thick of it, the task occupied the whole of his attention. He took it with full seriousness; there never was a scholar more immersed in research than was Henry James in the study of his chosen world.

There were times indeed when he might be thought to take it even more seriously than the case required. The world is not used to such deference from a rare critical talent, and it certainly has much less respect for its own standards than Henry James had, or seemed to have. His respect was, of course, very freely mingled with irony, and yet it would be rash to say that his irony preponderated. He probably felt that this, in his condition, was a luxury which he could only afford within limits. He could never forget that he had somehow to make up to himself for arriving as an alien from a totally different social climate; for his own satisfaction he had to wake and toil while others slept, keeping his ever-ready and rebellious criticism for an occasional hour of relief.

The world with which he thus sought to identify himself was a small affair, by most of our measurements. It was a circle of sensibilities that it might be easy to dismiss as hypertrophied and over-civilized, too deeply smothered in the veils of artificial life to repay so much patient attention. Yet the little world of urbane leisure satisfied him because he found a livelier interest, always, in the results and effects and implications of things than in the groundwork itself; so that the field of study he desired was that in which initial forces had traveled furthest from their prime, passing step by step from their origin to the level where, diffused and transformed, they were still just discernible to acute perception. It is not through any shy timidity that so often in his books he requires us to infer the presence of naked emotion from the faintest stirrings of an all but unruffled surface; it is because these monitory signals, transmitted from so far, tell a story that would be weakened by a directer method. The tiny movement that is the last expression of an act or a fact carries within it the history of all it has passed through on the way—a treasure of interest that the act, the fact in itself, had not possessed. And so in the social scene, wherever its crude beginnings have been left furthest behind, wherever its forms have been most rubbed and toned by the hands of succeeding generations, there he found, not an obliteration of sharp character, but a positive enhancement of it, with the whole of its past crowded into its bosom. The kind of life, therefore, that might have been thought too trifling to bear the weight of his grave and powerful scrutiny was exactly the life that he pursued for its expressive value. He clung to civilization, he was faithful throughout to a few yards of town-pavement, not because he was scared by the rough freedom of the wild, but rather because he was impatient of its insipidity. He is very often to be heard crying out against the tyrannous claims of his world, when they interfere with his work, his leisure, his health; but at the moment of greatest revulsion he never suggests that the claims may be fraudulent after all, or that this small corner of modernity is not the best and most fruitful that the age has to show.

It must be a matter of pride to an English reader that this corner happened to be found among ourselves. Henry James came to London, however, more by a process of exhaustion than by deliberate choice, and plenty of chastening considerations for a Londoner will appear in his letters. If he elected to live among thick English wits rather than in any nimbler atmosphere, it was at first largely because English ways and manners lay more open to an explorer than the closer, compacter societies of the mainland. Gradually, as we know well, his affection was kindled into devoted loyalty. It remained true, none the less, that with much that is common ground among educated people of our time and place he was never really in touch. One has only to think of the part played, in the England he frequented, by school and college, by country homes, by church and politics and professions, to understand how much of the ordinary consciousness was closed to him. Yet it is impossible to say that these limitations were imposed on him only because he was a stranger among strangers; they belonged to the conditions of his being from much further back. They were implied in his queer unanchored youth, in which he and his greatly gifted family had been able to grow in the free exercise of their talents without any of the foundations of settled life. Henry James's genius opened and flourished in the void. His ripe wisdom and culture seemed to have been able to dispense entirely with the mere training that most people require before they can feel secure in their critical outlook and sense of proportion. There could be no better proof of the fact that imagination, if only there is enough of it, will do the work of all the other faculties unaided. Whatever were the gaps in his knowledge—knowledge of life generally, and of the life of the mind in particular—his imagination covered them all. And so it was that without even acquiring a thousand things that go to the making of a full experience and a sound taste, he yet enjoyed and possessed everything that it was in them to give.

His taste, indeed, his judgment of quality, seems to have been bestowed upon him in its essentials like a gift of nature. From the very first he was sure of his taste and could account for it. His earliest writing shows, if anything, too large a portion of tact and composure; a critic might have said that such a perfect control of his means was not the most hopeful sign in a young author. Henry James reversed the usual procedure of a beginner, keeping warily to matter well within his power of management—and this is observable too in his early letters—until he was ready to deal with matter more robust. In his instinct for perfection he never went wrong—never floundered into raw enthusiasms, never lost his way, never had painfully to recover himself; he traveled steadily forward with no need of guidance, enriching himself with new impressions and wasting none of them. He accepted nothing that did not minister in some way to the use of his gifts; whatever struck him as impossible to assimilate to these he passed by without a glance. He could not be tempted by any interest unrelated to the central line of his work. He had enough even so, he felt, to occupy a dozen lives, and he grudged every moment that did not leave its deposit of stuff appropriate to his purpose. The play of his thought was so ample and ardent that it disguised his resolute concentration; he responded so lavishly and to so much that he seemed ready to take up and transform and adorn whatever was offered him. But this in truth was far from the fact, and by shifting the recollection one may see the impatient gesture with which he would sweep aside the distraction that made no appeal to him. It was natural that he should care nothing for any abstract speculation or inquiry; he was an artist throughout, desiring only the refracted light of human imperfection,

The Question of Henry James

never the purity of colorless reason. More surprising was his refusal, for it was almost that, of the appeal of music—and not wordless music only, but even the song and melody of poetry. It cannot be by accident that poetry scarcely appears at all in such a picture of a literary life as is given by his letters. The purely lyrical ear seems to have been strangely sealed in him— he often declared as much himself. And poetry in general, though he could be deeply stirred by it, he inclined to put away from him, perhaps for the very reason that it meant too forcible a deflection from the right line of his energy. All this careful gathering up of his powers, in any case, this determined deafness to irrelevant voices, gave a commanding warrant to the critical panoply of his later life. His certainty and consistency, his principle, his intellectual integrity—by all these the pitch of his opinions, wherever he delivered them, reached a height that was unforgettably impressive.

I have tried to touch, so far as possible, on the different strains in Henry James's artistic experience; but to many who read these letters it will be another aspect altogether that his name first recalls. They will remember how much of his life was lived in his relations with his countless friends, and how generously he poured out his best for them. But if, as I have suggested, much of his mind appears fitfully and obscurely in his letters, this side is fully irradiated from first to last. Never, surely, has any circle of friendship received so magnificent a tribute of expressed affection and sympathy. It was lavished from day to day, and all the resources of his art were drawn upon to present it with due honor. As time goes on a kind of personal splendor shines through the correspondence, which only becomes more natural, more direct a communication of himself, as it is uttered with increasing mastery. The familiar form of the letter was changed under his hand into what may really be called a new province of art, a revelation of possibilities hitherto unexplored. Perfect in expression as they are, these letters are true extemporizations, thrown off always at great speed, as though with a single sweep of the hand, for all their richness of texture and roundness of phrase. At their most characteristic they are like free flights of virtuosity, flung out with

Percy Lubbock

enjoyment in the hours of a master's ease; and the abundance
of his creative vigor is shown by the fact that there should
always be so much more of it to spare, even after the exhausting
strain of his regular work. But the greater wonder is that this
liberal gesture never became mechanical, never a fixed manner
displayed for any and all alike, without regard to the particular
mind addressed. Not for a moment does he forget to whom he
is speaking; he writes in the thought of his correspondent, always perceptibly turning to that relation, singled out for the
time from all the rest. Each received of his best, but some peculiar, inalienable share in it.

If anything can give to those who did not know him an impression of Henry James's talk, it will be some of the finest of
these later letters. One difference indeed is immediately to be
marked. His pondering hesitation as he talked, his search over
the whole field of expression for the word that should do justice to the picture forming in his mind—this gives place in the
letters to a flow unchecked, one sonorous phrase uncoiling itself
after another without effort. Pen in hand, or, as he finally preferred, dictating to his secretary, it was apparently easier for
him to seize upon the images he sought to detach, one by one,
from the clinging and populous background of his mind. In
conversation the effort seemed to be greater, and save in rare
moments of exceptional fervor—no one who heard him will
forget how these recurred more and more in the last year of
his life, under the deep excitement of the war—he liked to take
his time in working out his thought with due deliberation. But
apart from this, the letters exactly reflect the color and con-
tour of his talk—his grandiose courtesy, his luxuriant phrase-
ology, his relish for some extravagantly colloquial turn embedded in a Ciceronian period, his humor at once so majestic and
so burly. Intercourse with him was not quite easy, perhaps; his
style was too hieratic, too richly adorned and arrayed for that.
But it was enough to surrender simply to the current of his
thought; the listener felt himself gathered up and cared for—
felt that Henry James assumed all the responsibility and would
deal with the occasion in his own way. That way was never to

[67]

The Question of Henry James

give a mere impersonal display of his own, but to create and develop a reciprocal relation, to both sides of which he was more than capable of doing the fullest justice. No words seem satisfactory in describing the dominance he exerted over any scene in which he figured—yet exerted by no overriding or ignoring of the presence of others, rather with the quickest, most apprehending susceptibility to it. But better than by any description is this memory imparted by the eloquent roll and ring of his letters.

He grew old in the honor of a wide circle of friends of all ages, and of a public which, if small, was deeply devoted. He stood so completely outside the evolution of English literature that his position was special and unrelated, but it was a position at last unanimously acknowledged. Signs of the admiration and respect felt for him by all who held the belief in the art of letters, even by those whose line of development most diverged from his—these he unaffectedly enjoyed, and many came to him. None the less he knew very well that in all he most cared for, in what was to him the heart and essence of life, he was solitary to the end. However much his work might be applauded, the spirit of rapt and fervent faith in which it was conceived was a hermitage, so he undoubtedly felt, that no one else had perceived or divined. His story of the Figure in the Carpet was told of himself; no one brought him what he could accept as true and final comprehension. He could never therefore feel that he had reached a time when his work was finished and behind him. Old age only meant an imagination more crowded than ever, a denser throng of shapes straining to be released before it was too late. He bitterly resented the hindrances of ill health, during some of his last years, as an interruption, a curtailment of the span of his activity; there were so many and so far better books that he still wished to write. His interest in life, growing rather than weakening, clashed against the artificial restraints, as they seemed, of physical age; whenever these were relaxed, it leaped forward to work again. The challenge of the war with Germany roused him to a height of passion he had never touched before in the outer world; and

Percy Lubbock

if the strain of it exhausted his strength, as well it might, it gave him one last year of the fullest and deepest experience, perhaps, that he had ever known. It wore out his body, which was too tired and spent to live longer; but he carried away the power of his spirit still in its prime.

STUART P. SHERMAN

The Aesthetic Idealism of Henry James

[1917]

"NO one has the faintest conception of what I am trying for," says the celebrated author in *The Death of the Lion*, "and not many have read three pages that I've written; but I must dine with them first—they'll find out when they've time." The words are tinged with Henry James's own disdain of the fashionable world which wears, and wears out, a man of genius like a spangle on its robe. Perhaps twenty years ago everyone had read, or had attempted to read, a recent novel of his; but there has come up a generation of young people who have been permitted, with the connivance of critics, to concede the excellence of his earlier productions and the "impossibility" of his later ones without looking into either. Shortly before his death he emerged for the general public from his obscure memoir writing, and stood for a moment conspicuous on the skyline— a dark, august figure bowed in devout allegiance beneath the English flag; then with a thunder of ordnance not made for *his* passing he slipped below the horizon. In the hour of trial he had given to England a beautiful gesture which derived much of its interest from his lifelong refusal to commit himself to any cause but art. Though the adoption of English citizenship by an American would have excited in ordinary circumstances the profane wit of our paragraph writers, the gravity of this occasion chastened them; and when, a few months later, his death called for comment, many of them clutched at this transferal of allegiance as the last, if not the only, intelligible performance of his that was known to them. Some of them, to be sure, remembered, or said they remembered, *Daisy Miller* as a "perfect

Stuart P. Sherman

little thing of its kind," or professed a not unpleasant acquaintance with *The Portrait of a Lady,* or even exhibited a vague consciousness that the novelist had treated extensively the "international situation"; but in general they betrayed their "unpreparedness" for defining his talent and valuing his accomplishment.

Criticism should have declared by this time, and should have declared with emphasis and authority, what Henry James was "trying for." It should also have declared whether, when he slipped below the horizon, he sank into the deepening shadows of literary history, or whether he passed on into a widening world of light—the Great Good Place of a grateful and enlightened posterity which will not dine with him but which will read him. May we securely let him pass while we go on to something better; or shall we find, if we go on, that he is the something better to which we come at last? There are wide differences of opinion in the critical jury. Mr. Brownell, who has said a multitude of penetrating things about his mind and his art, and who is, one should suppose, the critic in America best qualified to enjoy and to value him, does not conceal his quiet hope and expectation that among the novelists of the future we shall not meet his like again. Professor Pattee, who is "out" for American local colors and big native American ideas, declares in so many words that Henry James's novels "really accomplish nothing." Recent English criticism strikes up in another key. Mr. Ford Madox Hueffer promises him immortality, if there is any immortality for extraordinarily fine work—a point about which he is doubtful; but he struggles to his handsome conclusion through such fantastic arguments, with such explosions of temper and erratic judgment, through such a stream of "God-forbid's" and "Thank-god's" and "God-knows's," with such ostentatious self-advertisement, and with such a display of the "new vulgarity," the new literary bad manners, that one wonders how he ever came to occupy himself with an author so dedicated to refinement. The little book of Miss Rebecca West, an acutely positive and intensely glowing young "intellectual," has delightful merits: its adverse criticism is cuttingly phrased if not always precisely keen, its appreciative passages are full of fresh

The Question of Henry James

ardor and luminous if not always illuminating imagery; it holds up a candle and swings a censer in the principal niches and chapels of the wide-arching cathedral upon which the builder toiled for half a century; but it rather evades the task of presenting a central and comprehensive view—of explaining, in short, in the honor of what deity the whole edifice was constructed.

I

Let us cut an avenue to the inner shrine by removing from consideration some of the objects for which most of Henry James's American and English compatriots profess a pious veneration. He has insulted all the popular gods of democratic society—for example, the three persons of the French revolutionary trinity and the "sovereign people" collectively. Captain Sholto, almost unique among his characters in uttering a political thought, must express pretty nearly his creator's position when he says, "I believe those that are on top the heap are better than those that are under it, that they mean to stay there, and that if they are not a pack of poltroons they will." It would be difficult to name an American author more nearly devoid of emotional interest in the general mass of humanity. His attitude toward the "submerged tenth" is chiefly established by his silence with regard to it. In *The Princess Casamassima,* one of the rare places in which he permits a view of the dark netherward of society to fall upon the eye of a sensitive observer, this is the reported reaction: "Some of the women and girls, in particular, were appalling—saturated with alcohol and vice, brutal, bedraggled, obscene. 'What remedy but another deluge, what alchemy but annihilation?' he asked himself as he went his way; and he wondered what fate there could be, in the great scheme of things, for a planet overgrown with such vermin, what redemption but to be hurled against a ball of consuming fire." The passage is a little deficient—is it not?—in warm fraternal feeling. Let us round out this impression with the reported reaction of a sensitive observer in *The Madonna of the Future* to a glimpse of free life in Rome: "Cats and monkeys, monkeys and cats; all human life is there!"

Stuart P. Sherman

These sensitive observers doubtless had cause for a shudder of
revulsion, and dramatic reason as well. Their behavior becomes
interesting when one compares it with James's personal account
in *London Notes* of his own attitude towards a very different
scene—the preparations for Victoria's Jubilee. "The foremost,
the immense impression is, of course, the constant, the permanent, the ever-supreme—the impression of that greatest
glory of our race, its passionate feeling for trade. . . . London
has found in this particular chapter of the career of its aged
sovereign only an enormous selfish advertisement." Later he reports that he has been taking refuge from the Jubilee in novel
reading. The great thing to be said for the novelists, he adds, is
"that at any given moment they offer us another world, another
consciousness, an experience that, *as effective as the dentist's
ether, muffles the ache of the actual* and, by helping us to an
interval, tides us over and makes us face, in the return to the
inevitable, a combination that may at least have changed." Was
it a pose to speak of fiction as an ethereal pause in the midst of
the perpetual toothache of the actual—and of a great patriotic
demonstration as a peculiarly sharp toothache? Or was it
"American humor"? I do not remember that anyone has
charged James with being a *poseur*. The pose at any rate is curiously of a piece with his saying to John Hay, who had been received with an "ovation" on his arrival in Southampton, "What
impression does it make in your mind to have these insects
creeping about you and saying things to you?"

A partial explanation of this disgust and this detachment
from the major interests of the majority of men may be found
in a half-dozen familiar facts of his biographical record. His
whole life was an evasion of circumstances. The ordinary road
to character in a democracy is through struggle and conflict.
The ordinary man is molded, battered, or squeezed into his shape
by struggling for an education, a livelihood, a wife, a family,
a "place in the world." As he approaches middle age he finds
himself becoming stable, adjusted, solid through the complex
pressure of commonplace responsibilities as husband, parent,
businessman, vestryman, property owner, and voter and payer
of taxes. In order to hold up his head he has had to put down

The Question of Henry James

his roots among all the institutional bases of society; he has had
to become vitally attached to the all-embracing not-himself.
The leading idea in the elder James's plan for his son's life seems
to have been to rescue him from the typical democratic process
in order to open to him some finer destiny: to provide him with
comfortable means and ample leisure, to save him from every
exacting pressure, to preserve him from the stamp of any definite educational system, by perpetual migrations to snap the
root of local attachments, to postpone for him as long as possible the choice of a career, so that at last the young man should
be whatever he was and do whatever he did by the free impulse
of his own spirit. The perfect working of this plan was probably marred by a physical accident at the time of the Civil War,
which, as Henry James circuitously explains, assigned him to
the role of an engrossed spectator. Whatever the significance of
this incident, the result of the plan of tasting life in New York,
Boston, Geneva, London, Paris, Rome, Florence, and Venice was
to set up an endless process of observation, comparison, discrimination, selection, and appreciation—a process which for this
highly civilized, highly sensitized young spirit, became all absorbing, and made of him a fastidious connoisseur of experience,
an artistic celibate to whose finer sense promiscuous mixing in
the gross welter of the world was wearisome and unprofitable.

There is no getting round the fact that he was as prodigiously
"superior" inside as he was outside the field of art. In his recent,
much-quoted essay on the new novel he has the air of a conscious old master condescending for the nonce to notice "the
rough and tumble 'output'" of the young vulgar democratic
herd. A false note in Miss West's treatment of his character is
her remark that he lacked "that necessary attribute of the good
critic, the power to bid bad authors to go to the devil." Mr.
Brownell, on the other hand, puts him at the head of American
criticism. He sent authors to their appropriate places so civilly
and suavely that they probably failed frequently to notice
where they were sent; but no critic ever more remorselessly sent
to the devil bad authors, mediocre authors, and even very distinguished authors. In his later years, he very blandly, very
courteously, sent the whole general public to the devil. He was

Stuart P. Sherman

mortally weary of the general public's obtuseness; he despaired
of the general public and despised it. At the same time he reit-
erated in his stories, his critical articles, and in the prefaces to
the New York edition of his work challenges and entreaties to
the critical few to come and find him.

II

In that fascinating work *The Figure in the Carpet* he depicts,
for criticism, what he would have called his own "case." He
presents there, amid various intensifications of interest, Hugh
Vereker, a master novelist, head and shoulders above his contemporaries; so that even his devoutest admirers and his most
studious critics miss the thing that he has written his books
"most *for*." "Isn't there," he says to one of them, "for every
writer a particular thing of that sort, the thing that most makes
him apply himself, the thing without the effort to achieve which
he wouldn't write at all, the very passion of his passion, the part
of the business in which, for him, the flame of art burns most
intensely? . . . There's an idea in my work without which I
wouldn't have given a straw for the whole job. . . . It
stretches, this little trick of mine, from book to book, and
everything else comparatively plays over the surface of it. The
order, the form, the texture of my books will perhaps constitute
for the initiated a complete representation of it. So it is naturally the thing for the critic to look for. It strikes me," Vereker
adds—smiling but inscrutable, "even as the thing for the critic
to find."

The thing which, as it seems to me, James hoped chiefly that
his critics would some day recognize is not that he is a great
stylist, or a learned historian of manners, or the chief of the
realists, or a master of psychological analysis. All these things
have been noted and asserted by various more or less irreligious
strollers through that cathedral-like edifice to which we have
likened his works. The thing which he, as the high priest sol-
emnly ministering before the high altar, implored someone to
observe and to declare is that he adored beauty and absolutely
nothing else in the world. To the discovery of beauty he dedi-

cates his observation, his analysis, his marvelous and all too little recognized imaginative energy. That is why he sends the rest of the world to the devil, that is his romance, that is his passion, that is why when he discusses his own creations he talks veritably like a soul in bliss. The intimate relation of his fiction to modern realities beguiles the uncritical reader into an erroneous notion that he is a "transcriber," a literal copyist, of life. What in his prefaces he begs us again and again to believe is that his stories originated in mere granules and germs of reality blown by chance breezes to the rich soil of the garden of his imagination, where they took root, and sprang up, and flowered; then they were transplanted with infinite art to the garden of literature. What he offers us, as he repeatedly suggests, is a thousand-fold better than life; it is an escape from life. It is an escape from the undesigned into the designed, from chaos into order, from the undiscriminated into the finely assorted, from the languor of the irrelevant to the intensity of the pertinent. It is not reality; he goes so far as to say quite expressly that it is poetry. If that is true, his novels should, in spite of Professor Pattee, "accomplish" something; they should give us on the one hand an ideal, and on the other hand a criticism; and they do give us both. Henry James's importance for Anglo-Saxons in general and for Americans in particular is that he is the first novelist writing in English to offer us on a grand scale a purely aesthetic criticism of modern society and modern fiction.

His special distinction among writers of prose fiction is in the exclusiveness of his consecration to beauty—a point which in this connection probably requires elucidation. To the religious consciousness all things are ultimately holy or unholy; to the moral consciousness all things are ultimately good or evil; to the scientific consciousness all things are ultimately true or not true; to Henry James all things are ultimately beautiful or ugly. In few men but fanatics and geniuses does any one type of consciousness hold undivided sway, and even among the geniuses and fanatics of the English race the pure aesthetic type was, till Ruskin's time, excessively rare. The normal English consciousness is, for purposes of judgment, a courthouse of several floors and courts, to each of which are distributed the cases proper

Stuart P. Sherman

to that jurisdiction. In the criticism of Matthew Arnold, for example, there are distinct courts for the adjudication of spiritual, ecclesiastical, moral, aesthetic, political, social, and scientific questions; but Ruskin handles all matters in the aesthetic chamber. In Shakespeare's criticism of life, to take the case of a creative artist, the discrimination of experience proceeds on clearly distinguishable levels of consciousness; the exquisite judgment of Sylvia—"holy, fair, and wise is she"—is a certificate of character from three distinct courts. But Henry James, on the contrary, receives and attempts to judge all the kinds of his experience on the single crowded, swarming, humming level of the aesthetic consciousness; the apartments above and below are vacant.

It is a much simpler task to indicate his position in literature with reference to the nature of his consciousness than with reference to the forms of his art. Critics attempting to "place" him have said the most bewildering things about his relationship to Richardson, Dickens, George Eliot, Trollope, George Meredith, Stevenson, Turgenev, Balzac, the Goncourts, Flaubert, Maupassant, Zola, and Daudet. To say that he is the disciple of this galaxy is to say everything and nothing. He knew intimately modern literature and many of its producers in England, France, Italy, and Russia, and he is related to them all as we are all related to Adam—and to the sun and the moon and the weather. He doubtless learned something of art from each of them, for he took instruction wherever he could find it—even from "Gyp," as he blushingly confesses in the preface to *The Awkward Age*. But what different gods were worshiped in this galaxy! Even Meredith, who resembles him in his psychological inquisitiveness, does not in nine-tenths of his novels remotely resemble him in form; moreover, Meredith is a moralist, a sage, a mystic, and a lyrical worshiper of Life, Nature, and other such loose divinities. James called Balzac "the master of us all," he called Turgenev "the beautiful genius," he sympathized intensely with Flaubert's dedication to perfection; but his total representation of life is not much more like that of any of his "masters" than George Eliot's is like Zola's.

It is a curious fact that, while American criticism tends to

The Question of Henry James

refer him to Europe, English criticism tends to refer him to America. A pretty argument, indeed, could be constructed to prove that he might have been very much what he was, if he had not gone body and soul to Europe, but had simply roved up and down the Atlantic Coast comparing the grave conscience of Boston and the open and skyey mind of Concord with the luxurious body and vesture of New York and the antique "gentility" of Richmond—comparing the harvested impressions of these scenes, and weaving into new patterns the finer threads which American tradition had put into his hands: Hawthorne's brooding moral introspection, his penetration of the shadowed quietudes of the heart, his love of still people and quiet places, his golden thread of imagery beaded with brave symbolism, the elaborated euphony of his style; Irving's bland pleasure in the rich surface of things, his delight in manorial dwellings, his sense of the glamour of history, his temperamental and stylistic mellowness and clarity, his worldly, well-bred air of being "at ease in Zion"; Poe's artistic exclusiveness, his artistic intelligence, his intensity, his conscious craftsmanship, his zest for discussing the creative process and the technique of literature. As a matter of fact, Henry James does "join on" to the eastern American traditions; he gathers up all these enumerated threads; he assimilates all these forms of consciousness. Hawthorne plays into his hands for depth and inwardness, Irving for outwardness and enrichment, and Poe for vividness and intensity.

The result of this fusion of types is a spacious and "richly sophisticated" type of the aesthetic consciousness of which the closest English analogue is the consciousness of Walter Pater. James is like Pater in his aversion from the world, his dedication to art, his celibacy, his personal decorum and dignity, his high aesthetic seriousness, his Epicurean relish in receiving and reporting the multiplicity and intensity of his impressions, and in the exacting closeness of his style. There are distinctions in plenty to be made by anyone curious enough to undertake the comparison; but on the whole there is no better sidelight on James's "philosophy" than Pater's conclusion to *The Renaissance* and his *Plato and Platonism;* no better statement of his general literary ideals than Pater's essay on style; no more interesting "parallel" to his later novels than *Marius, the Epicurean* and *Imaginary Portraits*. To make the matter a little more specific let the curious inquirer compare the exposure of Pater's consciousness, which is ordinarily known as his description of Mona Lisa, with the exposure of James's consciousness, which is ordinarily known as the description of a telegraph operator (*In the Cage*).

III

The reduction of all experience to the aesthetic level James himself recognized as a hazardous adventure. At the conclusion of his searching criticism of a fellow adventurer, Gabriele D'Annunzio, he raises the question whether it can ever hope to be successful. D'Annunzio's adventure he pronounces a dismal failure—that is, of course, an aesthetic failure; for in the quest of the beauty of passion the Italian, he declares, has produced the effect of a box of monkeys or, as he periphrastically puts it, "The association rising before us more nearly than any other is that of the manners observable in the most mimetic department of any great menagerie." But, he continues, the question is whether D'Annunzio's case is "the only case of the kind conceivable. May we not suppose another with the elements differently mixed? May we not in imagination alter the proportions within or the influences without, and look with cheerfulness for a different issue. *Need* the aesthetic adventure, in a word, organized for real discovery, give us no more comforting news of success? . . . To which probably the sole answer is that no man can say."

The last sentence is modest, but cannot have been wholly sincere; for James must have known that his own works answer all these questions in the affirmative. His own case is an altogether different variety of the species; his "news" is infinitely more comforting than D'Annunzio's. The particular ugliness, the morbid erotic obsession, on which D'Annunzio foundered, James, like Pater, sailed serenely by. His aesthetic vision had a far wider range and a far higher level of observation than that of almost any of the Latin votaries of "art for art"—Gautier or Flaubert, for example. And yet, let us admit it frankly once for all, his representation of life offends the whole-souled critical sense intensely in some particulars and on what is fundamentally the same ground as that on which these others offend it. His representation of life is an aesthetic flat; it sins against the diversity, the thick rotundity, the integrity of life. Its exquisitely arranged scenes and situations and atmospheres are not infrequently "ugly," as he would say, with the absence of moral energy and action. In *The Awkward Age,* for example, in that society which lives for "the finer things," which perceives, and compares, and consults, and so perfectly masters its instincts, the situation fairly shouts for the presence of at least one young man conceivably capable of bursting like Lochinvar through the circle of intriguing petticoats to carry off the heroine. The atmosphere of *The Golden Bowl* is ineffable—"There had been," says the author, "beauty day after day, and there had been for the spiritual lips something of the pervasive taste of it." The atmosphere is ineffably rich, still, golden, and, in the long run, stifling; the perceptive Mr. Verver, who is in it, gives a telling image of its effect: "That's all I mean at any rate—that it's 'sort of' soothing: as if we were sitting about on divans, with pigtails, smoking opium and seeing visions. 'Let us then be up and doing' —what is it Longfellow says? That seems sometimes to ring out; like the police breaking in—into our opium den—to give us a shake."

One may properly stress the point of his sin against the integrity of life because it is of the essence of the aesthetic case. It explains the vague but profound resentment which some readers who do not balk at James's difficulty feel when they have got "inside." Mr. Brownell, Mr. Hueffer, and Miss West all point towards but do not, I think, quite touch the heart of the matter when they say that James lacks "the historic sense." A part of the historic sense he indubitably has, and far more historical learning is implied in his work than is explicit in it; he loves the color and form of the past, he feels the "beauties" of history. But history to him, even the history of his own life, is a kind of magnificent picture gallery through which he strolls, delightedly commenting on the styles of different schools and periods, and pausing now and then for special expression of rapture before a masterpiece. Miss West beautifully flames with indignation at his "jocular" references to the Franco-Prussian War and at his unsympathetic treatment of the French Revolution, till she hits upon the explanation that he was out of Europe while the Franco-Prussian War raged, and that he was not born at the time of the French Revolution, so that he could no more speak well of it "than he could propose for his club a person whom he had never met." The explanation doesn't fit all the facts. He was not out of England when in his introduction to Rupert Brooke's letters he expressed his satisfaction that the English tradition "should have flowered *in a specimen so beautifully producible.*" The appreciation of Brooke is one of the most beautifully passionate tributes ever written; but the passion is purely aesthetic; the inveterate air of the connoisseur viewing a new picture in the gallery of masterpieces he cannot shake off. He was not speaking of events that took place before he was born when he said of the assassination of Lincoln in his *Notes of a Son and Brother:* "The collective sense of what had occurred was of a sadness too noble not somehow to inspire, and it was truly in the air that, whatever we had as a nation failed to produce, *we could at least gather round this perfection of classic woe.* True enough, as we were to see, the immediate harvest of our loss was almost too ugly to be borne—for nothing more sharply comes back to me than the tune to which the aesthetic sense, if one glanced but from *that* high window, recoiled in dismay from the sight of Mr. Andrew Johnson perched on the stricken scene."

Any good American will flame with indignation when he reads that passage; it so fails to present the subject; it is so horribly inadequate; it so affronts what Lord Morley would call "the high moralities" of life. With its stricken "scene," its aesthetic rapture, its aesthetic dismay, it insults the moral sense as a man would insult it who should ask one to note the exquisite slope of a woman's neck at the funeral of her husband. It sins against the integrity of life as, to take some distinguished examples, Renan's *Vie de Jésus* and Pater's *Plato and Platonism* sin against it. To present the Spartan boy as a nineteenth-century aesthete or to present the life of Jesus as essentially "delicious" is to miss in the quest of distinction the most vital and obvious of distinctions. It is a blunder into which simple, gross, whole-souled men like Fielding or Smollett or Dickens could never have fallen. It is a crudity of which only the most exquisite aesthete is capable; and he, perching exclusively in his high aesthetic window, absolutely cannot avoid it. It is of the pure aesthetic consciousness, not the intellect, that Emerson should have written his terse little couplet:

> Gravely it broods apart on joy
> And truth to tell, amused by pain.

IV

When all the discriminations already noted against the usurpations and blindnesses of the aesthetic sense have been made, it remains to be said that the infinitely seductive, the endlessly stimulating virtue of Henry James is the quintessential refinement, the intriguing complexity, the white-hot ardor of his passion for beauty. One feels the sacred flame most keenly, perhaps, in novels and tales like *The Figure in the Carpet*, *The Next Time*, *The Death of the Lion*, *The Lesson of the Master*, *Roderick Hudson*, and *The Tragic Muse*, in all of which he is interpreting the spirit of the artist or treating the conflict between the world and art. One feels it in the words of the young man in *The Tragic Muse* who abandons the prospect of a brilliant political career to become a portrait painter: "The cleanness and quietness of it, the independent effort to do something, to leave something which shall give joy to man long after the howling has died away to the last ghost of an echo—such a vision solicits me in the watches of the night with an almost irresistible force." One feels it in the described emotion of the young diplomat in the same novel, who is infatuated with a fine piece of acting: "He floated in the felicity of it, in the general encouragement of a sense of the perfectly *done*." One feels it in the words of the novelist in *The Lesson of the Master*, who says he has missed "the great thing"—namely, "the sense which is the real life of the artist and the absence of which is his death, of having drawn from his intellectual instrument the finest music that nature had hidden in it, of having played it as it should be played."

For a born man of letters the first effect of this passion for perfection is an immense solicitude for style; that is to say, for an exact verbal and rhythmical correspondence between his conception of beauty and his representation of it. Judgment upon style, then, involves two distinct points: first, the question whether the conception is beautiful, and, secondly, the question whether the representation is exact. In the case of Henry James there should not be much dispute about the exactness and completeness of the representation; no man ever strode more studiously or on the whole more successfully to reproduce the shape and color and movement of his aesthetic experience. The open question is whether his conceptions were beautiful; and on this point the majority of his critics have agreed that his earlier conceptions were beautiful, but that his later conceptions were not. To that, in the last analysis, one must reduce the famous discussion of his two, or three, or half a score of "styles." Anyone who reads the works through in chronological order can explode to his own satisfaction the notion that James in any book or year or decade deliberately changed his sentence structure. What changed from year to year was his conception of beauty, and that changed by an entirely gradual multiplication of distinctions through the enrichment of his consciousness and the intensification of his vision. To his youthful eye beauty appeared in clear light, clear colors, sharp outline, solid substance; accordingly the work of his earlier period abounds in figures distinct as an etching of the eighteenth century, grouping themselves as on a canvas of Gainsborough's, and conversing and interacting with the brilliant lucidity and directness of persons in a comedy of Congreve's. To his maturest vision beauty has less of body and more of mind; it is not so much in things as in the illimitable effluence and indefinable *aura* of things; it reveals itself less to eye and ear and hand—though these are its avenues of approach—than to some mysterious inner organ which it moves to a divine abstraction from sense, to an ecstasy of pure contemplation; accordingly late works like *The Sacred Fount* and

The Question of Henry James

The Golden Bowl present rather presences than persons—dim Maeterlinckian presences gliding through the shadow and shimmer of late Turneresque landscapes and Maeterlinckian country houses, and rarely saying or doing anything whatever of significance to the uninitiated ear and eye. The evolution of James's artistic interest may be summed up in this way: he begins with an interest in the visibly and audibly seen, said, and enacted; he ends by regarding all that as a nuisance—as an obstruction in the way of his latest and deepest interest, namely, the presentation of the unseen, the unsaid, the unacted—the vast quantity of mental life in highly organized beings which makes no outward sign, the invisible drama upon which most of his predecessors had hardly thought of raising the curtain. The difficulty of the later works is not primarily in the sentence structure, but in the point of view. The sentences in the most difficult of the novels, that psychical detective story, *The Sacred Fount*, are for the most part as neat, as terse, as alert as the sentences in *The Europeans*. When they are long and intricate, they generally imprison and precisely render some intricate and rewarding beauty of a moment of consciousness luxuriously full—for example, this moment of Strether's in *The Ambassadors:*

> How could he wish it to be lucid for others, for any one, that he, for the hour, saw reasons enough in the mere way the bright, clean, ordered water-side life came in at the open window?—the mere way Mme. de Vionnet, opposite him over their intensely white table-linen, their *omelette aux tomates,* their bottle of straw-colored chablis, thanked him for everything almost with the smile of a child, while her gray eyes moved in and out of their talk, back to the quarter of the warm spring air, in which early summer had already begun to throb, and then back to his face and their human questions.

Attend till this delicious moment of Strether's reproduces itself in your imagination, and you will not much complain of the difficult magic of the evocation.

Beyond almost all the English novelists of his time Henry James has applied his passion for beauty to the total form and composition of his stories. He cares little for the "slice of life," the loose episodic novel, the baggy autobiographical novel, so much in vogue of late, into which the author attempts to pitch the whole of contemporary life and to tell annually all that he knows and feels up to the date of publication without other visible principle of selection. With extremely few exceptions his subjects present themselves to him as "pictures" to be kept rigorously within the limits of a frame, or as "dramas" to be kept within the limits of a stage, or as alternations of "drama" with "picture." How he imposes upon himself the laws of painter and playwright, how he chooses his "center of composition," handles his "perspective," accumulates his "values," constructs his "stage," turns on the "lights"—all this he has told with extraordinary gusto in those prefaces which more illuminate the fine art of fiction than anything else—one is tempted to say, than everything else—on the subject. The point for us here is that he strives to make the chosen form and the intended effect govern with an "exquisite economy" every admitted detail. The ideal is to express everything that belongs in the "picture," everything that is *in* the relations of the persons of the drama, but nothing else.

V

Henry James's exacting aesthetic sense determines the field no less than the form of his fiction. A quite definite social ideal conceived in the aesthetic consciousness is implicit in his representation of a really *idle* leisure class—an ideal ultimately traceable to his own upbringing and to his early contact with the Emersonian rather than the Carlylean form of Transcendentalism. He has a positive distaste for our contemporary hero —"the man who does things"; the *summum bonum* for him is not an action, but a state of being—an untroubled awareness of beauty. Hence, his manifested predilection for "highly civilized young Americans, born to an easy fortune and a tranquil destiny"; for artists who amateurishly sketch and loiter through lovely Italian springs, though conscious of "social duties" that await them beyond the Alps; for diplomats devoted to the theater and members of Parliament who dabble in paint; for Italian princesses and princes free from the cares of state; for French counts and countesses who have nothing to keep up but the traditions of their "race"; for English lords with no occupation but the quest of a lady; for American millionaires who have left "trade" three thousand miles behind them to collect impressions, curios, and sons-in-law in Europe. Objectors may justly complain that he seems unable to conceive of a really fine lady or a really fine gentleman or a really decent marriage without a more or less huge fortune in the background or in the foreground of the picture; and it may be added that to the sense of a truly "Emersonian" mind the clink and consideration of gold in most of his crucial instances is a harsh and profound note of vulgarity vibrating through his noble society. He is entirely sincere when he says, in speaking of Balzac, that the object of money is to enable one to forget it. Yet fine ladies, fine gentlemen, and fine society as he understands these matters are, to tell the hard truth, impossible except in the conditions created by affluence and leisure. In comparative poverty one may be good; but one cannot, in the Jamesian sense, be beautiful!

Society cannot in the Jamesian sense be beautiful till the pressures of untoward physical circumstances, of physical needs, and of engagements with "active life" are removed, and men and women are free to live "from within outward," subjecting themselves only to the environment and entering only the relationships dictated by the aesthetic sense. Let us not undervalue the significance of this ideal, either with reference to life or with reference to literature. It is inadequate; but it has the high merit of being finely human. It has the precious virtue of utterly delivering Henry James from the riotous and unclean hands of the "naturalists." To it he owes the splendid distinction that when half the novelists of Europe, carried off their feet by the naturalistic drift of the age, began to go aslumming in the muck and mire of civilization, to explore man's simian relationships, to exploit *la bête humaine* and *l'homme moyen sensuel,* to prove the ineluctability of flesh and fate and instinct and environment —he, with aristocratic contempt of them and their formulas and their works, withdrew further and further from them, drew proudly out of the drift of the age, and set his imagination the task of presenting the fairest specimens of humanity in a choice, sifted society tremendously disciplined by its own

Stuart P. Sherman

ideals but generally liberated from all other compelling forces. Precisely because he keeps mere carnality out of his picture, holds passion rigorously under stress, presents the interior of a refined consciousness—precisely for these reasons he can produce a more intense pleasure in the reader by the representation of a momentary gush of tears or a single swift embrace than most of our contemporaries can produce with chapter after chapter of storms and seductions.

The controlling principle in Henry James's imaginary world is not religion nor morality nor physical necessity nor physical instinct. The controlling principle is a sense of style, under which vice, to adapt Burke's words, loses half its evil by losing all its grossness. In the noble society *noblesse,* and nothing else, obliges. Even in the early "international" novels we witness the transformation of Puritan morality, of which the sanction was religious, into a kind of chivalry, of which the sanctions are individual taste and class loyalty. Madame de Mauves, the lovely American married to a naughty French husband in that charming little masterpiece which bears her name, is not exhibited as preserving her "virtue" when she rejects her lover; she is exhibited as preserving her *fineness.* Her American lover acquiesces in his dismissal not from any sudden pang of conscience, but from a sudden recognition that if he persists in his suit he will be doing precisely what the vulgar French world and one vulgar spectator in particular expect him to do. In the earlier novels such as *Madame de Mauves, Daisy Miller,* and *The American,* the straightness, the innocence, the firmness of the American conscience are rather played up as beauties against the European background. Yet as early as 1878 he had begun, with the delightfully vivacious and witty *The Europeans,* his criticism of the intellectual dullness and emotional poverty of the New England sense of "righteousness"—a criticism wonderfully culminating in *The Ambassadors* (1903), in which the highly perceptive Strether, sent to France to reclaim an erring son of New England, is himself converted to the European point of view.

Noblesse in the later novels inspires beauties of behavior beyond the reaches of the Puritan imagination. It is astonishing to observe how many heroes and heroines of the later period are called upon to attest their fineness by a firm, clear-eyed mendacity. *The Wings of the Dove,* for example, is a vast conspiracy of silence to keep a girl who knows she is dying from knowing that her friends know that she knows. To lie with a wry face is a blemish on one's character. "*I* lie well, thank God," says Mrs. Lowder, "when, as sometimes will happen, there's nothing else so good." In the same novel poor Densher, who rather hates lying, rises to it: "The single thing that was clear in complications was that, whatever happened, one was to behave as a gentleman—to which was added indeed the perhaps slightly less shining truth that complications might sometimes have their tedium beguiled by a study of the question of how a gentleman would behave." When he is tempted to throw up his adventure in noble mendacity he is held to it in this way: as soon as he steps into the Palazzo Leporelli in Venice where the dying lady resides he sees "all the elements of the business compose, as painters called it, differently"—he sees himself as a figure in a Veronese picture, and he lives up to the grand style of the picture. He actively fosters the "suppressions" which are "in the direct interest of every one's good manners, every one's really quite generous ideal."

The most elaborate and subtle of all James's tributes to the aesthetic ideal in the conduct of life is *The Golden Bowl*—a picture in eight hundred pages of the relations existing between Maggie Verver and her husband the prince, between Maggie's father, Adam Verver, and his second wife, Charlotte, and between each one of the quadrangle and all the rest. Before the pair of marriages took place we are made to understand that an undefinedly intimate relation had existed between the prince and Charlotte, of which Maggie and her father were unaware; and after the marriages we are made to understand that the undefinedly intimate relation was resumed. All four of the parties to this complex relationship are thoroughly civilized; they are persons fit for the highest society; that is to say, they have wealth, beauty, exquisite taste, and ability to tell a lie with a straight face. What will be the outcome? The outcome is that, without overt act, or plain speech, or displayed temper on any hand, each one by psychic tact divines "everything," and Mr.

Stuart P. Sherman

and Mrs. Verver quietly return to America. Why is the *liaison* dissolved with such celestial decorum? It is dissolved because the "principals" in it perceive the aesthetic "impossibility" of continuing their relations in that atmosphere of silent but lucid "awareness"; and it is dissolved with decorum because all the persons concerned are infinitely superior to the vulgarity of rows, ruptures, and public proceedings. The "criticism of life" implicit in the entire novel becomes superbly explicit in Maggie's vision of the ugliness and barbarousness of the behavior of ordinary mortals in like circumstances.

She might fairly, as she watched them, have missed it [hot angry jealousy] as a lost thing; have yearned for it, for the straight vindictive view, the rights of resentment, the rages of jealousy, the protests of passion, as for something she had been cheated of not least; a range of feelings which for many women would have meant so much, but which for *her* husband's wife, for her father's daughter, figured nothing nearer to experience than a wild eastern caravan, looming into view with crude colours in the sun, fierce pipes in the air, high spears against the sky, all a thrill, a natural joy to mingle with, but turning off short before it reached her and plunging into other defiles.

Does not that description of Maggie's vision throb with a fine passion of its own—throb with the excitement of James's imaginative insight into the possible amenity of human intercourse in a society aesthetically disciplined and controlled?

VI

My thesis is simply that James's works throb with that fine passion from the beginning to the end—just as Pater's do. Criticism's favorite epithets for him hitherto have been "cold," "analytical," "scientific," "passionless," "pitiless" historian of the manners of a futile society. That view of him is doomed to disappear before the closer scrutiny which he demanded and which he deserves. He is not an historian of manners; he is a trenchant idealistic critic of life from the aesthetic point of view.

He is not pitiless except in the exposure of the "ugly," which to his sense includes all forms of evil; in that task he is remorseless whether he is exposing the ugliness of American journalism as in *The Reverberator,* or the ugliness of a thin, nervous, hysterical intellectualism and feminism as in *The Bostonians,* or the ugliness of murder as in *The Other House,* or the ugliness of irregular sexual relations as in *What Maisie Knew,* or the ugliness of corrupted childhood as in *The Turn of the Screw.* The deep-going uglinesses in the last three cases are presented with a superlative intenseness of artistic passion. If the effect is not thrilling in the first case and heartrending in the last two, it is because Anglo-Saxons are quite unaccustomed to having their deeps of terror and pity, their moral centers, touched through the aesthetic nerves. Granting the fact, there is no reason why they should deny the presence of a passion of antipathy in a man to whose singular consciousness the objectionable inveterately takes the shape of the ugly.

What, however, is more incomprehensible is the general failure of criticism to recognize the ardor of his quite unscientific attachment to the beautiful. His alleged deficiency in charm, it is asserted, is due to the fact that he does not sympathize with or love any of his characters. The alleged fact is not a fact. He sympathizes intensely with all his artists and novelists, with all his connoisseurs of life, with all his multitude of miraculously perceptive persons from the American homesick for England in *A Passionate Pilgrim* through the young woman aware of the fineness of old furniture in *The Spoils of Poynton* to Maggie and Mr. Verver in *The Golden Bowl.* And he dotes, devoutly dotes, dotes in idolatry upon the enriched consciousness, the general awareness, and the physical loveliness of his women. He cannot "abide" a plain heroine, even if she is to be a criminal. Of Rose, the murderess in *The Other House,* he says the most exquisite things—"She carries the years almost as you do, and her head better than any young woman I've ever seen. *Life is somehow becoming to her.*" In almost every novel that he wrote he touched some woman or other with the soft breath of pure aesthetic adoration—a refining and exalting emotion which is the note of Sherringham's relation to Miriam in *The Tragic Muse:*

Stuart P. Sherman

Beauty was the principle of everything she did. . . . He could but call it a felicity and an importance incalculable, and but know that it connected itself with universal values. To see this force in operation, to sit within its radius and feel it shift and revolve and change and never fail, was a corrective to the depression, the humiliation, the bewilderment of life. It transported our troubled friend from the vulgar hour and the ugly fact; drew him to something that had no warrant but its sweetness, no name nor place save as the pure, the remote, the antique.

This is the "very ecstasy of love"; and for this virtue, in the years to come, one adept after another reading the thirty or forty volumes of James which anyone can read with ease and the fifteen or twenty richer volumes which demand closer application—for this virtue one adept after another, till a brave company gathers, is certain to say, "I discriminate; but I adore him!"

JOSEPH WARREN BEACH

The Figure in the Carpet

[1918]

THERE is one group among the shorter stories of James that
has a peculiar interest for anyone seeking hints and revela-
tions of the personal experience, the temper and ideals of their
author. It comprises nearly a dozen tales dealing with writers
of fiction. It is of course a hazardous business making infer-
ences in regard to James from any of these stories. The information we may suppose ourselves to derive from them is neither so
substantial, so technical, nor so authoritative as what he offers
us in the prefaces. But it is not the less precious on that account.
If, with tact and discretion, we do learn something from these
stories about his attitude toward his art, it will be something of
an intimacy nowhere else to be felt. It will be something, say,
which modesty and pride forbade him to let us have straight
from himself; but something he might be willing for us to learn
by sympathetic inference, laying upon us the whole responsibility of assertion.

Most fascinating of all these tales, and the one which constitutes the greatest temptation for the interpreter of James, is
The Figure in the Carpet. For here he shows us a novelist of
rare distinction flinging down to the eager critic the challenge
of his secret. The critic is a clever fellow, a "demon of subtlety";
but he has failed, like everyone else, to discover the "little point"
the novelist most wishes to make. In fact he has to be informed
that there is any such little point to be discovered, that there is
a "particular thing" the novelist has "written his books most
for." "Isn't there for every writer," asks Hugh Vereker, in their
momentous midnight talk, "isn't there a particular thing of

Joseph Warren Beach

that sort, the thing that most makes him apply himself, the thing without the effort to achieve which he wouldn't write at all, the very passion of his passion, the part of the business in which, for him, the flame of art burns most intensely? Well, it's *that!*" And on a demand for more particularity he adds, "There's an idea in my work without which I wouldn't have given a straw for the whole job. It's the finest fullest intention of the lot, and the application of it has been, I think, a triumph of patience, of ingenuity. . . . It stretches, this little trick of mine, from book to book, and everything else, comparatively, plays over the surface of it. The order, the form, the texture of my books will perhaps some day constitute for the initiated a complete representation of it. So it's naturally the thing for the critic to look for. It strikes me . . . even as the thing for the critic to find." To the other's query, "You call it a little trick?" the novelist replies, "That's only my little modesty. It's really an exquisite scheme." It is later that the critic hits on the figure of speech by which this "little trick" is best to be described. "It was something, I guessed, in the primal plan; something like a complex figure in a Persian carpet. He [Vereker] highly approved of this image when I used it, and he used another himself. 'It's the very string,' he said, 'that my pearls are strung on.' "

"It's naturally the thing for the critic to look for," said Hugh Vereker of his "little trick." "It strikes me even as the thing for the critic to find." What head is cool enough to resist the suggestion that James had here in mind his own well-nigh desperate case? Was there not some "intention" of his own which had been regularly overlooked by reviewers in their hasty mention of his work? It was not that he *wished* to be difficult and esoteric. It was not so at least with Hugh Vereker. "If my great affair's a secret, that's only because it's a secret in spite of itself —the amazing event has made it one. I not only never took the smallest precaution to keep it so, but never dreamed of any such accident. If I had I shouldn't in advance have had the heart to go on. As it was, I only became aware little by little, and meanwhile I had done my work." But now his secret had become for him the great amusement of life. " 'I live almost to see if it will ever be detected.' He looked at me for a jesting challenge; something far within his eyes seemed to peep out. 'But I needn't worry—it won't!' " One cannot but wonder if Henry James, like Hugh Vereker, did pass away without ever having his secret put adequately into words.

We need not take this tale too gravely as a revelation of the artistic soul of Henry James. We need not set ourselves, with confident assumption, to solve the hinted riddle of his work. But we should be missing a rare occasion if we did not take up this metaphor and let it guide us in our summary of his art. Perhaps we should say there is not one, there are many figures in the carpet—as many figures as there are fond, discerning readers. For me the figure in the carpet is that which gives life to the whole work. It must be implied in all that we have found to be true of it; it must be the inner meaning and the motive of all that is included in his method. This, too, is suggested by what Hugh Vereker says of his "secret." It is not a "kind of esoteric message": at least it cannot be adequately described "in cheap journalese." He will not limit it by saying it is "something in the style or something in the thought, an element of form or an element of feeling." "Well," says Hugh Vereker, "you've got a heart in your body. Is that an element of form or an element of feeling? What I contend that nobody has ever mentioned in my work is the organ of life."

"Esoteric message" is "cheap journalese." The same red lantern warns off from any statement of James's "philosophy of life." It may be James has no philosophy of life. But he has something which will serve the purpose as well. He has a scale of values, a preference in human experience, an absorbing preoccupation. From first to last he is preoccupied not with men's lives but with the quality of their experience; not with the pattern but with the texture of life. Most novelists seem by comparison all taken up with the pattern. In Fielding and Scott, in Balzac and Zola, in Thackeray and Tolstoy, it is the adventures of the characters that we are bidden to follow. The contrast is the more remarkable when it is the English contemporaries of James that are brought into comparison. In Meredith and George Eliot, a matter of prime importance is what the characters bring to pass in a practical way. These authors may indeed reconcile themselves to the littleness of accomplishment on the part of their heroes; but it is accomplishment of some sort on which heroes and authors alike are determined. Meredith and George Eliot had both a philosophy of life. They were both strongly imbued with perfectionist and utilitarian ideals. They staked their all on the progress and improvement of humanity. A better world was the cry they had taken up from the lips of Rousseau and Voltaire, Bentham and Mill. The fact is deeply hidden under romance and sentiment of the later day; but George Eliot and Meredith are still in the practical and materialist tradition, of, say, Benjamin Franklin. It is another tradition, as we have seen, to which James owes allegiance; an idealist tradition deriving ultimately from romantic Germany and reaching its finest expression in Wordsworth, Emerson, and Hawthorne. Writing in the time of Gladstone and Bernard Shaw, James seems hardly to have given a thought to the political destinies of men or to the practical consequences and bearings of personal conduct. It is not in the relative terms of cause and effect that he considers human action. He is content, like some visionary Platonist, to refer each item of conduct to an absolute standard of the good and the beautiful. This is one reason why he is so strange a figure in our world all bent on getting results. We have, mostly, no such absolute standards. We know nothing of any Ideas in the mind of God.

In the stories of other writers, men and women are shown us obsessed with desires and ambitions and opposed by material difficulties. And our interest is absorbed in the process by which they overcome their difficulties and realize their desires. The characters of James, too, have ambitions and desires. But that is not the thing that strikes us most about them. What strikes us most about them is their capacity for renunciation—for giving up any particular gratification in favor of some fine ideal of conduct with which it proves incompatible. Common men and women have a more desperate grip on material values. There are things they insist on having. It may be money, or professional success, or social position, or some person indispensable to their happiness. And there is for them no immaterial substitute for these substantial goods. There is nothing in thought or feeling that can reconcile the lover to the loss of his mistress, nothing he will prefer to the woman he has set his heart upon. But the characters of James are not common men and women; and for the finest of them there is always something of more account than the substance of their experience, namely, its quality. They may, like other mortals, long for the realization of some particular desire; but they long still more fervently for the supreme comfort of being right with themselves. We know what a capacity for happiness was Isabel Archer's; but we know that happiness was far from being the thing she most sought, and we know with what deliberation she chose to embrace her fate when she was once made aware of "what most people know and suffer." We are gratified and appalled by the meekness with which these people accept their dole of misery and deprivation —this Mitchy and Nanda, this Christopher Newman and Fleda Vetch. It seems that we must not use words of unhappy connotation to describe such exalted fervency of renunciation. It is only because we ourselves require the objective realization of our desires that we so misrepresent them. They seem in point of fact to take some higher ground inaccessible to our feet. They seem to say: Lo, we have in not having. We were denied the shadow, but we have always possessed the real substance. One fantastic creature even ventures to contend that, in the realm of art, realization—concrete achievement—is inimical to the true life of the soul. Gabriel Nash is actually afraid Nick Dormer will prove a successful painter and so spoil the beauty of his testimony to the artistic faith. He prefers to "work in life" himself. Nick is so practical: he wishes Gabriel "had more to show" for his "little system." "Oh," says Gabriel, "having something to show's such a poor business. It's a kind of confession of failure." One does not need to measure one's acts by their consequences. "One is one's self a fine consequence." This is the very inner citadel of intransigent idealism. On this system we may interpret the story of Fleda Vetch as the triumph of Fleda. Let her cover her face in sorrow as she will. Her vulgar rival may have her lover, and the flames may have devoured the Spoils. But somehow we are given to understand that, of all

Joseph Warren Beach

the people in her world, she remains the wealthiest. She remains in substantial possession of beauty and of love.

What counts in the world of James is not the facts themselves—what one does or what happens to one, but the interpretation put upon the facts. James has a great fondness, especially in his tales, for subjects very slight and off the common track of observation. There is little in the circumstances themselves to attract attention, and the people are, on the surface, entirely wanting in romantic interest. The challenge is all the greater to an author who prides himself on seeing below the surface of human nature, who is like a naturalist delighted to bring home flowers of rare and neglected beauty from spots unnoted by vulgar eyes. Such a flower was the homely American kinswoman of Lady Beldonald, who was intended by that handsome woman to be her foil, her dull and unremarked companion, and who was declared by the portrait painter to be as distinguished and "beautiful" as a Holbein. It is himself that James describes in the words of the painter. "It's not my fault," he says, "if I am so put together as often to find more life in situations obscure and subject to interpretation than in the gross rattle of the foreground." This note is forever recurring both in the stories themselves and in the author's comment on them. We hear it in Miriam Rooth's naïve explanation to the great French actress that "there were two kinds of scenes and speeches: those which acted themselves, of which the treatment was plain, the only way, so that you had just to take it; and those open to interpretation, with which you had to fight every step, rendering, arranging, doing the thing according to your idea." The note is sounded more delicately and modestly in the case of Mrs. Blessingbourne and her romantic and at the same time Platonic feeling for Colonel Voyt. That gentleman, who is in full enjoyment of the love of another woman, is inclined to regard such merely Platonic love as but thin material for romance. But in his discussion of the matter with his own mistress, he agrees that the pathetic lady's very *consciousness* "*was,* in the last analysis, a kind of shy romance. Not a romance like their own, a thing to make the fortune of any author up to the mark . . . but a small scared starved subjective satisfaction that would do her

[97]

no harm and nobody else any good." We may be sure it was not the creator of Fleda Vetch and Milly Theale who is applying to Mrs. Blessingbourne's experience this supercilious description. As he says himself in the preface, "The thing is, all beautifully, a matter of interpretation and of the particular conditions; without a view of which latter some of the most prodigious adventures, as one has often had occasion to say, may vulgarly show for nothing."

The same point is made still more significantly in reference to the "adventures" of Isabel Archer, which he seems to think are but mild ones by the ordinary romantic measure. "Without her sense of them, her sense *for* them, as one may say, they are next to nothing at all; but isn't the beauty and the difficulty just in showing their mystic conversion by that sense, conversion into the stuff of drama or, even more delightful word still, of 'story'?" He vouchsafes two "very good instances of this effect of conversion." One of them is:

. . . in the long statement, just beyond the middle of the book, of my young woman's extraordinary meditative vigil on the occasion that was to become for her such a landmark. Reduced to its essence, it is but the vigil of searching criticism; but it throws the action further forward than twenty "incidents" might have done. It was designed to have all the vivacity of incident and all the economy of picture. She sits up, by her dying fire, far into the night, under the spell of recognitions on which she finds the last sharpness suddenly wait. It is a representation simply of her motionlessly *seeing*, and an attempt withal to make the mere still lucidity of her act as "interesting" as the surprise of a caravan or the identification of a pirate. It represents, for that matter, one of the identifications dear to the novelist, and even indispensable to him; but it all goes on without her being approached by another person and without her leaving her chair. It is obviously the best thing in the book, but it is only a supreme illustration of the general plan.

If Mr. James ever did trace out for us the Figure in the Carpet, it was in this passage, in which, concluding his review of the first book which really shows up the figure with any distinctness, he lets us know what is "obviously" the best thing in the book, and offers it to us as "only a supreme illustration of the general plan." We are reminded of the terms in which Hugh Vereker adumbrates for his young friend the "exquisite scheme," the "primal plan," not merely of his latest work, but of the whole series of his novels. We are further reminded of Hugh Vereker's attitude towards his public by Mr. James's apologetic and somewhat exasperated remark—it is in connection with his other instance of "the rare chemistry" of the character's sense for her adventures—"It is dreadful to have too much, for any artistic demonstration, to dot one's i's and insist on one's intentions, and I am not eager to do it now."

But however reluctant, he felt obliged on this one occasion to insist on his intentions. "The question here was that of producing the maximum of intensity with the minimum of strain. The interest was to be raised to its pitch and yet the elements to be kept in their key; so that, should the whole thing duly impress, I might show what an 'exciting' inward life may do for the person leading it even while it remains perfectly normal."

The Portrait of a Lady was the first book in which James plainly showed his "little trick," which he went on showing more and more plainly from that time out. His little trick was simply not to tell the "story" at all as the story is told by the Scotts and the Maupassants, but to give us instead the subjective accompaniment of the story. His "exquisite scheme" was to confine himself as nearly as possible to the "inward life" of his characters, and yet to make it as "exciting" for his readers as it was for the author, as exciting—were that possible—as it was for the characters themselves.

Such an interpretation of his "scheme" would conform very well, at any rate, to Hugh Vereker's comprehensive description of his own: "It's the finest fullest intention of the lot, and the application of it has been, I think, a triumph of patience, of ingenuity. . . . It stretches, this little trick of mine, from book to book, and everything else, comparatively, plays over the surface of it. The order, the form, the texture of my books will perhaps some day constitute for the initiated a complete representation of it." I don't know how the scheme I have indicated would be represented in the *order* of the books of James. But it might serve as an explanation of their form and texture, and

The Question of Henry James

of all the peculiarities of his method as we have made them out. Naturally, a book devoted to the inward life of a group of people would be nothing without its "idea." But the strict limitation of the action to the consciousness of these people would insure against undue abstractness in the idea, would transform idea into "picture." The succession of incidents in an ordinary story would in such a narrative be represented by the process of "revelation" of the picture. Suspense would have reference not to what might happen but to the subjective reverberation of what happens. In a record of inward life it is obvious how important must be the choice and maintenance of a point of view. It is almost absolutely essential that the center of interest should be a person of penetrating intelligence. It is plain how this subjective bias would affect the nature of the dialogue, making it less picturesque, more fine drawn and close knit, being the record of mental exploration carried on by several persons in concert. This is true of the dialogue even in those more dramatic situations involving tense oppositions of will, and gives its peculiar character to the "drama" of James. The exclusive interest in mental exploration explains to a large extent the wholesale "eliminations," which in turn relate themselves to the "neutral tone" of James's writing. And the almost complete abstraction from the world of common accident and circumstance, the confinement of attention to the realm of spiritual reactions, gives to the work of James its insubstantial, its romantic, even fantastic, character, which makes it the scorn of the "general," the despair of the conscientious, and the supreme entertainment of those who like it.

Above all does the exclusive concern with the inward life of his people explain the dominance of ethical considerations and at the same time perhaps the peculiar character of those involved. For the characters of James the faculty of supreme importance is the intelligence, or insight, the faculty of perceiving "values" beyond those utilities upon which everyone agrees. Of such immaterial values there are two general groups, both of great importance and of unfailing concern to the people of James. The first group includes social and aesthetic values, which I class together because of their close association in the char-

Joseph Warren Beach

acters' minds, and because of their being on a common level as contrasted with the other group of values—the spiritual.

Minor classifications we must here ignore. We must ignore those contrasts in social ideals which play so large a part in the earlier stories of James, but which in the long run prove to be of secondary importance. Social ideals may appear on the surface to be relative; but at bottom they show themselves, for this conservative philosopher, as absolute as any Platonic Ideas. Tact and discernment, fairness and modesty, the preference of the fine to the vulgar, the instinct for the nice and the proper, are after all traits in which practically all his favored characters agree, whether they be of Albany or London, Paris or "Woollett," "Flickerbridge" or Rome. There is one notable instance in which the contrast is drawn between a sense for social and a sense for aesthetic values. The drama of *The Tragic Muse* arises from the inability of Julia Dallow, socially so complete, to comprehend the aesthetic life of Nick Dormer; Nick Dormer is himself never quite able to make up his mind whether so thoroughly artistic a spirit as that of Gabriel Nash is capable of the refinements of gentility; and Peter Sherringham is in a similar perplexity as regards the character of Miriam Rooth. Generally however the social and the aesthetic senses are inseparable for the people of James. Mona Brigstock and her mother are as incapable of the social as of the aesthetic shibboleths of Fleda Vetch and Mrs. Gereth. Isabel Archer receives in one undivided flood her impressions of the aesthetic and the social qualities of Madame Merle and of Gilbert Osmond. The world of refinements typified to Hyacinth Robinson by the Princess Casamassima is a world in which he cannot distinguish the aesthetic from the social felicities. So that, on the whole, we should be justified in employing the hyphenated term of social-aesthetic to distinguish that type of intelligence which is shared by practically all the important characters of James. Or we might serve our purpose with the simpler, and equally comprehensive, term, good taste.

There is at least one important character who is lacking in good taste so understood. I mean Daisy Miller, whose peculiarity lies in her possession of a rare spiritual beauty quite unaccom-

The Question of Henry James

panied by social tact and artistic discernment. But Mr. James
has expressed doubts himself as to the reality of this charming
poetic creation; and the one romantic exception will but make
more notable the almost universal prevalence of good taste as a
qualification for admittance into the gallery of Henry James.
This is the first qualification—that is, the one first to be considered: one must successfully stand this test before being advanced to the higher one reserved for heroes and heroines. It is
good taste which unites in one great, shining company the
otherwise so various Gilbert Osmond and Isabel Archer, Mrs.
Brookenham and Nanda, Kate Croy and Milly Theale, Chad
Newsome and Lambert Strether.

The *ideal* of James is clearly a combination, or rather a *fusion*,
of good taste with spiritual discernment, and perhaps the most
complete, if not the most dramatic, instance of this fusion is
the last named, Lambert Strether. For him there seems to be no
such distinction between aesthetic and ethical as perplexes most
of us mortals. Madame de Vionnet has a claim upon Chad, he
thinks, because she has worked upon him so fine a transformation; and this character of Chad's, of her creation, is all described in terms of aesthetic and social connotation. No doubt
the idea of an *obligation* is a moral idea at bottom; but this
obligation is in direct opposition to the legal and religious code,
and never were greater pains taken to translate moral concept
into the language of simple good taste. In the mind of Lambert
Strether there seems to be no clear dividing line between the
categories of beauty and goodness.

Somewhat the same condition prevails in the psychology of
The Awkward Age; and the tendency is always in this direction in the stories of James. But in many cases the distinction
is much sharper between good taste and the moral sense. And
whenever the distinction appears, the moral sense is clearly preferred as the higher and rarer and as something added to the
other or built upon it. Fleda Vetch is preferred to Mrs. Gereth
as being capable of spiritual discernment in addition to possessing the mere good taste of which the latter is such a miracle.
We must do Mrs. Gereth the justice to acknowledge that her devotion to the Spoils was an ideal and unselfish devotion, alto-

gether different from the "crude love of possession," and that it gives a hint of spiritual quality. But in any other and more human connection, she was an unscrupulous because an unseeing woman. "She had no imagination about anybody's life save on the side she bumped against. Fleda was quite aware that she would have otherwise been a rare creature, but a rare creature was originally just what she had struck her as being. Mrs. Gereth had really no perception of anybody's nature—had only one question about persons: were they clever or stupid? To be clever meant to know the 'marks.' Fleda knew them by direct inspiration, and a warm recognition of this had been her friend's tribute to her character. The girl now had hours of sombre hope she might never see anything 'good' again; that kind of experience was clearly so broken a reed, so fallible a source of peace." Owen had no more sense for the "marks" than Mona or Mrs. Brigstock; but he was capable of rising to Fleda's spiritual bait. And so we are given the impression of him as really more clever than his mother, being in a class with Fleda. And Mrs. Gereth comes to recognize Fleda and Owen as "of quite another race and another flesh."

So it is that Milly Theale is preferred to the superb and socially incomparable Kate Croy; that Mitchy and Nanda are preferred to the infinitely clever and subtle mother of Nanda; that Isabel Archer is preferred to the charming and accomplished Madame Merle and to Osmond, who had both so long a start of her in social and aesthetic cultivation. In each case the one preferred has, in addition to the common good taste, the wit to distinguish moral beauty.

It is all, as we have seen, a matter of insight. The less favored characters, the false and the shady people, are morally colorblind. It is always the same story throughout the whole series of novels. It is so in *Roderick Hudson* at the beginning and in *The Golden Bowl* at the end. In *The Golden Bowl*, it is a question of whether the Prince Amerigo has enough discernment to perceive the superiority of his wife to his accomplished mistress. The "style" of Charlotte has indeed been "great" in the closing scenes of the drama, but great in a way far below the spiritual fineness of Maggie. Maggie is "great" enough to perceive the greatness of Charlotte. "Isn't she too splendid?" she asks her husband. "That's our help, you see." . . . "See?" says Amerigo, triumphantly meeting his final test, "I see nothing but *you*." Roderick Hudson is an artist of genius, with endowments infinitely superior to those of his friend and benefactor in every respect except this of spiritual discernment. It is only at the end of his life that he has a glimpse of what he has missed. It is in his last conversation with Rowland, in which the latter has finally told him of his own love for Mary. Roderick comes to see how "hideous" is the appearance he has made. "Do you really care," Rowland is prompted to ask, "for what you may have appeared?" "Certainly. I've been damnably stupid. Isn't an artist supposed to be a man of fine perceptions? I haven't, as it turns out, had *one*."

The stories of James are a continuous record of such "fine perceptions" had or missed. The stuff is as airy as gossamer: not at all "Things done, that took the eye and had the price." Hence the notorious difficulty and inaccessibility of James. And hence the romantic exhilaration of his work for so many denizens of a world in which the realization of ideals is so rare and hard of accomplishment. May this be the secret of his great following among women? His greatest appeal is perhaps to those whose lives have yielded the minimum of realization, to those who have the least control over the gross materials of life.

THOMAS BEER

Henry James and Stephen Crane

[1923]

WINTER brought to Stephen Crane bad colds and a trip to Harold Frederic's pet fishing village. On February 5, he dined with Frederic and Charles Griswold, an American tourist, at Richmond. To this matrix of a pleasant evening were suddenly added a nobleman then in alliance with a lady never certain as to her nationality, understood to be the honored subject of verses in *The Yellow Book* and reputed chaste though seldom sober. The party came back to Mr. Griswold's rooms in London and Madame Zipango—the name is certainly international—was imitating Yvette Guilbert when Henry James appeared to pay his young compatriot a call. The correct and the incorrect swam together in a frightful collision. Crane withdrew the elderly novelist to a corner and talked style until the fantastic woman poured champagne in the top hat of Henry James. Her noble lover had gone to sleep. Frederic was amused. The wretched host of this group was too young and too frightened to do anything preventative and Crane, coldly tactful, got the handsome creature out of the hotel, then came back to aid in the restoration of the abused hat.

Crane did not find this funny. In the next week he wrote: "I agree with you that Mr. James has ridiculous traits and lately I have seen him make a holy show of himself in a situation that —on my honour—would have been simple to an ordinary man. But it seems impossible to dislike him. He is so kind to everybody. . . ."

He was so kind. From the sacred fount of his self-adoration there yet welled on gifted folk those pools of tender corre-

The Question of Henry James

spondence and those courtesies a trifle tedious, one hears, but rendered with such grace. Ada Rehan might vexedly call him "my dear snob" across a luncheon table but she would repent for weeks that bit of unpremeditated, natural frankness. Another actress, in a forgetful breath, assured him that she found his friend Paul Bourget's novels vulgar and then shook as the deep voice stammered, "Vul—" to begin some sentence of pained expostulation that ended in mere syllables of affront. He was no longer a man. Henry James was a colored and complicated ritual that demanded of spectators a reverence unfailingly accorded. People who swooned under the burden of his final method sat and sat in pleasure while that astonishing egotism bared in slow phrases its detached and charming appreciation of its own singular skill. He had written plays incoherent and banal in exquisite English for the simple and admitted purpose of making money "as much and as soon as possible" and his votaries shuddered when the plebeians hooted *Guy Domville* from the stage. He committed in reviews consummate silliness such as his famous statement of tears shed over the butchered children of Rudyard Kipling's *Drums of the Fore and Aft* with its added comment on the dreadful dirtiness of the dead drummers. The sob balanced the snobbery and nobody jeered, save one remote and logical American. Critics mired themselves in verbal anguish over his successive novels. This plain and limited old bachelor commanded the world to respect him and the world obeyed. He was so kind.

Life waned for this man in his absurd and wonderful position, the patron of a cult. His books were so little read in America that he could be mentioned as "the late Henry James" in 1898 at a public banquet without exciting laughter. Americans invading England found, to their horror or secret relief, that nobody seemed to read his books in the territory assigned to his renown. But to no other writer in the Anglo-American field were attached such bristling adherents! He was holy and impeccable to the gaze of innumerable talented folk. Mrs. Humphry Ward fell speechless and scarlet when it was said, in her presence, that Mr. James had derived his tale *Paste* from De Maupassant, and another votary still living ordered from his house a heretic who chose to argue that the Master's preoccupation with refinements was a vulgar habit. He was prim and circumspect, as befitted the child grown old who was ordered at the age of seven to compose a note of apology for appearing barefoot on the porch of a seaside villa before callers, and he was the pet of cynical voluptuaries. He was a provincial sentimentalist touted by worshipers as the last flower of European culture while he recoiled in amazement from the profound civilization of Havelock Ellis who would and, "so successfully delicate in his attack on the matter of these abominations that one reads, I may say, almost painlessly," did write of sexual deflections and gross social phenomena without any sign of shock. This fading life of Henry James had passed in a series of recoils. Civilization, in his sight, seems to have been not the overthrow of empty inhibitions but an exaltation of limits. He had fled—and who blames him?—from a society that became, in his dreams, a tentacled beast ready always to overpower his individual trend, but he remained a Bostonian by every implication of his rare and scrupulous art. Even when in *The Turn of the Screw* he attempted to tell the story of "abominations" he must produce it with ghosts for sinners and the corrupted bodies must be those of children impossible and lovely as the babes of his predecessor Hawthorne. This master of groomed circumstance had found out a sunny garden where poisons blew as perfumes too heavy for a refined sense and crimes were shadows, not clouds, that swept across his shaved and watered turf.

T. S. ELIOT

On Henry James

[1918]

IN MEMORY

HENRY JAMES has been dead for some time. The current
of English literature was not appreciably altered by his
work during his lifetime; and James will probably continue to
be regarded as the extraordinarily clever but negligible curiosity. The current hardly matters; it hardly matters that very
few people will read James. The "influence" of James hardly
matters: to be influenced by a writer is to have a chance inspiration from him; or to take what one wants; or to see things
one has overlooked; there will always be a few intelligent people
to understand James, and to be understood by a few intelligent
people is all the influence a man requires. What matters least of
all is his place in such a Lord Mayor's show as Mr. Chesterton's
procession of Victorian literature. The point to be made is that
James has an importance which has nothing to do with what
came before him or what may happen after him; an importance
which has been overlooked on both sides of the Atlantic.

I do not suppose that anyone who is not an American can
properly appreciate James. James's best American figures in the
novels, in spite of their trim, definite outlines, the economy of
strokes, have a fullness of existence and an external ramification
of relationship which a European reader might not easily suspect. The Bellegarde family, for instance, are merely good outline sketches by an intelligent foreigner; when more is expected
of them, in the latter part of the story, they jerk themselves into
only melodramatic violence. In all appearance Tom Tristram is

an even slighter sketch. Europeans can recognize him; they have seen him, known him, have even penetrated the Occidental Club; but no European has the Tom Tristram element in his composition, has anything of Tristram from his first visit to the Louvre to his final remark that Paris is the only place where a white man can live. It is the final perfection, the consummation of an American to become, not an Englishman, but a European—something which no born European, no person of any European nationality, can become. Tom is one of the failures, one of nature's misfortunes, in this process. Even General Packard, C. P. Hatch, and Miss Kitty Upjohn have a reality which Claire de Cintré misses. Noémie, of course, is perfect, but Noémie is a result of the intelligent eye; her existence is a triumph of the intelligence, and it does not extend beyond the frame of the picture.

For the English reader, much of James's criticism of America must merely be something taken for granted. English readers can appreciate it for what it has in common with criticism everywhere, with Flaubert in France and Turgenev in Russia. Still, it should have for the English an importance beyond the work of these writers. There is no English equivalent for James, and at least he writes in this language. As a critic, no novelist in our language can approach James; there is not even any large part of the reading public which knows what the word "critic" means. (The usual definition of a critic is a writer who cannot "create"—perhaps a reviewer of books.) James was emphatically not a successful *literary* critic. His criticism of books and writers is feeble. In writing of a novelist, he occasionally produces a valuable sentence out of his own experience rather than in judgment of the subject. The rest is charming talk, or gentle commendation. Even in handling men whom he could, one supposes, have carved joint from joint—Emerson, or Norton—his touch is uncertain; there is a desire to be generous, a political motive, an admission (in dealing with American writers) that under the circumstances this was the best possible, or that it has fine qualities. His father was here keener than he. Henry was not a literary critic.

He was a critic who preyed not upon ideas, but upon living

beings. It is criticism which is in a very high sense creative. The characters, the best of them, are each a distinct success of creation: Daisy Miller's small brother is one of these. Done in a clean, flat drawing, each is extracted out of a reality of its own, substantial enough; everything given is true for that individual; but what is given is chosen with great art for its place in a general scheme. The general scheme is not one character, nor a group of characters in a plot or merely in a crowd. The focus is a situation, a relation, an atmosphere, to which the characters pay tribute, but being allowed to give only what the writer wants. The real hero, in any of James's stories, is a social entity of which men and women are constituents. It is, in *The Europeans,* that particular conjunction of people at the Wentworth house, a situation in which several memorable scenes are merely timeless parts, only occurring necessarily in succession. In this aspect, you can say that James is dramatic; as what Pinero and Mr. Jones used to do for a large public, James does for the intelligent. It is in the chemistry of these subtle substances, these curious precipitates and explosive gases which are suddenly formed by the contact of mind with mind, that James is unequaled. Compared with James's, other novelists' characters seem to be only accidentally in the same book. Naturally, there is something terrible, as disconcerting as a quicksand, in this discovery, though it only becomes absolutely dominant in such stories as *The Turn of the Screw.* It is partly foretold in Hawthorne, but James carried it much further. And it makes the reader, as well as the *personae,* uneasily the victim of a merciless clairvoyance.

James's critical genius comes out most tellingly in his mastery over, his baffling escape from, Ideas; a mastery and an escape which are perhaps the last test of a superior intelligence. He had a mind so fine that no idea could violate it. Englishmen, with their uncritical admiration (in the present age) for France, like to refer to France as the Home of Ideas; a phrase which, if we could twist it into truth, or at least a compliment, ought to mean that in France ideas are very severely looked after; not allowed to stray, but preserved for the inspection of civic pride in a Jardin des Plantes, and frugally dispatched on occasions of

T. S. Eliot

public necessity. England, on the other hand, if it is not the Home of Ideas, has at least become infested with them in about the space of time within which Australia has been overrun by rabbits. In England ideas run wild and pasture on the emotions; instead of thinking with our feelings (a very different thing) we corrupt our feelings with ideas; we produce the political, the emotional idea, evading sensation and thought. George Meredith (the disciple of Carlyle) was fertile in ideas; his epigrams are a facile substitute for observation and inference. Mr. Chesterton's brain swarms with ideas; I see no evidence that it thinks. James in his novels is like the best French critics in maintaining a point of view, a viewpoint untouched by the parasite idea. He is the most intelligent man of his generation.

The fact of being everywhere a foreigner was probably an assistance to his native wit. Since Byron and Landor, no Englishman appears to have profited much from living abroad. We have had Birmingham seen from Chelsea, but not Chelsea seen (really *seen*) from Baden or Rome. There are advantages, indeed, in coming from a large flat country which no one wants to visit: advantages which both Turgenev and James enjoyed. These advantages have not won them recognition. Europeans have preferred to take their notion of the Russian from Dostoevski and their notion of the American from, let us say, Frank Norris if not O. Henry. Thus, they fail to note that there are many kinds of their fellow countrymen, and that most of these kinds, similarly to the kinds of *their* fellow countrymen, are stupid; likewise with Americans. Americans also have encouraged this fiction of a general type, a formula or idea, usually the predaceous square jawed or thin lipped. They like to be told that they are a race of commercial buccaneers. It gives them something easily escaped from, moreover, when they wish to reject America. Thus, the novels of Frank Norris have succeeded in both countries; though it is curious that the most valuable part of *The Pit* is its satire (quite unconscious, I believe; Norris was simply representing faithfully the life he knew) of Chicago society after business hours. All this show of commercialism which Americans like to present to the foreign eye James quietly waves aside; and in pouncing upon his

[111]

fellow countryman after the stock exchange has closed, in tracking down his vices and absurdities across the Atlantic and exposing them in their highest flights of dignity or culture, James may be guilty of what will seem to most Americans scandalously improper behavior. It is too much to expect them to be grateful. And the British public, had it been more aware, would hardly have been more comfortable confronted with a smile which was so far apart from breaking into the British laugh. Henry James's death, if it had been more taken note of, should have given considerable relief "on both sides of the Atlantic," and cemented the Anglo-American entente.

THE HAWTHORNE ASPECT

My object is not to discuss critically even one phase or period of James, but merely to provide a note, *Beitrage,* toward any attempt to determine his antecedents, affinities, and "place." Presumed that James's relation to Balzac, to Turgenev, to anyone else on the continent is known and measured—I refer to Mr. Hueffer's book and to Mr. Pound's article—and presumed that his relation to the Victorian novel is negligible, it is not concluded that James was simply a clever young man who came to Europe and improved himself, but that the soil of his origin contributed a flavor discriminable after transplantation in his latest fruit. We may even draw the instructive conclusion that this flavor was precisely improved and given its chance, not worked off, by transplantation. If there is this strong native taste, there will probably be some relation to Hawthorne; and if there is any relation to Hawthorne, it will probably help us to analyze the flavor of which I speak.

When we say that James is "American," we must mean that this "flavor" of his, and also more exactly definable qualities, are more or less diffused throughout the vast continent rather than anywhere else; but we cannot mean that this flavor and these qualities have found literary expression throughout the nation, or that they permeate the work of Mr. Frank Norris or Mr. Booth Tarkington. The point is that James is positively a continuator of the New England genius; that there is a New England genius,

T. S. Eliot

which has discovered itself only in a very small number of people in the middle of the nineteenth century—and which is *not* significantly present in the writings of Miss Sara Orne Jewett, Miss Eliza White, or the Bard of Appledore, whose name I forget. I mean whatever we associate with certain purlieus of Boston, with Concord, Salem, and Cambridge, Massachusetts: notably Emerson, Thoreau, Hawthorne, and Lowell. None of these men, with the exception of Hawthorne, is individually very important; they all can, and perhaps ought to be made to look very foolish; but there is a "something" there, a dignity, above the taint of commonness about some English contemporary, as, for instance, the more intelligent, better-educated, more alert Matthew Arnold. Omitting such men as Bryant and Whittier as absolutely plebeian, we can still perceive this halo of dignity around the men I have named, and also Longfellow, Margaret Fuller and her crew, Bancroft and Motley, the faces of (later) Norton and Child pleasantly shaded by the Harvard elms. One distinguishing mark of this distinguished world was very certainly leisure; and importantly not in all cases a leisure given by money, but insisted upon. There seems no easy reason why Emerson or Thoreau or Hawthorne should have been men of leisure; it seems odd that the New England conscience should have allowed them leisure; yet they *would* have it, sooner or later. That is really one of the finest things about them, and sets a bold frontier between them and a world which will at any price avoid leisure, a world in which Theodore Roosevelt is a patron of the arts. An interesting document of this latter world is the *Letters* of a nimbly dull poet of a younger generation, of Henry James's generation, Richard Watson Gilder, Civil Service Reform, Tenement House Commission, Municipal Politics.

Of course leisure in a metropolis, with a civilized society (the society of Boston was and is quite uncivilized but refined beyond the point of civilization), with exchange of ideas and critical standards, would have been better; but these men could not provide the metropolis, and were right in taking the leisure under possible conditions.

Precisely this leisure, this dignity, this literary aristocracy, this unique character of a society in which the men of letters

The Question of Henry James

were also of the best people, clings to Henry James. It is some consciousness of this kinship which makes him so tender and gentle in his appreciations of Emerson, Norton, and the beloved Ambassador. With Hawthorne, as much the most important of these people in any question of literary art, his relation is more personal; but no more in the case of Hawthorne than with any of the other figures of the background is there any consideration of influence. James owes little, very little, to anyone; there are certain writers whom he consciously studied, of whom Hawthorne was not one; but in any case his relation to Hawthorne is on another plane from his relation to Balzac, for example. The influence of Balzac, not on the whole a good influence, is perfectly evident in some of the earlier novels; the influence of Turgenev is vaguer, but more useful. That James was, at a certain period, more moved by Balzac, that he followed him with more concentrated admiration, is clear from the tone of his criticism of that writer compared with the tone of his criticism of either Turgenev or Hawthorne. In *French Poets and Novelists,* though an early work, James's attitude toward Balzac is exactly that of having been very much attracted from his orbit, perhaps very wholesomely stimulated at an age when almost any foreign stimulus may be good, and having afterwards reacted from Balzac, though not to the point of injustice. He handles Balzac shrewdly and fairly. From the essay on Turgenev there is on the other hand very little to be got but a touching sense of appreciation; from the essay on Flaubert even less. The charming study of Hawthorne is quite different from any of these. The first conspicuous quality in it is tenderness, the tenderness of a man who had escaped too early from an environment to be warped or thwarted by it, who had escaped so effectually that he could afford the gift of affection. At the same time he places his finger, now and then, very gently, on some of Hawthorne's more serious defects as well as his limitations.

"The best things come, as a general thing, from the talents that are members of a group; every man works better when he has companions working in the same line, and yielding the stimulus of suggestion, comparison, emulation." Though when he says that "there was manifestly a strain of generous indolence in his [Hawthorne's] composition" he is understating the fault of laziness for which Hawthorne can chiefly be blamed. But gentleness is needed in criticizing Hawthorne, a necessary thing to remember about whom is precisely the difficult fact that the soil which produced him with his essential flavor is the soil which produced, just as inevitably, the environment which stunted him.

In one thing alone Hawthorne is more solid than James: he had a very acute historical sense. His erudition in the small field of American colonial history was extensive, and he made most fortunate use of it. Both men had that sense of the past which is peculiarly American, but in Hawthorne this sense exercised itself in a grip on the past itself; in James it is a sense of the sense. This, however, need not be dwelt upon here. The really vital thing, in finding any personal kinship between Hawthorne and James, is what James touches lightly when he says that "the fine thing in Hawthorne is that he cared for the deeper psychology, and that, in his way, he tried to become familiar with it." There are other points of resemblance, not directly included under this, but this one is of the first importance. It is, in fact, almost enough to ally these two novelists, in comparison with whom almost all others may be accused of either superficiality or aridity. I am not saying that this "deeper psychology" is essential, or that it can always be had without loss of other qualities, or that a novel need be any the less a work of art without it. It is a definition; and it separates the two novelists at once from the English contemporaries of either. Neither Dickens nor Thackeray, certainly, had the smallest notion of the "deeper psychology"; George Eliot had a kind of heavy intellect for it (Tito) but all her genuine feeling went into the visual realism of *Amos Barton*. On the continent it is known; but the method of Stendhal or of Flaubert is quite other. A situation is for Stendhal something deliberately constructed, often an illustration. There is a bleakness about it, vitalized by force rather than feeling, and its presentation is definitely visual. Hawthorne and James have a kind of sense, a receptive medium, which is not of sight. Not that they fail to make you *see*, so far as necessary, but sight is not the essential sense. They per-

The Question of Henry James

ceive by antennae; and the "deeper psychology" is here. The deeper psychology indeed led Hawthorne to some of his absurdest and most characteristic excesses; it was forever tailing off into the fanciful, even the allegorical, which is a lazy substitute for profundity. The fancifulness is the "strain of generous indolence," the attempt to get the artistic effect by meretricious means. On this side a critic might seize hold of *The Turn of the Screw*, a tale about which I have many doubts; but the actual working out of this is different from Hawthorne's, and we are not interested in approximation of the two men on the side of their weakness. The point is Hawthorne was acutely sensitive to the situation; that he did grasp character through the relation of two or more persons to each other; and this is what no one else, except James, has done. Furthermore, he does establish, as James establishes, a solid atmosphere, and he does, in his quaint way, get New England, as James gets a larger part of America, and as none of their respective contemporaries get anything above a village or two, or a jungle. Compare, with anything that any English contemporary could do, the situation which Hawthorne sets up in the relation of Dimmesdale and Chillingworth. Judge Pyncheon and Clifford, Hepzibah and Phoebe, are similarly achieved by their relation to each other; Clifford, for one, being simply the intersection of a relation to three other characters. The only dimension in which Hawthorne could expand was the past, his present being so narrowly barren. It is a great pity, with his remarkable gift of observation, that the present did not offer him more to observe. But he is the one English-writing predecessor of James whose characters are *aware* of each other, the one whose novels were in any deep sense a criticism of even a slight civilization; and here is something more definite and closer than any derivation we can trace from Richardson or Marivaux.

The fact that the sympathy with Hawthorne is most felt in the last of James's novels, *The Sense of the Past*, makes me the more certain of its genuineness. In the meantime, James has been through a much more elaborate development than poor Hawthorne ever knew. Hawthorne, with his very limited culture, was not exposed to any bewildering variety of influences. James,

[116]

in his astonishing career of self-improvement, touches Hawthorne most evidently at the beginning and end of his course; at the beginning, simply as a young New Englander of letters; at the end, with almost a gesture of approach. *Roderick Hudson* is the novel of a clever and expanding young New Englander; immature, but just coming out to a self-consciousness where Hawthorne never arrived at all. Compared with *Daisy Miller* or *The Europeans* or *The American* its critical spirit is very crude. But *The Marble Faun* (*Transformation*), the only European novel of Hawthorne, is of Cimmerian opacity; the mind of its author was closed to new impressions though with all its Walter Scott-*Mysteries of Udolpho* upholstery the old man does establish a kind of solid moral atmosphere which the young James does not get. James in *Roderick Hudson* does very little better with Rome than Hawthorne, and as he confesses in the later preface, rather fails with Northampton.[1]

He does in the later edition tone down the absurdities of Roderick's sculpture a little, the pathetic Thirst and the gigantic Adam; Mr. Striker remains a failure, the judgment of a young man consciously humorizing, too suggestive of *Martin Chuzzlewit*. The generic resemblance to Hawthorne is in the occasional heavy facetiousness of the style, the tedious whimsicality how different from the exactitude of *The American Scene,* the verbalism. He too much identifies himself with Rowland, does not see through the solemnity he has created in that character, commits the cardinal sin of failing to "detect" one of his own characters. The failure to create a situation is evident: with Christina and Mary, each nicely adjusted, but never quite set in relation to each other. The interest of the book for our present purpose is what he does *not* do in the Hawthorne way, in the instinctive attempt to get at something larger, which will bring him to the same success with much besides.

The interest in the "deeper psychology," the observation, and

[1] Was Hawthorne at all in his mind here? In criticizing *The House of the Seven Gables* he says "it renders, to an initiated reader, the impression of a summer afternoon in an elm-shaded New England town," and in the preface to *Roderick Hudson* he says "what the early chapters of the book most 'render' to me today is not the umbrageous air of their New England town."

the sense for situation, developed from book to book, culminate in *The Sense of the Past* (by no means saying that this is his best), uniting with other qualities both personal and racial. James's greatness is apparent both in his capacity for development as an artist and his capacity for keeping his mind alive to the changes in the world during twenty-five years. It is remarkable (for the mastery of a span of American history) that the man who did the Wentworth family in the eighties could do the Bradhams in the hundreds. In *The Sense of the Past* the Midmores belong to the same generation as the Bradhams; Ralph belongs to the same race as the Wentworths, indeed as the Pyncheons. Compare the book with *The House of the Seven Gables* (Hawthorne's best novel after all); the situation, the "shrinkage and extinction of a family," is rather more complex, on the surface, than James's with (so far as the book was done) fewer character relations. But James's real situation here, to which Ralph's mounting the step is the key, as Hepzibah's opening of her shop, is a situation of different states of mind. James's situation is the shrinkage and extinction of an idea. The Pyncheon tragedy is simple; the "curse" upon the family a matter of the simplest fairy mechanics. James has taken Hawthorne's ghost sense and given it substance. At the same time making the tragedy much more ethereal: the tragedy of that "Sense," the hypertrophy, in Ralph, of a partial civilization; the vulgar vitality of the Midmores in their financial decay contrasted with the decay of Ralph in his financial prosperity, when they precisely should have been the civilization he had come to seek. All this watched over by the absent but conscious Aurora. I do not want to insist upon the Hawthorneness of the confrontation of the portrait, the importance of the opening of a door. We need surely not insist that this book is the most important, most substantial sort of thing that James did; perhaps there is more solid wear even in that other unfinished *Ivory Tower*. But I consider that it was an excursion which we could well permit him, after a lifetime in which he had taken talents similar to Hawthorne's and made them yield far greater returns than poor Hawthorne could harvest from his granite soil; a permissible exercise, in which we may by a legitimately cognate fancy seem to detect Hawthorne coming to a mediumistic existence again, to remind a younger and incredulous generation of what he really was, had he had the opportunity, and to attest his satisfaction that that opportunity had been given to James.

VAN WYCK BROOKS

Two Phases of Henry James

[1925]

I

A HISTORIAN of manners, a critic of manners, a mind at home with itself, alert, witty, instructed, in its own familiar domain. Yes, and in the foreground of life, the ground of the typical, the general. Turgenev said of Flaubert's Monsieur Homais that the great strength of such a portrait consisted in its being at once an individual, of the most concrete sort, and a type. James [1] creates these types again and again: they are not universal but they are national—there are scarcely half a dozen figures in American fiction to be placed beside them. Christopher Newman remains for all time the wistful American businessman who spends his life hankering after the fine things he has missed. Daisy Miller's character, predicament, life, and death are the story of a whole phase of the social history of America. Dr. Sloper, that perfect embodiment of the respectability of old New York; Miss Birdseye, the symbol of the aftermath of the heroic age of New England; Mrs. Burrage, the eternal New York hostess; Gilbert Osmond, the Italianate American—these are all veritable creations: indeed one has only to recall Winterbourne, in *Daisy Miller*, the American who has lived abroad so long that he has ceased to understand the behavior of his fellow countrywoman, to perceive with what an unfailing resourcefulness James infuses into the least of his characters the element of the typical. It goes without saying that all this, together

[1] In the novels written prior to about 1890. It is Brooks's contention, in *The Pilgrimage of Henry James*, from which these passages are taken, that the later work deteriorated because James was at home in neither the United States nor Europe. *Ed.*

with the tenderness and the benevolent humor that bathe the primitive Jamesian scene, indicates the sort of understanding that is born only of race. These novels are the work of a man who was so sure of his world that he could play with it as all the great novelists have played with their worlds. The significant theme came to him with a natural inevitability, for he shared some of the deepest and most characteristic desires of his compatriots. And this relation, as long as he maintained it, endowed him with the notes of the great tellers of tales, the note of the satirist, the note of the idyllist, the note of the tragedian.

And "how does he feel about life? What, in the last analysis, is his philosophy? When vigorous writers have reached maturity," James remarks in *Partial Portraits*, "we are at liberty to look in their works for some expression of a total view of the world they have been so actively observing." Nothing could be clearer than his own view, the point, as it might be called, of these gathered novels and tales. Mr. Hueffer says that James's chief mission was to civilize America; and if by civilizing one means the development of individuality, the development of consciousness, one can hardly find a happier phrase. He is the friend of all those who are endeavoring to clarify their own minds, to know their own reasons, to discover their real natures, to make the most of their faculties, to escape from the lot of mere passive victims of fate. His tragedies are all the tragedies of *not knowing;* and those against whom he directs his shafts are the representatives and advocates of mass opinion and of movements that mechanize the individual. He was the first novelist in the distinctively American line of our day: the first to challenge the herd instinct, to reveal the inadequacy of our social life, to present the plight of the highly personalized human being in the primitive community. And James succeeds, where so many later novelists have failed, succeeds in presenting the struggle for the rights of personality—the central theme of all modern American fiction—because he is able to conceive personalities of transcendent value.

Yes, his own race, even his own soil—the soil to which he had remained for so long uneasily attached, the soil in which, in response to his own desire, he was brought back to be buried at last—was for James, in spite of all, the Sacred Fount. It was the spring of his own unconscious being; and the world to which it gave birth in his mind was a world that he saw with a level eye, as it was, as it should be, that he loved, hated, possessed, caressed, and judged. Judged it humanely, in the light of essential standards, of the "scale of mankind," in Dostoevski's phrase, and by so doing created values for it. . . . As long as he retained a vital connection with it. But later? . . . "The world," says Mr. Lubbock, referring to his life in England, "is not used to such deference from a rare critical talent, and it certainly has much less respect for its own standards than Henry James had, or seemed to have. His respect was of course very freely mingled with irony, and yet it would be rash to say that his irony preponderated. He probably felt that this, in his condition, was a luxury which he could only afford within limits." That is discreetly put, but what it was to mean we can divine from one of his own early letters from London: "You will have read this second part [of *An International Episode*] by this time," he writes to his mother, "and I hope that you won't, like many of my friends here (as I partly know and partly suspect) take it ill of me as against my 'British entertainers.' It seems to me myself that I have been very delicate; but I shall keep off dangerous ground in future. It is an entirely new sensation for them (the people here) to be (at all delicately) *ironized* or satirized, from the American point of view, and they don't at all relish it." That is also discreetly put; nevertheless, it marks the beginning of the gradual metamorphosis of James's mind. He had seen life, in his own way, as all the great novelists have seen it, *sub specie aeternitatis;* he was to see it henceforth, increasingly, *sub specie mundi*—for had he not subscribed, as only a probationer can subscribe, to the codes and scruples, the conventions and prejudices, the standards (held so lightly by everyone else) of the world he longed to possess? In adapting himself to this world he was to lose his instinctive judgment of men and things; and this explains his "virtuosity of vision," as Mr. Brownell describes it, the gradual decomposition, more and more marked the more his talent grew, of his sense of human values.

Van Wyck Brooks

II

He had entered thus early [2] on that period of life when, as Taine says, feeling vanishes before science and the mind especially delights in overcoming difficulties. "I find our art, all the while," he was to write betimes to Howells, "more difficult of practice, and want, with that, to do it in a more and more difficult way; it being really, at bottom, only difficulty that interests me." *Only* difficulty—and not the life he desired to represent? Only the way to do a thing that would make it undergo most doing? The day had not yet come, perhaps, when he was to forget the names of his characters, when he was to refer in his scenarios to "my first young man" and "my second young man," to "the Girl" and "Aurora What's-her-name," when he was to speak of the need of individuals simply of a particular size and weight; nevertheless, it is significant that the first novel in his later manner, *The Spoils of Poynton*, should have been, as he said, conceived as a story of "things." His people were to grow dimmer and dimmer, like the flame of a lamp in which the oil is exhausted; but he had found another object for his interest. He had found—*The Awkward Age* had proved it to him—that a novel might be "fundamentally organized."

That was the figure in the carpet, that was the joy of his soul; that was the very string his pearls were strung on. "By my little point I mean—what shall I call it?" says Hugh Vereker. "The particular thing I've written my books most *for*. Isn't there for every writer a particular thing of that sort, the thing that most makes him apply himself, the thing without the effort to achieve which he wouldn't write at all, the very passion of his passion, the part of the business in which, for him, the flame of art burns most intensely? Well, it's *that!*" It was the point Mr. Wells observed when he said that "James begins by taking it for granted that a novel is a work of art that must be judged by its oneness, judged first by its oneness"; and we have only to turn to our author's prefaces to perceive with what fervor he developed it. "A form all dramatic and scenic" was what he

[2] In his middle fifties. *Ed.*

contemplated for *The Awkward Age,* "of presented episodes, architecturally combined and each making a piece of the building," and he began by drawing a diagram of "a circle consisting of a number of small rounds disposed at equal intervals about a central object"—the central object being his "situation." By such means he obtained his "rope, the rope of the direction and march of the subject, the action, pulled, like a taut cable between a steamer and a tug, from beginning to end." And he achieved his unity of effect by still another ingenious expedient. He defines this as his "preference for dealing with my subject-matter, for 'seeing' my story, through the opportunity and the sensibility of some more or less detached, some not strictly involved, though thoroughly initiated and intelligent, witness or reporter." In other words, the characters are presented to the reader as they are seen by one of them, the mind of the latter being alone presented directly.

Such was the general intention, the buried treasure, in the scheme of his books, upon which the creator of Hugh Vereker looked back with so much pride. He had reason to do so, for what craft, what cunning, what prodigies of deliberation, what arts of the chase had contributed to produce it! And this was only one of those innumerable "secrets of the kitchen" upon which he dwells in his later letters and essays. The "saturation and possession, the fact of the particular experience, the state and degree of acquaintance incurred," these elements, he says, constitute the circumstances of the interest of a novel: the interest itself lies where but in the "doing"? It lies, in short, not in the "matter" but in the "method"—and who had ever contrived such a method as his?

He had emerged as an impassioned geometer—or, shall we say, some vast arachnid of art, pouncing upon the tiny airblown particle and wrapping it round and round. And now a new prodigy had appeared, a style, the style that was the man Henry James had become. He had eschewed the thin, the sharp, the meager; he had desired the rich, the round, the resonant, and all these things had been added unto him; everything that he had thought and felt and tasted and touched, the fabrics upon which his eyes had feasted, the colors that he had loved, the soft sounds, the delicate scents, had left their stamp upon the house of his spirit. The house?—he had "thrown out extensions and protrusions, indulging even, all recklessly, in gables and pinnacles and battlements, things that had transformed the unpretending place into a veritable palace, an extravagant, bristling, flag-flying structure that had quite as much to do with the air as with the earth." His sense, like Adam Verver's, had been kept sharp, year after year, by the collation of types and signs, the comparison of fine object with fine object, of one degree of finish, of one form of the exquisite with another; and type and object and form had molded his style. Metaphors bloomed there like tropical air plants, throwing out branches and flowers; and every sound was muted and every motion vague.

For other things had passed into this style—the evasiveness, the hesitancy, the scrupulosity of an habitually embarrassed man. The caution, the ceremoniousness, the baffled curiosity, the nervousness and constant self-communion, the fear of committing himself—these traits of the self-conscious guest in the house where he had never been at home had fashioned with time the texture of his personality. They had infected the creatures of his fancy, they had fixed the character of his imaginative world; and behind his novels, those formidable projections of a geometrical intellect, were to be discerned now the confused reveries of an invalid child. For in his prolonged association with people who had merely glimmered for him, in the constant abrogation of his moral judgment, in these years of an enchanted exile in a museum world—for what else had England ever been for him?—Henry James had reverted to a kind of childhood. Plots thronged through his mind, dim figures which, like his own Chad and Strether, "passed each other, in their deep immersion, with the round, impersonal eye of silent fish"; and with these figures, as with pawns or paper soldiers, he devised his labyrinthine games. What interested him was not the figures but their relations, the relations which alone make pawns significant.

Glance at these stories. Do they "correspond with life . . . life without rearrangement"? A man procures as a private preserve an altar in a Catholic church (*The Altar of the Dead*). A great author dies in a country house because he is afraid to offend his hostess by going home (*The Death of the Lion*). A young man breaks his engagement to marry a girl he is in love with in order to devote his life to the discovery of the "intention" of a great author (*The Figure in the Carpet*). A young man who is described as a "pure, passionate, pledged Radical" agrees to act against his beliefs, stand as the Tory candidate, and marry a girl he dislikes in order to keep his family estate (*Covering End*). The guests in a country house devote themselves for three days to "nosing about for a relation that a lady has her reasons for keeping secret" (*The Sacred Fount*). A French countess who is presented to us as the type of the great lady loses her self-command when she is discovered in an equivocal situation, thrusts her daughter forward as a scapegoat, and joins in a conspiracy not to hear the name of a certain undistinguished toilet article (Madame de Vionnet in *The Ambassadors*). A young man who is represented as "a gentleman, generally sound and generally pleasant," straightway appears without any adequate explanation as engaged in the most atrocious of conspiracies (Merton Densher in *The Wings of the Dove*). Two young men put away in a drawer without opening it a will which they have every right to open only to discuss for hours what the will probably contains (*The Ivory Tower*). A young man who is deeply in love abandons his betrothed because he is more deeply in love with a house he had inherited in London (*The Sense of the Past*). The reason we find these stories so oppressive is that they do not follow the lines of life. The people act out of character (Merton Densher), or in a fashion that belies their author's professions for them (the Countess de Vionnet), or in violation of the nature of things (the man who monopolizes the altar in the Catholic church), or as characters can only act with impunity to the author when they are presented ironically. It is intolerable to be asked to regard as "great" the Lion who is so afraid of his hostess, or as honorable the young politician who changes his party to save his house, or as worthy of our serious attention the lover who prefers his furniture to his mistress. Reset in the key of satire all these themes would be plausible; but James gathers grapes of thorns and figs of thistles.

No, the behavior of his characters bears no just relation to the motives that are imputed to them. They are "great," they are "fine," they are "noble"—and they surrender their lovers and their convictions for a piece of property. They are "eminent" —and their sole passion is inquisitiveness. Magnificent pretensions, petty performances!—the fruits of an irresponsible imagination, of a deranged sense of values, of a mind working in the void, uncorrected by any clear consciousness of human cause and effect. This is the meaning of Mr. Richard Curle's remark that James had become the "victim of his own personality." The general impression these writings give us—to quote a phrase from *The Spectator,* is "that of a world in which a brilliant conjuror manipulates puppets of his own invention, not one in which the experience of real life is transmuted in the crucible of creative genius."

VERNON LOUIS PARRINGTON

Henry James and the Nostalgia of Culture

[1930]

THERE is a suggestion of irony in the fact that one of our earliest realists, who was independent enough to break with the romantic tradition, should have fled from the reality that his art presumably would gird itself up to deal with. Like his fellow spirit Whistler, Henry James was a lifelong pilgrim to other shrines than those of his native land, who dedicated his gifts to ends that his fellow Americans were indifferent to. Life, with him, was largely a matter of nerves. In this world of sprawling energy it was impossible to barricade himself securely against the intrusion of the unpleasant. His organism was too sensitive, his discriminations too fine, to subject them to the vulgarities of the Gilded Age, and he fled from it all. He early convinced himself that the American atmosphere was uncongenial to the artist.[1] The grotesqueries of the frontier irruption, the crude turmoil released by the new freedoms, were no materials to appeal to one in search of subtleties, to one who was a lover of nocturnes in gray. And so, like Whistler, he sought other lands, there to refine a meticulous technique, and draw out ever thinner the substance of his art.

The explanation of the curious career of Henry James, seeking a habitation between worlds and finding a spiritual home nowhere, is that he was never a realist. Rather he was a self-deceived romantic, the last subtle expression of the genteel, who

[1] "Civilization at its highest pitch was the master passion of his mind, and his preoccupation with the international aspects of character and custom issued from the conviction that the rawness and rudeness of a young country were not incapable of cure by contact with more developed forms." Pelham Edgar, *Henry James, Man, Author*, pp. 40-41.

Vernon Louis Parrington

fell in love with culture and never realized how poor a thing he worshiped. It was the first mistake of Henry James that he romanticized Europe, not for its fragments of the medieval picturesque, but for a fine and gracious culture that he professed to discover there. With the naïveté of the Age of Innocence he assumed that an aristocratic society—shall we say that of Mayfair or the Quartier Saint-Germain?—is a complex of subtle imponderables that one comes to understand and embody only through heritage; and it was an assumption even more romantic that these imponderables were so subtly elusive as to escape any but the subtlest art. Like Edith Wharton he erected this suppositious culture into an abstract *tertium quid*, something apart from social convention or physical environment, something embodied in the choicer spirits of a class that for generations presumably had cherished them. Born of an unconscious inferiority complex in presence of a long-established social order to which he was alien, this romanticization of European culture worked to his undoing, for it constrained the artist to a lifelong pursuit of intangible realities that existed only in his imagination. The gracious culture that James persistently attributed to certain choice circles in Europe was only a figment of his romantic fancy—a fact that after long rambling on the continent and nearly forty years' unbroken residence in England, he came finally to recognize. It was this failure to find the substance of his dream that imparted to his work a note of wistfulness. He had quitted the land of his birth to seek his spiritual home elsewhere, yet increasingly he came to question the wisdom of his act. He suffered the common fate of the *déraciné;* wandering between worlds, he found a home nowhere. It is not well for the artist to turn cosmopolitan, for the flavor of the fruit comes from the soil and sunshine of its native fields.

The spirit of Henry James marks the last refinement of the genteel tradition, the completest embodiment of its vague cultural aspirations. All his life he dwelt wistfully on the outside of the realm he wished to be a free citizen of. Did any other professed realist ever remain so persistently aloof from the homely realities of life? From the external world of action he withdrew to the inner world of questioning and probing; yet even in his subtle psychological inquiries he remained shut up within his own skull-pan. His characters are only projections of his brooding fancy, externalizations of hypothetical subtleties. He was concerned only with *nuances*. He lived in a world of fine gradations and imperceptible shades. Like modern scholarship he came to deal more and more with less and less. It is this absorption in the stream of psychical experience that justifies one in calling Henry James a forerunner of modern expressionism. Yet how unlike he is to Sherwood Anderson, an authentic product of the American consciousness!

EDNA KENTON

Henry James in the World

[1934]

WHY did Henry James leave America in his young manhood and go to England to live? This question—it is a
good one, for it strikes straight at the motivation of an act
which determined the whole trend of his life—has in recent
years been played with and worried over by more than one
intensely American-minded critic. An answer of sorts has come
out of the welter of worry but it is not, I think, quite the right
one. It is too much colored by a resentment against overt or
covert criticism of America which is so typically American, and
by the new psychology which is still in a hypothetical stage.

The early answers to this question—it has, of course, been
asked and answered before—were not based on hypothetical
psychology new or old; they implied where they did not directly charge that the choice was born of snobbery, toadyism,
sycophancy, shame of his country and countrymen. His stric-
tures on the bleak, provincial, American background in his
Hawthorne and the "outrage on American girlhood" perpe-
trated in *Daisy Miller* were almost coincident; they roused antagonism whose bitterness we can hardly realize today unless we
go back and steep ourselves for a while in the period. Henry
James is the most unrepresented and misrepresented figure in
letters; the misrepresentation of him began then, exactly, in
1879, and reverberations of that old contemporary criticism are
still sounding today.

But we are more civil today. We have sunk the unlovely old
epithets into a single word, "expatriate." Unfortunately, we
have not sunk with them their old connotations which rise to

[131]

The Question of Henry James

the surface like oil. The gist of our modern thesis is, to begin with, and all flatly, that James was a failure because he was an expatriate, and so, in accordance with every psychological law of cause and effect, the answer to the good question of why he chose to live abroad is colored at once by that foregone dark conclusion. Under its shadow and in the none too steady light of the new psychology the answer appears to be that he fled from nightmare to sweet dream; from the sinister symbol of failure and destruction (America) to the symbol of success through rebirth in the "great world" (Europe); that he fought there his lifelong battle against a foe he clearly perceived—the self-exiled American's superstitious valuation of Europe—but none the less died beguiled, deluded, still a child living in a fantasied world. This modern elaboration is founded on what are, I think, really false premises: The first one, "All expatriates are failures!" But are they? The second, "Henry James was an expatriate!" But was he?

"Expatriate" as a synonym for James's whole attitude toward America has become a favorite critical *cliché*. But is it the right word? As a noun, it is a bastard word; if we use coined words we should use them for sole sake of expressing exactly what we are intending to say. This word carries with it the idea either of forced banishment, or of self-banishment, or of voluntary renouncement of citizenship in order to become citizen of another country. "Expatriate" covers James's situation during the last few months of his life; to the long backward stretch of his English residence it simply doesn't apply. And it may be said, almost omnisciently, that if the Great War had not forced regulations for aliens which made simple trips from Rye to London highly irritating, James would never have surrendered his American citizenship. He liked it; it was never a problem.

We have only to look about us a little, however, to find the word which does describe his status as a permanent absentee from his country. James gives it to us himself, in a brief though exceedingly meaty essay which has been drawn on to prove him a regretful, discouraged, repentant "expatriate." In *The Story-teller at Large: Mr. Henry Harland* (a bit of fugitive prose of 1898 never reprinted), which deals directly with Harland, a

[132]

Edna Kenton

self-exiled American in Europe, and indirectly throughout with the case—James's case—of "a citizen of the world," James speaks of *dis*patriation and subtly defines it as a kind of detachment in viewpoint of, not severance of interest in, the birthland. It is a coined word, coined deliberately as he coined others at need for expressing fine shades and coined in this case from need of the prefix. A *dis*patriated point of view takes its place alongside that kind of curiosity he held so essential for appreciation, curiosity supremely *dis*interested, disentangled from personal bias, and so at white heat, intent only on arriving at the truth of a particular case, whatever the truth might be.

His small quarrel with Harland was that Harland's point of view was not dispatriated, disinterested, detached; that, with no strong impressions of America or Europe, with only a most acute sense of "the 'Europe'—(synthetic symbol!)—of the American mind," simply surrender of surface to surface, he was merely skimming over the synthetic land, rooted nowhere, pausing nowhere to dig. This essay appeared thirty-six years ago, before most of what has since made the world a mere neighborhood was more than a dream. But thirty-six years ago, glancing at the old notion that a writer to have his own quality "must needs draw his sap from the soil of his origin," James pointed out that, since the days of Dickens, Scott, Balzac, Hawthorne, the "globe is fast shrinking, for the imagination, to the size of an orange that can be played with," and that soon, successfully to emulate the old local concentration so involuntary in Dickens or Balzac, would be a rare and possibly beautiful *tour de force*. One "went abroad" in spite of oneself, and the good point of view for the artist was born of dispatriation, the point of view of "a citizen of the world." This is the full sense of *The Story-teller at Large*; it is poor stuff to quote in support of the theory that James regretted his long residence abroad.

Full discussion of this moot question of "country" is contained in a single group of James's writings and there lies the answer to the whole affair. One of this group is the portrait of Hawthorne; another is the portrait of Story; the third is the portrait of an artist painted by himself. In his *Hawthorne* (1879) James diagnosed the case of an American artist who

[133]

stayed at home, even when he went abroad; an artist "become one by being just American *enough*, by the felicity of how the artist in him missed nothing, suspected nothing, that the ambient air [of America] didn't affect him as containing." (That sentence is James at his best, deftly protecting his subject by way of praise and hosannas.) In *William Wetmore Story and His Friends* (1903) he analyzed, once for all, in two close-packed volumes, the case of an American artist who, missing everything in America's ambient air, both what it contained and what it didn't, and turning therefore in aesthetic disgust a permanent back on his country, lacked enough sap drawn from his native soil to survive transplantation. In the autobiographies and prefaces (and in the *Letters*) James gave us the case of an artist American enough, as Story was not, to take a natively developed vigor with him to Europe; and artist enough, as Hawthorne was not, to feel need of free range through other cultures and manners. Hawthorne, pure provincial, pure native, flowered into eternal, native, provincial charm just because his aesthetic demands were not too much for his slender aesthetic equipment. He drank from his own small glass. Story, rooted neither in Salem nor Boston, in Italy branched and leaved in a dozen directions but never flowered in one. The victim of mere beguilement, hagridden by a superstitious valuation of Europe, his career was "a sort of beautiful sacrifice to a noble mistake," the mistake being, all simply, "the frank consent to be beguiled." James, too much the artist not to miss what America didn't contain, but also too much the artist to miss anything and everything it did hold, turned only his literal back on his literal country. There are pages in plenty, in *Notes of a Son and Brother,* where the process of his realization both of his Americanism and of its high value to be is intimately disclosed. We can stand by, can watch it unfold. America *plus* Europe equals what?—this was the sum he set about adding up. America minus Europe was Hawthorne's simple problem; as Europe minus America was Story's more complicated one. The solutions of these formulae, what they "equal," lie before us in the body of work of each of the dissimilar three.

Without his "American subject" James would have been, as

he somewhere frankly confesses, nowhere at all; on it his long
career opened and closed. In this group of his writings, then,
since the relation between artist and subject is the paramount
one, the general idea that most interested Hawthorne, Story,
and James plays a part as important as country. In the Story
biography the case of the American artist at large in Europe
is the theme, illustrated by more examples than Story's. Its aesthetic moral—the core of its more than seven hundred pages
is this:—that the artist must have a country of his own and that
his relation to his subject is that country. If his subject is purely
American, as was Hawthorne's; if his relation to it is purely
American, as was Hawthorne's (and never so much as in *The
Marble Faun*), then he is no citizen of the great world. If he
has no subject; if, like Story, he never lacks *a* subject, is facile
but is never possessed by or in possession of *the* subject about
which everything centers, then he has no country of his own.
If, on the other hand, his subject is one which must feed on
comparisons and contrasts, as James's avowedly and provably
was, then, so long as his relation to it is constant, he is always
at "home." All this and much more lies under the surface of a
long letter to Edith Wharton of 1912, where, after discussing
her latest "international" novel, *The Reef,* the meanwhile protecting his disinterested opinion of it with admirable finesse,
he said: ". . . your only drawback is not having the homeliness
and the inevitability and the happy limitation and the affluent
poverty, of a Country of your Own (*comme moi, par ex-
emple!*)."

Since James's American subject was an integral part of his
general one, his projected treatment of it could not be Hawthorne's close, confined, local kind—the treatment, so to say,
of the village doctor, operating instinctively, with primitive in-
struments, by a single, American light. James's treatment demanded dispatriation as a *sine qua non;* disattachment from any
single measure of values; the Spartan virtue, constantly practiced for disinterested curiosity's sake, of triumph over distaste.
It demanded—nothing less—the elimination of provincialism
not only in attitude but in expression.

Provincialism is, of course, not a matter of literacy or illiteracy; it is a matter of attitude to the world at large. In its last analysis it is nothing more nor less than an *unawareness* of the process and kind of life in other orders. In this sense, as James ironically indicates in the Story biography, Judge Story, who never left his native soil, was both New Englander and man of the world; while his son, disdaining his New England heritage and living a lifetime in Europe, remained a provincial always. Certainly, it was not to take on Story's kind of Europeanized provincialism that James went abroad to shed his own. And nothing is clearer than that he had not abandoned America once for all when he went over to live, in 1875. Entirely too much has been made of this "struggle," this "conflict"; most of it is mere hangover of sentimentality from that most sentimental decade. Within three years he was writing his brother William of a plan to return in a couple of years for a twelvemonth, "and see everything of the country I can, including Washington." This is the letter in which occurs the much-quoted line: "I know what I am about, and I have always my eyes on my native land." He carried out this plan; he did come back in 1881; spent weeks in Washington, near Henry Adams; ". . . had a plan of travelling all about the country this winter." Howells wrote John Hay early in 1882; but the plan was broken by his mother's sudden death the February after his return.

Half a dozen years later, in another much-quoted letter to William, he set down his conclusions on the relations between the two great English-speaking countries: they were more like than unlike, were but different chapters of the same general subject with which fiction could magnificently deal under one great condition. "I have not," he wrote, "the least hesitation in saying that I aspire to write in such a way that it would be impossible to an outsider to say whether I am at a given moment an American writing about England or an Englishman writing about America (dealing as I do with both countries,) and far from behing ashamed of such an ambiguity I should be exceedingly proud of it, for it would be highly civilized." It would be the last, fine product of deliberate dispatriation—expression from which every last dreg of provincialism, American *or* English, had been filtered out, with the great mother tongue left pure. It constituted an attitude in itself, it must be admitted, for Henry James consciously in his youth to have set about the attainment of such a point of view and such a rendering of it. So he went to England to live, to observe, to register notes and impressions. Because he was "foreign," his observation was keener; he noticed things Englishmen didn't; of English usage, manners, modes of thought and action. The English talk in his novels is better than the English talk in English novels; it is English talk itself in its finest shades. Amazed Englishmen noted it and at times resented it; *An International Episode* they resented extremely. Their reactions to this particular tale gave James more notes, more insight. ". . . for a Bostonian nymph to reject an English duke," he replied to one challenge, "is an adventure only less stirring, I should say, than for an English duke to be rejected by a Bostonian nymph. I see dramas within dramas in that, and innumerable points of view." Englishmen noted, too, the American talk in his novels. It was not English talk but neither was it the American talk in English novels. Without other expedient James turned up English provincialism before English eyes. He represented Englishmen to Englishmen, Americans to Americans, and each to the other, as no novelist before or since has succeeded in doing. It is as if he had lived his life as unrecognized, unauthorized, undreamed-of ambassador of letters at large. America, England, France, Italy, Germany, Russia—he rounded them all and included them in his mission. In this light, in the light of the biographies and the autobiographies we have glanced at, the tears shed over his so-called, lifelong struggle between countries must strike us as slightly mawkish. Life is a struggle, wherever we are. But Henry James *was* "between" countries. There lay his subject and his relation to it, and there was his home.

CONSTANCE ROURKE

The American

[1931]

THE Civil War has been considered a prime destructive agent in the life of the nation, warping or even destroying a native culture. But the literature of the fifties had never been truly complete. Uncalculating digressions might have followed even though there had been no catastrophe. In spite of the disruption of the war a determined experiment continued through the sixties, seventies, and eighties. The international scene became a great American scene, even in a sense *the* great American scene.

Few ideas had disturbed the American mind more acutely than those which had to do with the European relationship. In the sixties the early commentaries of European travelers still rankled: Tuckerman gathered them into a compendious volume, with rejoinders. But the old fable had undergone a change. In its last notable version, *Our American Cousin,* the nationalistic hero had exhibited his character and enjoyed his adventures in England, and possessed an English heritage. He was in fact one of those "dispossessed princes and wandering heirs" of whom Henry James was to write. In spite of the burlesque the gesture of disseverance had grown less positive in Mark Twain's long skits. The American went abroad, often to stay; sentiment overspread his return to "our old home," and that preoccupation with art which had been satirized in *Innocents Abroad* became one of his larger preoccupations.

This was mixed with a consideration which had long since been borne in upon the American mind by British criticisms. Culture was an obvious proof of leisure, of long establishment, of half a hundred desirable assurances that had been lacking in American life; it even seemed to resolve the vexing problem of manners. Culture was sought abroad as a tangible emblem. The resultant "pillage of the past" was to mount to monstrous proportions, and to include the play of many unworthy instincts—ostentation, boredom, a morbid inversion of personal desires; often, no doubt, it represented a natural response to the fine accumulations of time. Yet surely on the wide scale it was something more than these. Fumbling and fantastic, the restless habit seemed an effort to find an established tradition, with the solidity, assurance, and justification which traditions may bring. The American wish for establishment had often seemed a fundamental wish, with all the upheaval.

Many Americans continued to make the extravagant denials of *Innocents Abroad*, but the exodus was unbroken, and found an interpreter in Henry James. His talk of "dispossessed princes and wandering heirs" was not without a personal connotation. As a young man, considering Europe, he had wondered how he was to come into his "own." "The nostalgic poison had been distilled for him," he declared, speaking of himself. James became indeed, as Van Wyck Brooks has said, "an immortal symbol." Strangely enough in this connection, he was something more: an American artist who worked within native sequence.

Henry James has been pictured as a troubled evasionist without a country; and the charge has been turned to a militant charge against American civilization. Yet this theory can hardly account for the long engagement of a major talent. Such talent usually has only one great subject; the choice of that subject will be instinctive, resting upon innumerable elements of heritage and of intimate experience. The consciousness of the European relationship had been binding in America. Given favoring observation, some considerable artist was bound to use the international scene and to find its richest content.

But even a major talent will need the impetus which may come from other imaginative approaches. As formal literary expression of the time is scanned nothing arises to account for the scope and intention of James. He had none of those slightly inferior forerunners in his own medium by which the great writer is often heralded. He wrote as from a fresh impulse; yet the way for his achievement had been opened by a popular vanguard with whose efforts he had some contact. As a small boy he frequented Barnum's, where the Yankee farces were often performed, where the whole American legend was racily sketched, with the backwoodsman and the minstrel as occasional figures, and with melodrama well to the fore. *Our American Cousin* achieved its first great success when James was a lad of fifteen; the play created an immense volume of talk, and was continued for many years. During James's boyhood the streets of New York were alive with the color of the California adventure, with its outlining of the composite American character.

Somewhere James has spoken of the novelist's aptitude for judging the whole piece by a small bit of pattern. Such hints as those abroad in New York during the fifties could go far with a sensitive young mind like his; and others existed to complement them, in the London magazines read before the fire in the New York house, in the visits of Thackeray there, in the glimpses of the great foreign world afforded by the constant voyaging of the family to Europe. James never lost the sense of romance with which his youthful apprehensions of Europe were tinged. He was to write of the European scene with warmth and luster and enchantment; even his dull passages have their inner glow. But he began on humble, even primitive ground in his consideration of the American character as this appeared within the European scene; and he kept throughout his life convictions which he must have drawn from the fund of a common native experience.

II

James was bent upon a purpose that had absorbed many American fabulists, that of drawing the large, the generic, American character. Deliberately, it seems, he abandoned the portrayal of local figures, though for this he had a singular genius: in regions familiar to him he caught the local speech, the manner, the inevitable effect of background. Barring the char-

acters in *The Europeans* and *The Bostonians* and a scattering
few elsewhere, his Americans are nomadic and rootless; even
when they are seen on American soil they belong to no special
locality; they are the composite type; the broad lineaments are
unmistakable. He wrote of an American "confidence that broke
down . . . a freedom that pulled up nowhere . . . an idyllic
ease that was somehow too ordered for a primitive social consciousness and too innocent for a developed." In drawing Roderick Hudson, with his "instinctive quickness of observation
and his free appropriation of whatever might serve his purpose,"
James seemed to have in mind something more than a character:
his young sculptor becomes a national type. "His appetite for
novelty was insatiable, and for everything characteristically foreign, as it presented itself, he had an extravagant greeting; but
in half an hour the novelty had faded, he had guessed the secret,
he had plucked out the heart of the mystery, and was clamor-
ing for a keener sensation. . . . The boy was living too fast
. . . and giving alarming pledges of ennui in his later
years. . . ."

James was candid, as the early fabulists had been candid. He
wrote of Americans who treated Europe "collectively, as a vast
painted and gilded holiday toy, serving its purpose on the spot,
but to be relinquished, sacrificed, broken and cast away, at the
dawn of any other convenience." Using the familiar symbolism
of the comic name, he pictured the conquering Mrs. Headway,
who by a gross energy and with impenetrable surfaces achieved
an external European triumph.

He pictured Mr. Leavenworth, "a tall, expansive, bland gentleman, with a carefully brushed whisker and a spacious, fair,
well-favored face, which seemed somehow to have more room
in it than was occupied by a smile of superior benevolence, so
that (with his smooth white forehead) it bore resemblance to
a large parlor with a very florid carpet but no pictures on the
walls." Mr. Leavenworth was in fact the pretentious consummation of a dominating American idea. "You may be sure that
I have employed a native architect for the large residential
structure that I am erecting on the banks of the Ohio," he said
to Roderick Hudson. "In a tasteful home, surrounded by the

memorials of my wanderings, I hope to recover my moral tone. I ordered in Paris the complete appurtenances of a dining-room. Do you think you could do something for my library? It is to be filled with well-selected authors, and I think a pure white image in this style"—he pointed to one of Roderick's statues—"standing out against the morocco and gilt, would have a noble effect. The subject I have already fixed upon. I desire an allegorical representation of Culture. Do you think now," Mr. Leavenworth inquired, "you could rise to the conception?"

These questing Americans—James showed some of them full of an eager pathos, others as indifferent and lost, moving about the world for lack of another occupation. He made an inclusion that went far beyond the efforts of any American before his time, except that of Hawthorne in *The Scarlet Letter*. He drew American women at full length. With the exception of Christopher Newman and Roderick Hudson and a few others the most significant of James's characters are women: it is they who engage in disastrous encounters abroad, they who embody diverse and contradictory American elements. Isabel Archer, Milly Theale, Mary Garland—their number could be extended: their close and delicate portraiture seemed James's greatest preoccupation. Some of his lesser feminine figures reveal hardy American habits; it is they who most often indulge in the monologue. "I don't apologize, Lord Lambeth," said Mrs. Westgate; "some Americans are always apologizing; you must have noticed that. We've the reputation of always boasting and 'blowing' and waving the American flag; but I must say that what strikes me is that we're perpetually making excuses and trying to smooth things over. The American flag has quite gone out of fashion; it's very carefully folded up, like a tablecloth the worse for wear. Why should we apologize? The English never apologize—do they? No, I must say *I* never apologize. You must take us as we come—with all our imperfections on our heads. Of course we haven't your country life and your old ruins and your great estates and all that. . . ." On she went at immense length, this pretty lady, then and later, "with a mild merciless monotony, a paucity of intonation, an impartial flatness that suggested a flowery mead scrupulously 'done over' by a steam roller that had reduced its texture to that of a drawing-room carpet."

The true heroines of James usually possess a bias of temperament which had appeared more than once in the fable of the contrast and casually elsewhere: Poe had stressed it. "Morella's erudition was profound." "I have spoken of the learning of Ligeia: it was immense—such as I have never known in women." The shadow is not deep in James's novels, but it exists. Mrs. Westgate's sister was little Bessie Alden, a great reader, who united native inquisitiveness with a sturdy integrity. There was Mary Garland, a prim and pretty bluestocking. The young women in *The Europeans*—the true Americans—appear against a background of high thinking; and those in *The Bostonians* form a galaxy absorbed in esoteric knowledge. When these women are not directly absorbed in books they are likely to fulfill the general intention by a definite leaning toward the arts: Isabel Archer walked blindly to her fate because of her belief in the fine accumulations of time. Occasionally James pictured the child of nature—fully feminine at last—as in Daisy Miller or Pandora Day, thus following another tradition; but in the main the women with whom he was most deeply engaged took the aloof, the conscious, the slightly studious part.

Portrait after portrait becomes clear in the great range of his novels and short stories. An entire gallery of characters is created to which Americans may well turn for knowledge and social experience and enlargement, or even for a sense of renewal. They are more than types: they are a whole society of typical individuals: they appear with narrow aggressions and an insular nobility, a careless honesty, a large and delicate purpose. Their ambitions are often blind, or have grown hard and unerring. This society of migratory Americans was a provincial society, transcending provincialism only by fine character. Race, history, even a sense of the future, is upon these people; they still remain singularly inclusive. They offer indeed a legible critique of the American character for those who care to read it; and in the end they reveal more than one unmistakable bias which had appeared in earlier years.

The wilderness and the farm had gone: only their faint traces

The Question of Henry James

were discernible in these narratives. James noted in Mr. Westgate a face of toil, a voice of leisure; he remarked a peculiar
blankness on the faces of older women who may have belonged
to a pioneer society. But for the most part the level has changed;
these are people of leisure; they are distinctly urban. The range
was wide, the innovation profound; the accomplishment of
James, who began to write soon after the Civil War, seems little
short of miraculous when set against the spare and simple portraiture of earlier years. Yet his illumination of the American
character may have grown bright and deep because he accumulated energy from that portraiture, because he possessed the
momentum which a tradition may give. He was grounded in
the Yankee fable; his basic apprehension of the American character was that which had been drawn there. He was acutely sensitive to foreign criticism, as a long line of popular writers had
been before him.

"It was not in the least of American barbarism that she was
afraid," he wrote of Lady Barberina. "Her dread was all of
American civilization." The satirical recognition included the
familiar foreign charge. In *Pandora* the German envoy was on
his way "to explore a society abounding in comic aspects"—
an American society comic to the European. Repeatedly James
set the wickedness or subtlety or deceit of Europeans against
American innocence. The contrast is clear in the small encounters of *Four Meetings;* it lies at the basis of *An International Episode;* it is dramatically posed, with all the implications of a wounding British scorn, in *The Modern Warning.*
Even such fine characters as Kate Croy and Merton Densher reveal an ancestral blackness, against which is drawn the touching
and exquisite nobility of Milly Theale, an American.

In later years James denied that the innocent Americans in
The Wings of the Dove and *The Golden Bowl* were exhibited
as Americans; yet the contrast remains. James never presented
its opposite terms with imaginative force; and the pattern was
repeated too often to be anything but the outgrowth of a profound conviction. He was captivated by the vision of American
innocence. In *The Europeans* the American characters appear
as the very perfection of a delicate and straitened purity—those

indigenous Americans who were being contrasted with vagrant others born and bred in Europe. They were "charming," these true characters, as Felix said, "in a style of their own. How shall I describe it? It's primitive; it's patriarchal; it's the *ton* of the golden age." In one of his later prefaces James wrote with an almost hysterical emphasis of "the comparative *state of inno-cence* of my country folk."

Truly enough, this preoccupation may have been strengthened by influences outside the old view. The endowment of innocence for heroes and heroines alike had been present in the English novels of his period in a fanciful extreme, and it was not unnatural for the son of the elder Henry James to be concerned with moral and ethereal qualities. Truly enough, too, his portrayals often reach far beyond simple effects of contrast and comprise a revelation of moral beauty transcending national considerations altogether; and the pattern was often broken by gross contradictions and incongruities. Yet innocence as drawn by Henry James remains rooted in an established idea. In *The American* he wrote the complete fable, with an altered ending.

III

Even the title was a fulfillment. Who ever heard of a significant English novel called *The Englishman* or an excellent French novel called *Le Français?* The simple and aggressive stress belonged to an imagination perennially engaged by the problem of the national type. The name Newman had significance, faintly partaking of that comic symbolism by which a hero in one of the Yankee fables was called Jedidiah Homebred.

At the opening of the story, as Newman strolled through the Salon Carré examining masterpieces, James declared that no one with an eye for types could have failed to perceive that he was an American. "Indeed such an observer might have made an ironic point of the almost ideal completeness with which he filled out the mold of race. . . . He had the flat jaw and firm, dry neck which are frequent in the American type. . . . Long, lean, and muscular, he suggested an intensity of unconscious resistance. . . . His usual attitude and carriage had a liberal looseness; but when, under a special intensity of inspiration, he straightened himself, he looked like a grenadier on parade." Newman was of the familiar build; he had the familiar consciousness of costume; in an ensuing scene he appeared in a blue satin cravat of too light a shade and with a shirt front obtrusively wide. But according to James it was the eye, of a clear, cold gray, that told the final story: "an eye in which the unacquainted and the expert were singularly blended"—the innocent and the shrewd. "I can't make you out," said Mrs. Tristram, "whether you are very simple or very deep."

Newman's local origin was never given; though he stemmed from the Yankee, he was not of New England, certainly not of Boston. The Pacific Coast had been the scene of his financial successes; and these were fixed as occurring before 1868, that is, during the period of the gold rush. He might have been in San Francisco or Virginia City with Mark Twain; he had habits of the time and place. "He had sat with western humorists in circles around cast-iron stoves and had seen tall stories grow taller without toppling over, and his imagination had learnt the trick of building straight and high." Young Madame de Bellegarde said that if she had not known who Newman was she could have taken him for a duke—an American duke, the Duke of California. "The way you cover ground!" said Valentin de Bellegarde. "However, being as you are a giant, you move naturally in seven league boots. . . . You're a man of the world to a livelier tune than ours."

Fabulous stories were told about Newman. At the great ball given by the Bellegardes he was presented to the Duchess, whose nodding tiara and triple chins and vast expanse of bosom troubled him, and who looked at him "with eyes that twinkled like a pair of polished pin-heads in a cushion." "With her little circle of admirers this remarkable woman reminded him of a Fat Lady at a fair." "I've heard all sorts of extraordinary things about you," she said, fixing her small, unwinking gaze upon him. "*Voyons,* are they true? . . . Oh, you've had your *légende.* You've had a career of the most chequered, the most *bizarre.* What's that about your having founded a city some ten years ago in the great West, a city which contains today half a million inhabitants? Isn't it half a million, messieurs? You're exclusive proprietor of the wonderful place and are consequently fabulously rich, and you'd be richer still if you didn't grant land and houses free of rent to all newcomers who'll pledge themselves never to smoke cigars. At this game, in three years, we're told, you're going to become President of all the Americas."

"He liked doing things that involved his paying for people," said James; "the vulgar truth is he enjoyed 'treating' them. . . . Just as it was a gratification to him to be nobly dressed, just so it was a private satisfaction (for he kept the full flavor of it quite delicately to himself) to see people occupied and amused at his pecuniary expense and by his profuse interposition. To set a large body of them in motion and transport them to a distance, to have special conveyances, to charter railway-carriages and steamboats, harmonized with his relish for bold processes and made hospitality the potent thing it should ideally be."

Newman preserved a negligent air in such enterprises just as he casually gave an order for copies of half a dozen masterpieces to Mademoiselle Noémie in order to provide money for her *dot*. But he clearly saw the direction of Mademoiselle Noémie's purpose when she announced to him that her paintings were daubs in the hope that her candor might bring her a more considerable profit. He passed over her declaration with his customary blankness, dropping into some hidden cavern of his mind the revelation that his taste had been at fault. "You've got something it worries me to have missed," said Valentin. "It's not money, it's not even brains, though evidently yours have been excellent for your purpose. It's not your superfluous stature, though I should have rather liked to be a couple of inches taller. It's a sort of air you have of being imperturbably, being irremovably and indestructibly (that's the thing) at home in the world. When I was a boy my father assured me it was by just such an air that people recognized a Bellegarde. He called my attention to it. He didn't advise me to cultivate it; he said that as we grew up it always came of itself. . . . But you who, as I understand it, have made and sold articles of vulgar household use—you strike me—in a fashion of your own, as a man who stands about at his ease and looks straight over ever so many high walls. I seem to see you move everywhere like a big stockholder on his favorite railroad. You make me feel awfully my want of shares. And yet the world used to be supposed to be ours. What is it I miss?"

Newman's reply was resounding, and might have been taken out of many an American oration of the past. "It's the proud consciousness of honest toil, of having produced something yourself that somebody has been willing to pay for—since that's the definite measure. Since you speak of my washtubs—which were lovely—isn't it just they and their loveliness that make up my good conscience?"

"Oh, no; I've seen men who had gone beyond washtubs, who had made mountains of soap—strong-smelling yellow soap, in great bars; and they've left me perfectly cold."

"Then it's just the regular treat of being an American citizen," said Newman. "That sets a man right up."

The tone, as one knows Newman, was jocose, with an admixture of serious conviction. It was the comic belligerent tone that had spread through the assertive nationalism of the Yankee fables; and James seemed to enjoy the mixed quality. He glossed over nothing, writing with gusto of Newman's early preoccupation with money, which had also been dominant in Yankee swapping and bargaining. He admitted that his hero considered "what he had been placed in the world for was . . . simply to gouge a fortune, the bigger the better, out of its hard material. This idea completely filled his horizon and contented his imagination. Upon the uses of money, upon what one might do with a life into which one had succeeded in injecting the golden stream, he had up to the eve of his fortieth year very scantly reflected."

"I cared for money-making, but I have never cared so very terribly about money," Newman told Madame de Cintré with expansive confidence, launching into self-revelation. As he sat in her drawing room he stretched his legs; his questions had a simple ease. "Don't you find it rather lifeless here," he inquired, "so far from the street?" "Your house is tremendously old then?" he asked a little later. When Valentin had found the

Constance Rourke

date, 1627, over the mantelpiece, Newman announced roundly, "Your house is of a very fine style of architecture." "Are you interested in questions of architecture?" asked Valentin. "Well, I took the trouble this summer to examine—as well as I can calculate—some four hundred and seventy churches. Do you call that interested?" "Perhaps you're interested in religion," answered his host. Newman considered for a moment. "Not actively." He spoke as though it were a railroad or a mine; and he seemed quickly to feel the apparent lack of nicety. To correct this he turned to Madame de Cintré and asked whether she was a Roman Catholic.

Satire invaded the portrait—a deep satire—but James loved Newman. Toward the end of his life he spoke of his young "infatuation" with his subject, and though by this he particularly meant an artistic absorption, his personal devotion was likewise plain. He revealed his hero as a man whom Madame de Cintré could love—that creature "tall, slim, imposing, gentle, half *grande dame* and half an angel; a mixture of 'type' and simplicity, of the eagle and the dove." It was Newman's goodness which drew her; but this alone would not have sufficed for the daughter of an old race if goodness had not been joined with an essential dignity.

But while Madame de Cintré and Valentin perceived the genuine stature of Newman others of his family remembered their prejudices. When Madame de Bellegarde first received Newman, knowing his wish to marry her daughter, she sat small and immovable. "You're an American," she said presently. "I've seen several Americans." "There are several in Paris," said Newman gaily. "Oh, really? It was in England I saw these, or somewhere else; not in Paris. I think it must have been in the Pyrenees many years ago. I'm told your ladies are very pretty. One of these ladies was very pretty—with such a wonderful complexion. She presented me with a note of introduction from some one—I forget whom—and she sent with it a note of her own. I kept her letter a long time afterwards, it was so strangely expressed. I used to know some of the phrases by heart. But I've forgotten them now—it's so many years ago. Since then I've

[149]

seen no more Americans. I think my daughter-in-law has; she's a great gadabout; she sees every one."

Even the gentle Madame de Cintré furthered the critical note, perhaps from a mild notion that Newman would be amused. "I've been telling Madame de la Rochefidèle that you're an American," she said as he came up to her in her salon. "It interests her greatly. Her favorite uncle went over with the French troops to help you in your battles in the last century, and she has always, in consequence, wanted greatly to see one of your people. But she has never succeeded until tonight. You're the first—to her knowledge—that she has ever looked upon." Madame de la Rochefidèle lifted an antique eyeglass, looked at Newman from head to foot, and at last said something to which he listened with deference but could not understand, for Madame de la Rochefidèle had an aged and cadaverous face with a falling of the lower jaw that impeded her utterance. Madame de Cintré offered an interpretation. "Madame de la Rochefidèle says she's convinced that she must have seen Americans without knowing it." Newman considered that she might have seen many things without knowing it; and the French visitor, again speaking in an inarticulate guttural, said that she wished she *had* known it. This interchange was followed by the polite approach of a very elderly gentleman who declared that almost the first person he had looked upon after coming into the world was an American, no less than the celebrated Doctor Franklin. But he, too, in the circumstances, could hardly have known it.

The animus of James, who has so often been pictured as a happy expatriate, mounted as such episodes recurred. At the great reception given by the Bellegardes for Newman after the announcement of his engagement to Madame de Cintré, he was introduced to their friends by her elder brother. "If the Marquis was going about as a bear-leader," wrote James stormily, "the general impression was that the bear was a very fair imitation of humanity." James even made a comment on worldly society which might have derived from one of the early wise, wandering Yankees; its like had been heard in *Fashion*. "Every one gave Newman extreme attention: every one lighted up for him regardless, as he would have said, of expense: every one looked at him with that fraudulent intensity of good society which puts out its bountiful hand but keeps the fingers closed over the coin." Nearly fifty years later James could betray an enduring bitterness. "Great and gilded was the whole trap set, in fine, for his wary freshness and into which it would blunder upon its fate."

When the catastrophe came, when the Bellegardes broke their word and Claire was commanded to withdraw from her engagement, Newman was rejected and publicly humiliated because he was American: they found themselves unable to tolerate that circumstance in relation to their family. He was rejected on the score of manners—the old and vexing score. He should have known that to ask the old Marquise to parade through her own rooms on his arm the evening of the ball would be almost an affront. When the journey was accomplished and she said, "This is enough, sir," he might have seen the gulf widening before his eyes. His commercial connections were held against him; and James pointed the irony of the objection. The Bellegardes were shown as sordidly commercial; in shrewdness they far outdistanced Newman. He was beaten, indeed, because he was incapable of suspecting the treachery accumulating against him. At the end Newman was unable to maintain his purpose of revenge against the Bellegardes; he destroyed the scrap of evidence which would have proved their earlier inhuman crime. His act is not overstressed; a deep-lying harshness gave stringency to Newman's generous impulses. But the contrast is firmly kept.

With all the preordained emphasis these characters are rounded and complete. The integrity of Valentin was placed against the unscrupulous coldness of his older brother. Claire, with her lovely purity, lights the black picture created by the Marquise. If the balance seems to be tipped down by the inclusion of Mademoiselle Nioche and her deplorable father, there is always Mrs. Bread. As a great artist James had moved immeasurably beyond the simple limits of the original fable. A genuine tragedy was created whose elements were tangled deep in inalienable differences. At the last Newman was unable to understand either the character or the decision of the woman he so deeply loved. Circling across the sea and the American continent, he returned again to Paris by an irresistible compulsion, and at twilight one evening, a gray time, walked to the convent of the Carmelite order in the Rue d'Enfer and gazed at the high blank wall which surrounded it. Within, his beloved was forever enclosed, engaged in rites which he could never understand, withdrawn for reasons which he could not fathom. He could never pass beyond that wall, in body or in spirit. The image was final, and became a dramatic metaphor: in the spelling of the old fable the outcome had changed from triumph to defeat. Defeat had become at last an essential part of the national portraiture.

IV

Almost invariably the opening moods and even the later sequences of James's novels were those of comedy. He instinctively chose the open sunny level; the light handling of his early *Confidence*, uncomplicated by the international situation, shows what he could do in maintaining this when his materials permitted. He ran indeed through a wide gamut of humor, from that of the happy and easy view and a delicate satire to a broad caricature and irony. Social comedy appeared in Henry James. For the first time an American writer drew a society and infused his drawing with an acute sense of human disparities. Yet the aggregation of his novels does not spell comedy, but a kind of *tragédie Américaine*, which was in large part a tragedy of manners. "I have the instincts—have them deeply—if I haven't the forms of a high old civilization," Newman told Claire de Cintré; but the instincts, if he possessed them, were not enough. *Daisy Miller*, bringing down a storm of angry reproof upon James's head, was a classic instance which he multiplied with variations of subtlety and range.

Defeat for the American adventurer was new, at least in wide transcription. Triumph had hitherto been the appointed destiny in American portraiture, except for vagabonds and common adventurers. Yet with all the tragic implications the ultimate ending of these latter-day fables was not that of tragedy. In

Constance Rourke

the midst of his final encounters with the forces of opposition
Newman gathered his energies; his spirits rose. When he confronted the Marquis de Bellegarde he "had a singular sensation;
he felt his sense of wrong almost brim into gaiety." He could
laugh during the momentous interview with Mrs. Bread; at one
moment in their plotting his face "lighted with the candor of
childhood." The mood was unreasoning, beyond reason: it was
a typical mood, that of resilience under opposition or criticism.
Finally, after all the conflict, after his searching and baffled effort to understand inscrutable forces, this mood was resolved
into something subtler and more enduring than resilience. When
Newman stood before the wall that forever enclosed Claire de
Cintré "the barren stillness of the place represented somehow
his own release from ineffectual desire." Touching the nadir of
despair and disillusionment, he was "disburdened"—free at last
from those dark personalities by whom he had been cruelly
wronged. He reached a moment of profound recognition, not
perhaps of the inner character of the forces that worked against
him—these he could never understand—but of his own final
plight. He achieved that laden balance of mind and feeling from
which an enduring philosophical comedy may spring. As one
sees Newman beyond the end of the book he has become a far
graver character, but for him something of humor might play
quietly once more.

Again and again James pictured this low-keyed humor of
defeat. For Isabel Archer more than one way of escape lay open;
fronting these possibilities, she made the choice which meant
renunciation; and the outcome is not tragic, for all the wrench
which it produces at the end, since James has revealed that free
poise and nobility of her character which made renunciation inevitable and acceptance of her lot tolerable. Even *The Wings
of the Dove* cannot be called tragedy. Milly Theale learned the
worst there was to know of those to whom she was attached,
their betrayal, their base purpose; yet with knowledge she still
could keep a magnanimous love. James repeated this stress again
in the recognition which finally lay between Kate Croy and
Merton Densher. Each had plumbed a deep and even dangerous
knowledge of the other; yet an indissoluble acceptance remained

between them; and their final alliance had a touch of the secure, upward swing which belongs to comedy.

In comedy reconcilement with life comes at the point when to the tragic sense only an inalienable difference or dissension with life appears. Recognition is essential for the play of a profound comedy; barriers must be down; perhaps defeat must lie at its base. Yet the outcome in these novels was in a sense the traditional outcome, for triumph was comprised in it; but the sphere had altered from outer circumstance to the realm of the mind and spirit; and triumph was no longer blind and heedless, but achieved by difficult and even desperate effort.

In this outcome James transcended the nationalistic altogether —that obsession which had had so long a history. Yet in the aggregate of his novels he repeated a significant portion of the old fable. He showed that the American was in truth what the belligerent Yankee had always declared him to be, a wholly alien, disparate, even a new character. In the end the primary concern of James was with that character; and he kept a familiar touch of the fabulous in his narratives. "I had been plotting arch-romance without knowing it," he said of *The American;* and by romance he meant what Hawthorne had meant, life with a touch of the marvelous, an infusion which can be apprehended only imperfectly by the sense of fact. Romance appeared in the generality and scale which James gave to his characters and to his situations. Such titles as *The Wings of the Dove* and *The Golden Bowl* suggest a poetized conception completing the romantic character of the themes; and his handling is kept free from complicated circumstance. Poetry indeed overspread much of James's writing. Like that of the popular fabulists, it was packed with metaphor. "The morning was like a clap of hands." "She carried her three and thirty years as a light-wristed Hebe might have carried a brimming wine-cup." His figures could also be ironical; the romantic feeling is constantly enclosed by a close drawing. Recognition is fundamental in all of James's portraiture; yet a basic poetry of outline and expression remains clear, most of all in his later novels. Few writers have had so deep a sense of the poetry of character; and his poetical penetration was the rarer achievement because his approaches were not those of the primary emotions.

In commentary James once spoke of one of the women whom he had drawn as "unaware of life." Elsewhere he wondered "what it might distinguishably be in their own flourishing Order that could *keep* them, the passionless pilgrims, so unaware?" "Passionless" surely was not meant to include his major characters; yet even they could not be called passionate in the sense that the characters in *Wuthering Heights* are passionate; it is significant of his obsessions that elsewhere James could give the attribute "passionate" to a pilgrim in quest of the past. For the most part emotion in these Americans in his wide gallery is frustrated, buried, or lost. Instead, renunciation, tenderness, pity, are likely to be dominant among them. The finest of these feelings do not belong to the primary emotions; they are restrained or delicate or withdrawn. These characters indeed are of an established native mold; this diminution had prevailed elsewhere. In a fashion James himself revealed the same qualities; a profound tenderness suffuses the greatest of his writing, but not the compulsion of a deep and natural, simple emotion. He gains power by integrity, by a close intensity of view, often by intensity of the mind. His portrayals gain every possible concentration from the high art by which they are revealed. "Dramatize! dramatize!" he said again and again; and the dramatic quality belonged to his writings at every point, in the ready immediacy of the talk, in the swift juxtapositions, in swift and daring ellipses, particularly in his later novels. At one point he considered that the drama was his true form. "I feel at last as if I had found my *real* form, which I am capable of carrying far, and for which the pale little art of fiction, as I have practiced it, has been, for me, but a limited and restricted substitute." James failed in writing drama; nothing of true dramatic expression had appeared in American literature, and he was not to transcend its tendency. He necessarily failed, lacking a depth of simple emotion; the approach to the drama had been made before without completion, perhaps for the same reason. James returned to the novel, and kept the dramatic organization.

The Question of Henry James

The highly conscious artist was uppermost in Henry James; and he joined in the traditional bias toward the inward view. Strangely enough, though he had no New England ancestry and was likely to be positive in his declarations to the contrary, he came closer than any of the earlier American writers to that introspective analysis which had belonged to the Puritan, closer even than Hawthorne. His scrutiny of motives, while delicate, was intense. He never used that direct revelation of elements in the stream of consciousness which had been ventured by Whitman and Hawthorne before him; yet his later novels are full of the unsaid and understated; they are full of complex moods and states of inner feeling revealed by the slightest and most ephemeral of notations. Whether or not James was subject to some untraceable Puritan influence, whether he touched popular sources, whether perhaps he gained greatly from the initial experiments of Hawthorne and Poe, his novels vastly amplified this new subject of the mind lying submerged beneath the scope of circumstance, which had long engaged the American imagination.

V

Nearly always the mark of that era in which an artist is young will in some way lie upon his work, however far he may advance into the future. Henry James bore the mark of that deeply experimental era which came to a culmination in the late forties and early fifties. Like Poe, Hawthorne, Melville, Whitman, he performed that difficult and elliptical feat by which a writer both invades a province and occupies it. Like them he was in a sense a primary writer.

No American before him had made a full imaginative approach to living characters and the contemporary scene; the view hitherto had been mainly the retrospective view. He greatly extended the areas of native comedy; he all but created a new subject for the novel in his stress upon the inward view; he discovered the international scene, as Van Wyck Brooks has said, "for literature." There is irony in the fact that so wide and subtle an accomplishment should have been produced within a tradition that still bore the print of the pioneer. There is a further irony in the circumstance that the American character should first have been fully realized within the European scene. This remoteness has been considered a flight and a loss; and truly enough to have perceived that character with equal amplitude against the native background would have meant an immense gain in imaginative understanding. Yet James's choice fulfilled the consciousness of a fundamental relationship; only the denial had been abortive.

The great experimental writer is like to betray signs of incompletion, to cover more than one era, to show hesitation as well as an unmistakable insecurity. James showed some of these signs. They are apparent in the great division between his later and his earlier writing, and in the incalculable abysms of his later style. In a strange fashion after the middle of his career he showed a partial reversal of his sense of language, which took on an extreme gentility even while it attempted that colloquialism which had been part of the American tradition. He strove for elegances like a minor writer of the thirties who sought to prove that Americans, too, could enter the stately domain of English literature. He used quotation marks to set off such phrases as "detective story," and the attempted grace of his movements through the great morass of his words was often elephantine. In his final revisions of the earlier novels he often emasculated a vigorous speech. The result was a form of writing which was neither English nor American in character. Yet few experimental writers have maintained so fine an artistry or encompassed with that artistry so great a scope. His failures are minor failures within a great original accomplishment.

Howells was the only other measurable American writer of this time to employ the novelistic form; the concerns of Howells were largely regional; he was engaged by small portions of the American scene and of the American character; he never fused these into an unmistakable and moving whole. The real situation in *Silas Lapham* lay between the Yankee and the Bostonian, between Lapham and the Coreys, between Penelope and young Corey. Here were elements of social comedy or tragedy, which Howells pictured in one scene which remains a high scene in American humor, full of comedy indeed, full of pathos and hurt—the scene of the Coreys' dinner party. But Howells evaded the full scope of the indicated differences, packing Lapham off to Vermont and Penelope and young Corey to South America. He made the same evasion in *The Lady of the Aroostook,* never showing Lydia in any prolonged contact with the superior Americans with whom her destinies were linked, never exploring the social situation beyond its superficial aspects, and again at the end sending his two major characters to far parts, where the manners and speech of the country girl need trouble nobody, and where Howells, at any rate, was not troubled by ensuing complications.

In spite of lapses in local observation, Howells had a striking aptitude for seizing essential elements in the native tradition: he knew the Yankee, the backwoodsman, the itinerant revivalist. His narratives are full of prime comic sketches, full of a racy contemporary and local speech. They reveal, too, that acute and expressive awareness with which the American constantly viewed himself, his fellow countrymen, his nation. His young men are always theorizing about America, and often have superior attitudes. "What a very American thing!" exclaims one of them when he heard Lydia saying "I want to know." "It's incredible," he continued. "Who in the world can she be?" The American quarrel with America, the product of a long self-consciousness, was beginning.

Howells had it in his power to draw social comedy of breadth and the first order, for disparities of background were included within his view; he was grounded within the comic tradition. He might have been the great artist to picture the American against the native scene, complementing the portrayals of James abroad. He had all the gifts except a passionate concern with his subject. Whether from lassitude or from a fundamental lack of imagination he never truly explored his materials; not one of his novels can be put beside *The Portrait of a Lady* or *The American.* He veered from one theme to another, from one locale to another. His novels were in the end not novels at all but an invaluable collection of minor notations on the American character.

Henry James stands alone in his time, not wholly to be accounted for, not in any immediate sense productive as an influence. He began writing in the sixties; his work was hardly a force among other writers for nearly half a century. In later years other American writers have followed him in using the international scene; yet his other great achievement, that of portraying the inner mind, cannot be said to have given any notable impetus to the American novel. It is abroad that the implications of his work have been pushed to their furthest boundaries. Proust and Joyce, Dorothy Richardson and Virginia Woolf, may or may not have been influenced by James; but they have carried the whole stress of an American intention far beyond anything achieved by American writers, in their portrayal of the inner consciousness.

The fate of Henry James has been that of other primary writers within the American tradition. Each of these had stormed some battlement without a following sequence of writers. The prolific energies that create an entire literature were lacking in this long period, though a widely flung pattern had been created which had freshness and even magnificence.

EDMUND WILSON

The Ambiguity of Henry James

[1934-38]

A DISCUSSION of Henry James's ambiguity may appropri-
ately begin with *The Turn of the Screw*. This story, which
seems to have proved more fascinating to the general reading
public than anything else of James's except *Daisy Miller*, apparently conceals another horror behind the ostensible one. I
do not know who first propounded the theory; but Miss Edna
Kenton, whose insight into James is profound, has been one of
its principal exponents, and the late Charles Demuth did a set
of illustrations for the story based on this interpretation.

According to this theory, the young governess who tells the
story is a neurotic case of sex repression, and the ghosts are not
real ghosts at all but merely the hallucinations of the governess.

Let us go through the story from the beginning. It opens with
an introduction. The man who is presenting the governess's
manuscript tells us first who she is. She is the youngest daughter of a poor country parson, but "the most agreeable woman
I've ever known in her position," who would have been "worthy
of any whatever." She had come up to London and answered
an advertisement and found a man who wanted a governess for
his orphaned nephew and niece. "This prospective patron proved
a gentleman, a bachelor in the prime of life, such a figure as
had never risen, save in a dream or an old novel, before a flut-
tered, anxious girl out of a Hampshire vicarage." It is made
clear that the young woman has become thoroughly infatuated
with her employer. He is charming to her and lets her have the
job on condition that she will never bother him about the chil-

dren; and she goes down to the house in the country where they
have been left with a housekeeper and some other servants.

The boy, she finds, has been sent home from school for reasons into which she does not inquire but which she colors, on
no evidence at all, with a significance somehow sinister. She
learns that the former governess left, and that she has since
died, under circumstances which are not explained but which
are made in the same way to seem ominous. She is alone with the
illiterate housekeeper, a good and simple soul, and the children,
who seem innocent and charming. As she wanders about the
estate, she thinks often how delightful it would be to come
suddenly round the corner and find that the master had arrived: there he would stand, smiling, approving, and handsome.

She is never to meet her employer again, but what she does
meet are the apparitions. One day when his face has been vividly
in her mind, she comes out in sight of the house and sees the
figure of a man on the tower, a figure which is not the master's.
Not long afterward, the figure appears again, toward the end of
a rainy Sunday. She sees him at closer range and more clearly:
he is wearing smart clothes but is not a gentleman. The housekeeper, meeting the governess immediately afterward, behaves
as if the governess herself were a ghost: "I wondered why she
should be scared." The governess tells her about the apparition
and learns that it answers the description of one of the master's
valets who had stayed down there and used to wear his clothes.
The valet had been a bad character, who used "to play with the
boy . . . to spoil him"; he had been found dead, having slipped
on the ice coming out of a public house: it is impossible to say
that he wasn't murdered. The governess believes that he has
come back to haunt the children.

Not long afterward, she and the little girl are out on the
shore of a lake, the little girl playing, the governess sewing.
The latter becomes aware of a third person on the opposite side
of the lake. But she looks first at the little girl, who is turning
her back in that direction and who, she notes, has "picked up a
small flat piece of wood, which happened to have in it a little
hole that had evidently suggested to her the idea of sticking in
another fragment that might figure as a mast and make the

thing a boat. This second morsel, as I watched her, she was very markedly and intently attempting to tighten in its place." This somehow "sustains" the governess so that she is able to raise her eyes: she sees a woman "in black, pale and dreadful." She concludes that it is the former governess. The housekeeper tells her that her predecessor, though a lady, had had an affair with the valet. The boy used to go off with the valet and then lie about it afterwards. The governess concludes that the boy must have known about the valet and the woman—the boy and girl have been corrupted by them.

Observe that there is never any real reason for supposing that anybody but the governess sees the ghosts. She believes that the children see them, but there is never any proof that they do. The housekeeper insists that she does not see them; it is apparently the governess who frightens her. The children, too, become hysterical; but this is evidently the governess's doing, too. Observe, also, from the Freudian point of view, the significance of the governess's interest in the little girl's pieces of wood and of the fact that the male apparition first appears on a tower and the female apparition on a lake. There seems here to be only a single circumstance which does not fit into the hypothesis that the ghosts are hallucinations of the governess: the fact that the governess's description of the first ghost at a time when she has never heard of the valet should be identifiable as the valet by the housekeeper. And when we look back, we see that even this has been left open to a double interpretation. The governess has never heard of the valet, but it has been suggested to her in a conversation with the housekeeper that there has been some other male somewhere about who "liked everyone young and pretty," and the idea of this other person has been ambiguously confused with the master and with the master's possible interest in her, the present governess. And has she not, in her subconscious imagination, taking her cue from this, identified herself with her predecessor and conjured up an image who wears the master's clothes but who (the Freudian "censor" coming into play) looks debased, "like an actor," she says (would he not have to stoop to love her!)? The apparition had "straight, good features" and his appearance is described in detail. When we look back, we find that the master's appearance has never been described at all: we have merely been told that he was "handsome." It is impossible for us to know how much the ghost resembles the master—certainly the governess would never tell us.

The apparitions now begin to appear at night, and the governess becomes convinced that the children get up to meet them, though they are able to give plausible explanations of their behavior. The housekeeper tells the governess that she ought to report these phenomena to the master, if she is so seriously worried about them. The governess, who has promised not to bother him, is afraid he would think her insane; and she imagines "his derision, his amusement, his contempt for the breakdown of my resignation at being left alone and for the fine machinery I had set in motion to attract his attention to my slighted charms." The housekeeper threatens to send for the master herself; the governess threatens to leave if she does. After this, for a considerable period, the visions no longer appear.

The children become uneasy: they begin to wonder when their uncle is coming down; they want to write to him—but the governess suppresses their letters. The boy finally asks her frankly when she is going to send him to school, intimates that if he had not been so fond of her he would have written to his uncle long ago about her failure to do so, threatens to write him at once.

This upsets her; she thinks for a moment of leaving, but decides that this would be deserting them. She is apparently now in love with the boy. The ghost of the other governess immediately appears again, looking "dishonored and tragic," full of "unutterable woe." The new governess feels now—the morbid half of her split personality is getting the upper hand of the other—that it is she who is intruding upon the spirit instead of the spirit who is intruding upon her: "You terrible miserable woman!" she cries. The apparition disappears. She tells the housekeeper, who looks at her oddly, that the soul of the former governess is damned and wants the little girl to share her damnation. She finally agrees to write to the master, but no sooner has she sat down to the paper than she gets up and goes to the

boy's bedroom, where she finds him lying awake. When he demands to go back to school, she embraces him and begs him to
tell her why he was sent away; appealing to him with what
seems to her desperate tenderness but what must seem queer and
disquieting to the child, she insists that all she wants is to save
him. There is the sudden gust of wind—it is a windy night outside—the casement rattles, the boy shrieks. She has been kneel-
ing beside the bed: when she gets up, she finds the candle ex-
tinguished. "It was I who blew it, dear!" says the boy. For her,
it has been the evil spirit disputing her domination. It does not
occur to her that the boy may really have blown the candle
out in order not to have to tell her with the light on about his
disgrace at school. (Here, however, occurs the only detail which
is not readily susceptible of double explanation: the governess
has *felt* a "gust of frozen air" and yet sees that the window is
"tight." Are we to suppose she merely fancied that she felt it?)

The next day, the little girl disappears. They find her beside
the lake. The young woman now for the first time speaks openly
to one of the children about the ghosts. "Where, my pet, is Miss
Jessel?" she demands—and immediately answers herself. "She's
there, she's there!" she cries, pointing across the lake. The housekeeper looks with a "dazed blink" and asks where she sees anything; the little girl turns upon the governess "an expression of
hard, still gravity, an expression absolutely new and unprecedented and that appeared to read and accuse and judge me."
The governess feels her "situation horribly crumble." The little
girl breaks down, becomes feverish, begs to be taken away from
the governess; the housekeeper sides with the child, and hints
that the governess had better go. But the young woman forces
her, instead, to take the little girl away; and she tries to make it
impossible, before their departure, for the children to see each
other.

She is now left alone with the boy. A strange and dreadful
scene ensues. "We continued silent while the maid was with us
—as silent, it whimsically occurred to me, as some young couple
who, on their wedding-journey, at the inn, feel shy in the presence of the waiter." When the maid has gone, and she presses
him to tell her why he was expelled from school, the boy seems

suddenly afraid of her. He finally confesses that he "said things" —to "a few," to "those he liked." It all sounds very harmless: there comes to her out of her "very pity the appalling alarm of his being perhaps innocent. It was for the instant confounding and bottomless, for if he *were* innocent, what then on earth was *I?*" The valet appears at the window—it is "the white face of damnation." (But is the governess condemning the spirits to damnation or is she succumbing to damnation herself?) She is aware that the boy does not see it. "No more, no more, no more!" she shrieks to the apparition. "Is she *here?*" demands the boy in panic. (He has, in spite of the governess's efforts, suc- ceeded in seeing his sister and has heard from her of the inci- dent at the lake.) No, she says, it is not the woman; "But it's at the window—straight before us. It's *there!*" . . . "It's *he?*" then. Whom does he mean by "he"? " 'Peter Quint—you devil!' His face gave again, round the room, its convulsed supplication. 'Where?' " "What does he matter now, my own?" she cries. "What will he *ever* matter? *I* have you, but he has lost you for- ever!" Then she shows him that the figure has vanished: "There, *there!*" she says, pointing toward the window. He looks and gives a cry; she feels that he is dead in her arms. From her point of view, the disappearance of the spirit has proved too terrible a shock for him and "his little heart, dispossessed, has stopped"; but if we study the dialogue from the other point of view, we see that he must have taken her "There, *there!*" as an answer to his own "Where?" Instead of persuading him that there is noth- ing to be frightened of, she has, on the contrary, finally con- vinced him either that he has actually seen or that he is on the point of seeing something. He gives "the cry of a creature hurled over an abyss." She has literally frightened him to death.

When one has once been given this clue to *The Turn of the Screw*, one wonders how one could ever have missed it. There is a very good reason, however, in the fact that nowhere does James unequivocally give the thing away: almost everything from beginning to end can be read equally in either of two senses. In the preface to the collected edition, however, as Miss Kenton has pointed out, James does seem to want to put him- self on record. He asserts here that *The Turn of the Screw* is "a fairy-tale pure and simple"—but adds that the apparitions are of the order of those involved in witchcraft cases rather than of those in cases of psychic research. And he goes on to tell of his reply to one of his readers, who had complained that he had not characterized the governess sufficiently. At this criticism, he says, "One's artistic, one's ironic heart shook for the instant almost to breaking"; and he answered: "It was '*déjà très-joli*' . . . please believe, the general proposition of our young woman's keeping crystalline her record of so many intense anomalies and obscurities—*by which I don't of course mean her explanation of them, a different matter.* . . . She has 'authority,' which is a good deal to have given her. . . ." The italics above are mine: these words seem impossible to explain except on the hypothesis of hallucination. And note, too, in the collected edition that James has not included *The Turn of the Screw* in the volume with his other ghost stories but in a volume of stories of another kind, between *The Aspern Papers* and *The Liar*—this last the story of a pathological liar, whose wife protects his lies against the world, acting with very much the same sort of deceptive "authority" as the governess in *The Turn of the Screw.*

When we look back in the light of these hints, we become convinced that the whole story has been primarily intended as a characterization of the governess: her visions and the way she behaves about them, as soon as we look at them from the obverse side, present a solid and unmistakable picture of the poor country parson's daughter, with her English middle-class class consciousness, her inability to admit to herself her sexual impulses and the relentless English "authority" which enables her to put over on inferiors even purposes which are totally deluded and not at all to the other people's best interests. Add to this the peculiar psychology of governesses, who, by reason of their isolated position between the family and the servants, are likely to become ingrown and morbid. The writer knows of an actual case of a governess who used to frighten the servants by opening doors and smashing mirrors and who tortured the parents by mythical stories of kidnapers. The poltergeist, once a figure of demonology, is now a recognized neurotic type.

Edmund Wilson

When we examine *The Turn of the Screw* in this light, we understand for the first time its significance in connection with Henry James's other fiction—(the story, on any other hypothesis, would be, so far as I remember, the only thing James ever wrote which did not have some more or less serious point). We see now that it is simply a variation on one of James's familiar themes: the frustrated Anglo-Saxon spinster; and we remember that he has presented other cases of women who deceive themselves and others about the sources and character of their emotions. The most obvious example is that remarkable and too-little-read novel, *The Bostonians*. The subject of *The Bostonians* is the struggle for the attractive daughter of a poor evangelist between a young man from the South who wants to marry her and a well-to-do Boston lady with a Lesbian passion for her. The strong-minded and strong-willed spinster is herself apparently quite in the dark as to the real reason for her interest in the girl; she is convinced that her desire to dominate her, to make her live with her, to teach her to make speeches on women's rights, to prevent the eligible young Southerner from marrying her, is all ardor for the feminist cause. But James does not leave the reader in doubt—and he presents Olive Chancellor in a setting of other self-deluded New England idealists.

There is a theme of the same kind in the short story called *The Marriages*, which amused Robert Louis Stevenson so hugely. But here the treatment is comic. A young English girl, described by one of the characters as of the unmarriageable type, much attached to an attractive father and obsessed by the memory of a dead mother, breaks up her father's projected second marriage. She goes to his fiancée and tells her that her father is an impossible character who had made her late mother miserable. When her brother calls her a raving maniac, she remains serene in the conviction that, by ruining the happiness of her father, she has been loyal to her duty to her mother.

James's world is full of these women. They are not always emotionally perverted. Sometimes they are emotionally apathetic—like the amusing Francie Dosson of *The Reverberator*, who, though men are always falling madly in love with her, seems never really to understand what courtship and marriage mean and is apparently quite content to go on all her life eating *marrons glacés* with her father and sister in their suite in a Paris hotel. Sometimes they are emotionally starved—like the pathetic Milly Theale of *The Wings of the Dove,* who wastes away in Venice and whose doctor recommends a lover.

II

James's men are not precisely neurotic; but they are the masculine counterparts of his women. They have a way of missing out on emotional experience, either through timidity or caution or through heroic renunciation.

The extreme and fantastic example is the hero of *The Beast in the Jungle,* who is finally crushed by the realization that his fate is to be the man in the whole world to whom nothing at all is to happen. Some of these characters are presented ironically: Mr. Acton of *The Europeans,* so smug and secure in his neat little house, deciding not to marry the baroness who has proved such an upsetting element in the community, is a perfect comic portrait of a certain kind of careful Bostonian. Others are made sympathetic: the starved and weary Lambert Strether of *The Ambassadors,* who comes to Paris too late in life.

Sometimes, however, the effect is ambiguous. Though the element of irony in Henry James is often underestimated by his readers, there are stories which leave us in doubt as to whether or not the author knew how his heroes would strike his readers. Is the fishy Bernard Longueville of the early novel *Confidence* really intended for a sensitive and interesting young man or is he a prig in the manner of Jane Austen? And some of James's later heroes are just as unsympathetic. The very late short story *Flickerbridge,* in which a young American painter decides not to marry a young newspaper woman (the men are always deciding *not* to marry the women in Henry James) because he is afraid she will spoil by publicizing it a delightful old English house, the property of her own family, in which he has greatly enjoyed living without her, affects us in the same unpleasant way.

But *Flickerbridge* seems merely a miscue: evidently James in-

Edmund Wilson

tends it to be taken seriously. How is *The Sacred Fount* to be taken? This short novel, surely one of the curiosities of literature, which inspired the earliest parody—by Owen Seaman—I ever remember to have seen of James and which apparently marked his passing over some borderline into a region where he was to become for the public unassimilably exasperating and ridiculous, was written not long after *The Turn of the Screw* and is a sort of companion piece to it. There is the same setting of an English country house, the same passages of a sad and strange beauty, the same furtive and disturbing goings on in an atmosphere of clarity and brightness, the same dubious central figure, the same almost inscrutable ambiguity. As in the case of *The Turn of the Screw,* the fundamental question presents itself and never seems to get definitely answered: what is the reader to think of the protagonist?—who is here a man instead of a woman.

It would be tedious to analyze *The Sacred Fount* as I have done with *The Turn of the Screw*—and it would be a somewhat more difficult undertaking. *The Sacred Fount* is mystifying, even maddening. But I believe that if anyone really got to the bottom of it, he would throw a good deal of light on Henry James. Rebecca West has given a burlesque account of this novel as the story of how "a week-end visitor spends more intellectual force than Kant can have used on *The Critique of Pure Reason* in an unsuccessful attempt to discover whether there exists between certain of his fellow-guests a relationship not more interesting among these vacuous people than it is among sparrows." A gentleman, who tells the story, goes to a week-end party in the country; there he observes that certain of his friends appear to have taken a new lease on life whereas others seem to have been depleted. He evolves a theory about them: the theory is that the married couples have been forming new combinations and that the younger individuals have been feeding the older individuals from the sacred fount of their youth at the price of getting used up themselves.

This theory seems obviously academic: older people feed younger people with their vitality quite as often as younger people feed older ones—and does James really mean us to accept it? Are not the speculations of the narrator intended to characterize the narrator as the apparitions characterize the governess? As this detached and rather eerie individual proceeds to spy on and cross-examine his friends in order to find out whether the facts fit his theory, we decide, as we do in *The Turn of the Screw,* that there are two separate things to be kept straight: a false hypothesis which the narrator is putting forward and a reality which we are supposed to guess from what he tells us about what actually happens. We remember the narrator of *The Aspern Papers,* another inquisitive and annoying fellow, who is finally foiled and put to rout by the old lady whose private papers he is trying to get hold of. In the case of *The Aspern Papers,* there is no uncertainty about James's attitude toward the narrator: James lets us know that the papers were none of the journalist's business and that the rebuff served him right. And the amateur detective of *The Sacred Fount* is foiled and rebuffed in precisely the same manner by one of his recalcitrant victims. "My poor dear, you *are* crazy, and I bid you good-night!" she says to him at the end of the story. "Such a last word," the narrator remarks, "the word that put me altogether nowhere—was too inacceptable not to prescribe afresh that prompt test of escape to other air for which I had earlier in the evening seen so much reason. I *should* certainly never again, on the spot, quite hang together, even though it wasn't really that I hadn't three times her method. What I too fatally lacked was her tone." But why *did* he lack her tone?—why *would* he never again hang together? What are we supposed to conclude about his whole exploit?

Mr. Wilson Follett, the only writer on James who has given *The Sacred Fount* special attention (in "Henry James's Portrait of Henry James," *New York Times Book Review,* August 23, 1936), believes that the book is a parable—even a conscious parody—of James's own role as an artist. The narrator may or may not have been right as to the actual facts of the case. The point is that, in elaborating his theory, he has constructed a work of art, and that it is a mistake to make the validity of works of art depend on a correspondence with actuality. Art

Edmund Wilson

has only its own kind of validity, and a collision with actuality would destroy it and put an end to the activities of the artist.

Certainly James has put himself into *The Sacred Fount*, and certainly he has intended some sort of fable about the imaginative mind and the material with which it works. But it seems to me that Mr. Follett's theory assumes on James's part a conception of artistic truth which would hardly be worthy of him. After all, the novelist must know what people are actually up to, however much he may rearrange actuality; and it is not clear in *The Sacred Fount* whether the narrator really knew what he was talking about. If *The Sacred Fount* is a parody, what is the point of the parody? Why should James have represented the artist as defeated by the breaking in of life?

The truth is, I believe, that Henry James was not clear about the book in his own mind. Already, with *The Turn of the Screw*, he has carried his ambiguous procedure to a point where it seems almost as if he did not want the reader to get through to the hidden meaning. See his curious replies in his letters to correspondents who write him about the story: to what seem to have been leading questions, he seems to have given evasive answers, dismissing the tale as a mere "pot-boiler," a mere "*jeu d'esprit*." Olive Chancellor in *The Bostonians*, though tragic perhaps, is horrid, and she is vanquished by Basil Ransom. But he was willing to leave his readers in doubt as to whether the governess was horrid or nice. And now in *The Sacred Fount*, we do not know whether the week-end guest, though he was unquestionably obnoxious to the other guests, is intended to be taken as one of the élite, a fastidious, highly civilized sensibility, or merely as a little bit cracked and a bore. The man who wanted to get the Aspern papers was fanatically inquisitive and a nuisance; but many of James's inquisitive observers who never take part in the action are presented as most superior people. James confessed to being this sort of person himself. Ambiguity was certainly growing on James. It was to pass all bounds in those scenes in his later novels (of which the talks in *The Turn of the Screw* between the housekeeper and the governess are only comparatively mild examples) in which the characters are able to carry on long conversations with each consistently mistaking the other's meaning and neither ever yielding to the impulse to say any of the obvious things which would clear the situation up.

What if the hidden theme of *The Sacred Fount* is simply sex again? What if the real sacred fount, from which the people observed by the narrator have been drawing their new vitality, is love instead of youth? They have something which he has not had, know something which he does not know; and, lacking the clue of love, he can only pedantically misunderstand them. And they, since they have the forces of life on their side, are able to frighten him away.

This theory may be dubious, also; but there is certainly involved in *The Sacred Fount* the conception of a man shut out from love and doomed to barren speculation on human relations, who will be shocked by direct contact with reality.

Hitherto, it has usually been quite plain what James wanted us to think of his characters; but now there appears in his work a morbid element which is not always handled objectively but has invaded the storyteller himself. He seems to be dramatizing the frustrations of his own life without quite being willing to confess it, without always fully admitting it to himself.

But before we pursue this line of inquiry, let us look at him in a different connection.

III

Who *are* these characters of Henry James's about whom we come to be less and less certain as to precisely what he means us to think?

The type is the cultivated American bourgeois, like Henry James himself, who lives on an income derived from some form (usually left extremely vague) of American business activity but who has taken no part in the achievements which made the income possible. These men turn their backs on business; they attempt to enrich their experience through the society and art of Europe. But they bring to it the bourgeois qualities of timidity, prudence, primness, the habits of mind of a narrow morality which, even when they wish to be open-minded, cause them to be easily shocked. They wince alike at the brutalities of the aristocracy and at the vulgarities of the working class; they shrink most of all from the "commonness" of the less cultivated bourgeoisie, who, having acquired their incomes more recently, are not so far advanced in self-improvement. The women have the corresponding qualities: they are innocent, conventional, and rather cold—sometimes they suffer from Freudian complexes or a kind of arrested development, sometimes they are neglected or cruelly cheated by the men to whom they have given their hearts. And even when James's heroes and heroines are English, they assimilate themselves to these types.

It is illuminating in this connection to compare James's attitude to Flaubert's. The hero of *L'Education sentimentale* is a perfect Henry James character: he is sensitive, cautious, afraid of life, he lives on a little income and considers himself superior to the common run. But Flaubert's attitude toward Frédéric Moreau is devastatingly ironic. Frédéric has his aspects of pathos, his occasional flashes of spirit: but Flaubert is quite emphatic in his final judgment of Frédéric. He considers Frédéric a worm.

Now James has his own kind of irony, but it is not Flaubert's kind. Frédéric Moreau is really the hero of most of James's novels, and you can see very plainly how James's estimate of him usually differs from Flaubert's if you compare certain kinds of scenes which tend to recur in Henry James with scenes in *L'Education sentimentale* from which James has evidently imitated them: those situations of a sensitive young man immersed in some kind of gathering or having a succession of meetings with various characters without being able in his innocence precisely to figure out what they are up to. The reader is able to guess that they are more worldly and unscrupulous persons than the hero and that they are talking over his head, acting behind his back. You have this pattern, as I say, both in Flaubert and in James; but the difference is that, whereas in James the young man is made wondering and wistful and is likely to turn out a pitiful victim, in Flaubert he is made to look like a fool and is as ready to double-cross these other people who seem to him so inferior to himself as they are to double-cross him.

In this difference between Flaubert's attitude toward Frédéric

The Question of Henry James

and James's attitude toward, say, Hyacinth Robinson of *The Princess Casamassima* is to be discovered, I believe, the real reason for James's peculiar resentment of Flaubert. Flaubert interested James deeply: they had in common that they were both trying to give dignity to the novel of modern life by bringing it to intense aesthetic form. And James returned to Flaubert again and again, wrote three essays on him at different periods. But though he obviously cannot help admiring Flaubert, he usually manages in the long run to belittle him—and is especially invidious on the subject of *L'Education sentimentale*. His great complaint is that Flaubert's characters are so ignoble that they do not deserve to have so much art expended on them and that there must have been something basically wrong with Flaubert ever to have supposed that they did. James never seems to understand that Flaubert intends all his characters to be "middling" and that the greatness of his work arises from the fact that it constitutes a criticism of something bigger than they are. James praises the portrait of Madame Arnoux: Thank God, at least, he exclaims, that here Flaubert was able to muster the good taste to deal delicately with a pure and fine-grained woman! He seems completely unaware that Madame Arnoux is treated as ironically as any of the other characters—that the virtuous bourgeois wife with her inhibitions and superstitions is pathetic only as a part of the bigger thing of which Flaubert is showing the failure. Henry James mistakes Madame Arnoux for a refined portrait of an American lady and he is worried because Frédéric isn't a quietly vibrating young American. Yet at the same time he must have his uneasy suspicion that young Americans of that kind are being made fun of. I believe that James's antagonism to Flaubert may be primarily due to the fact that Flaubert's criticism of the pusillanimity of the bourgeois has really touched James himself. James's later heroes are always regretting having lived and loved too meagerly; and James distills from these sensitive nonparticipants all the sad, self-effacing nobility, all the fine and thin beauty, he can get out of them. Whereas Flaubert extracts something quite different and bitter: when Frédéric recalls in middle age his first clumsy and fright-

ened visit to a brothel as the best that life has had to offer him,
it is a damnation of a whole society.

But there was another kind of modern society which Flau-
bert did not know and which Henry James did know. Henry
James was that new anomalous thing, an American. He is an
American who has spent much of his childhood and youth in
Europe, and he is imbued to a considerable extent with the
European point of view. The monuments of feudal and ancient
Europe, the duchesses and princesses and princes who seem to
carry on the feudal tradition, are still capable of making modern
life look to him dull, undistinguished, and tame. But the past
for him does not completely dwarf the present, as the vigil of
Saint Anthony and the impacts of pagan armies dwarf Flaubert's Frédéric Moreau. The American in Henry James insistently asserts himself against Europe. After all, Frédéric Moreau
and Madame Arnoux are the best people of Albany and Boston!—but they are not characters in Flaubert there. There
their scruples and their renunciations possess a real value—for
Frédéric Moreau at home possesses a real integrity; and when
they visit Europe, they judge the whole thing in a new way.
Henry James speaks somewhere of his indignation at an English-
woman's saying to him in connection with something: "That is
true of the aristocracy, but in one's own class it is quite different." As an American, it had never occurred to him that he
could be described as a middle-class person. When Edith Wharton accused him in his later years of no longer appreciating
Flaubert and demanded of him why Emma Bovary was not as
good a subject for a novel as Anna Karenina, he replied: "Ah,
but one paints the fierce passions of a luxurious aristocracy;
the other deals with the petty miseries of a little bourgeoise in a
provincial town!" But if Emma Bovary is small potatoes, what
about Daisy Miller? Why, Daisy Miller is an American girl!
Emma Bovary has her debts and adulteries, but she is otherwise
a conventional person, she remains in her place in the social
scheme, even when she dreams of rising out of it: when she goes
to visit the château, the sugar seems to her whiter and finer than
elsewhere. Whereas Daisy Miller represents something which has
walked quite out of the frame of Europe. When it comes back

The Question of Henry James

to Europe again, it disregards the social system. Europe is too much for Daisy Miller: she catches cold in the Coliseum, where according to European conventions she oughtn't to have been at that hour. But the great popularity of her story was certainly due to her creator's having somehow conveyed the impression that her spirit went marching on.

In Henry James's mind, there disputed all his life the European and the American points of view; and their debate, I believe, is closely connected with his inability sometimes to be clear as to what he thinks of a certain sort of person. It is quite mistaken to talk as if James had uprooted himself from America in order to live in England. He had traveled so much from his earliest years that he never had any real roots anywhere. His father had himself been a wandering intellectual, oscillating back and forth between the United States and Europe. And even in America, the Jameses oscillated back and forth between Boston and New York. They were not New Englanders but New Yorkers, and they had none of the tight local ties of New Englanders—they always came to Boston from a larger outside world and their attitude toward it was critical and objective.

To James's critical attitude toward Boston was probably partly due the failure in America of *The Bostonians;* and to this failure is possibly due his discouragement with his original ambition of becoming the American Balzac. At any rate, it marks the moment of his taking up his residence in England and of his turning from the Americans to the English.

He was in London, and he found he liked living in London better than living in Boston or New York. His parents in the States had just died, and his sister came over to join him.

IV

And this brings us to what seems to have been the principal crisis in Henry James's life and work. We know so little about his personal life that it is impossible to give any account of it save as it reflects itself in his writings.

Up to the period of his playwriting his fiction has been pretty plain sailing. He has aimed to be a social historian, and, in a

Edmund Wilson

rather limited field, he has succeeded. His three long novels of the later eighties—*The Bostonians, The Princess Casamassima,* and *The Tragic Muse*—are, indeed, as social history, his most ambitious undertakings and, up to a point, his most brilliant. The first hundred pages of *The Bostonians,* with the arrival of the Mississippian in Boston and the crowded picture of the meeting of reformers is, in its way, one of the most masterly things that Henry James ever did. *The Princess Casamassima,* with its prison and its revolutionary exiles in London, deals with issues and social contrasts of a kind that James had never before attempted. The familiar criticism of Henry James—the criticism made by H. G. Wells—does not, in fact, hold true of these books. Here his people do have larger interests and functions aside from their personal relations: they have professions, missions, practical aims; and they also engage in more drastic action than in his novels of any other period. Basil Ransom pursues Verena Tarrant and rescues her from the terrible Olive Chancellor; Hyacinth Robinson pledges himself to carry out a political assassination, then kills himself instead; Miriam Rooth makes her career as a great actress. Here there is a genuine will to do rather than a mere disposition to observe. Up to a point these three books are quite triumphant.

But there *is* a point—usually about halfway through—at which every one of these novels begins strangely to run into the sands; the excitement seems to lapse at the same time that the color fades from the picture; and the ends are never up to the beginnings. This is most obvious, and even startling, in *The Tragic Muse,* the first volume of which, when we read it, makes us think that it must be James's best novel, so solid and alive does it seem. There are in it a number of things which he has never given us before: a wonderful portrait of a retired parliamentarian with an implied criticism of British Liberal politics, a real scene—what one might have thought he could never do—between a man and a woman (Nick Dormer and Julia Dallow) instead of the polite conversations to which he has accustomed us; and Miriam Rooth, the Muse herself, comes nearer to carrying Henry James out of the enclosure of Puritan scruples and prim prejudices onto the larger stage of human creative effort than any other character he has drawn. Here at last we seem to find ourselves with real people, who have the same appetites and ambitions as other people—in comparison, the characters of his earlier works are real only in a certain convention. Then suddenly the story stops short: after the arrival of Miriam in London, *The Tragic Muse* is an almost total blank. Of the two young men who have been preoccupied with Miriam, one renounces her because she will not leave the stage and the other apparently doesn't fall in love with her. Miriam, to be sure, makes a great success as an actress, but we are never taken into her life, we know nothing at first hand about her emotions. And with nothing but these negative decisions in sight, the author himself seems to lose interest.

The first half of *The Tragic Muse* is the high point of the first part of James's career, after which something snaps. He announces that he will write no more long novels, but only fiction of shorter length. He may have been aware that a long novel demands a mounting up to a point of intensity and revelation of a kind which he was unable to give it, whereas a short story need not go so deep. At any rate, he set himself to write plays, and for five years he produced little else.

Why did he do this? He complained at this time that he had difficulty in selling his fiction, and he confessed that his plays were written in the hope of a popular success, that they were intended merely to entertain and were not to be taken too seriously. Yet this is surely an inadequate explanation of the phenomenon of a novelist of the first order giving up the art in which he has perfected himself to write plays which do not even aim to be serious.

That there was something incomplete and unexplained about James's emotional life seems to appear unmistakably from his novels. I believe it may be said that up to this point there are no consummated love affairs in his fiction—that is, none among the principal actors and during the action of the story; and this fact must certainly have contributed to his increasing loss of hold on his readers. It is not merely that he gave in *The Bostonians* an unpleasant picture of Boston, and in *The Tragic Muse* an equally unpleasant picture of the English; it is not

Edmund Wilson

merely that *The Princess Casamassima* treated a social-revolutionary subject from a point of view which gave neither side best. It was not merely that he was thus at this period rather lost between America and England. It was also that you cannot long hold an audience with stories about men wooing women in which the parties either never get together or are never seen as really functioning as lovers. And you will particularly discourage your readers with a story about two men and a girl in which neither man ever gets her and in which she marries a third person, totally uninteresting. There is, as I have said, in *The Tragic Muse,* a much more convincing man-and-woman relationship. Julia Dallow is really female and she really behaves like a woman with Nick Dormer; but here her political ambitions get between Nick and her, so that this, too, never comes to anything: here the man, again, must renounce. (In James's later novels, these healthily female women are always invested with a value frankly sinister and usually animated by evil designs: Kate Croy and Charlotte Stant.) Years later, Henry James explained in his preface to *The Tragic Muse* that he had been prevented from allowing Miriam Rooth to have a genuine love affair with anybody by the prudery of the American magazines; and certainly the skittishness of a reading public which was scandalized by *Jude the Obscure* is not to be underestimated. But, after all, Hardy and Meredith did write about Jude and Lord Ormont and his Aminta and let the public howl; and it would certainly have enhanced rather than diminished Henry James's reputation—as to which his ambitions seem by no means to have been modest—if he had done the same thing himself. Problems of passion in conflict with convention and law were coming to be subjects of burning interest; but James could not deal with that kind of passion and was much too honest to try to fake it.

One feels about the episode of his playwriting that it was an effort to put himself over, an effort to make himself felt, as he had never succeeded in doing before. His brother William James wrote home in the summer of 1889, at the beginning of Henry's playwriting period, that Henry, beneath the "rich sea-weeds and rigid barnacles and things" of "strange heavy alien manners and

[179]

customs" with which he had covered himself like a "marine crustacean," remained the "same dear old, good, innocent and at bottom very powerless-feeling Harry." He had injured his back in an accident in his boyhood, and it was still necessary for him to lie down for regular rests. And it is as if he were putting his back into playwriting as he had never been able to put it into a passion. His heroine Miriam Rooth in the novel has turned away from the Philistine English world, which rejects her, and taken into the theater the will of the artist, which will enable her to conquer that world; and her creator is now to imitate her.

But his plays were not produced or did not go. At the first night of *Guy Domville,* he ran foul of a hissing and booing British audience (the play contained another of his confounded renunciations); and these five years put him under a severe strain. When he recovers from his disappointment, he is seen to have passed through a kind of crisis.

Now he enters upon a new phase, of which the most obvious feature is a subsidence back into himself. And now sex *does* appear in his work—in a queer and left-handed way. We have *The Turn of the Screw* and *The Sacred Fount*—and *What Maisie Knew* and *In the Cage.* There are plenty of love affairs now and plenty of irregular relations, but there are always barriers between them and us; they are the chief object of interest, but they are seen from a distance.

For the Jamesian central observer, through whose intelligence the story is usually relayed to us, has undergone a strange diminution. This observer is no longer a complete and interesting person more or less actively involved in the events, but a small child, a telegraph operator who lives vicariously through the senders of telegrams, a week-end guest who seems not to exist in any other capacity except that of a week-end guest and who lives vicariously through his fellow visitors. The people who surround this observer tend to take on the diabolic value of the specters of *The Turn of the Screw,* and this diabolic value is almost invariably connected with their concealed and only guessed at sexual relations. The innocent Nanda Brookenham of *The Awkward Age,* a work of the same period and group, has a whole host of creepy creatures around her. James is ceasing to sustain the objectivity which has kept the outlines of his stories pretty definite up through his middle novels: he has relapsed into a dreamy, inner world, where values are often uncertain and where it is not even possible for him any longer to judge the effect of his stories on his audience—that audience which, as a matter of fact, has almost ceased to exist. One is dismayed in reading his comments on *The Awkward Age,* which he seems to have considered highly successful, to realize that he is unaware of the elements in the book which, in spite of the technical virtuosity displayed in it, make it unpleasant and irritating. The central figure of *The Sacred Fount* may perhaps have been presented ironically; but James could never have known how we should feel about the gibbering, disemboweled crew who hover about one another with sordid, shadowy designs in *The Awkward Age.*

This is accompanied by a kind of expansion of the gas of the psychological atmosphere—an atmosphere which has now a special odor. With *What Maisie Knew,* as F. M. Ford says, the style first becomes a little gamey; and then, dropping off its old formality and what sometimes amounted to a mechanical hardness, it becomes progressively, in the conventional sense, more poetic.

With all this, his experience of playwriting has done him no good in his fiction. He had set himself to emulate the most stultifying models of the mechanically well-made play. He turned certain of these pieces into novels—*Covering End* and *The Other House*—and dreadful novels they made; and in *The Awkward Age* and other works of this period, an artificial dramatic technique persists. It is one of the elements that make some of them so exasperating. They combine a lifeless trickery of logic with the ambiguous subjectivity of a nightmare.

In this period certainly originates that tendency on James's part to exploit the mysteries of technique for the purpose of diverting attention from his shortcomings which has imposed on some of his critics and which must of course have imposed on himself. One can see from his comments of various periods how a method like that of Tolstoy in *War and Peace* became more and more distasteful to him. Tolstoy, he insisted, was all over the shop, entering the minds of far too many of his characters and failing to exercise the principle of selection. He speaks in the preface to *The Tragic Muse* of his own difficulty in handling a complex subject—though here it is a question of going into the minds of only two of the characters. But, obviously, the question of whether the novelist enters into a variety of points of view has nothing to do with his technical proficiency or even with his effect of concentration. One trouble with *The Tragic Muse* is that James does not show us the inside of Miriam Rooth; and if he fails to do so, it is because, here as elsewhere, he does not know, as Tolstoy did, what the insides of such people are like. So, in *The Wings of the Dove,* the "messengering," as the drama courses say, of Kate Croy's final scene with Merton Densher is evidently due to James's increasing incapacity for dealing directly with scenes of emotion rather than to the esoteric motives he alleges. And so his curious, constant complaint that he is unable to do certain things because there is no longer space within the prescribed limits of the story is certainly only another hollow excuse: he never seems to be aware of the amount of space he is wasting through the roundabout locutions or quite gratuitous verbiage with which he habitually pads out his sentences—and which is itself a form of staving off his main problems. His censure of Tolstoy for his failure to select is a defensive reflex action on Henry James's part for his own failure to fill in his picture.

V

What happens after this, however, is interesting. In *The Ambassadors, The Wings of the Dove,* and *The Golden Bowl* the psychological atmosphere thickens, fills up the stories with the Jamesian gas instead of with detail and background. The characters (though usually apprehended as convincing personal entities) are seen dimly through a phantasmagoria of dreamlike metaphors and similes, which seem sometimes, as Rebecca West has said, more vivid and solid than the settings.

But a positive element reappears. The novels of *The Awkward Age* period were written not merely from James's international limbo between the United States and Europe but under the oppression of defeat and self-doubt. But in these queer and neu-

Edmund Wilson

rotic stories—(some of them, of course—*The Turn of the Screw* and *What Maisie Knew*—among James's masterpieces)—moral values begin to assert themselves again. They sprout first in the infantile form of Maisie and Nanda Brookenham, whose innocence is the test of the other characters. Then in the longer novels that follow, in figures of a more mature innocence, they completely take the field; and these figures are now invariably Americans. We are back to the pattern of his earlier novels, where the typical conflict was between glamorous people who were also worldly and likely to be wicked, and people of superior scruples who were likely to be more or less homely, and where the former usually represented Europe and the latter the United States. In these novels, it was sometimes the Americans—as in *The Portrait of a Lady*—who were left with the moral advantage; sometimes—as in *The Europeans*—the Europeans. But in these late novels it is always the Americans who have the better of it from the moral point of view—scoring heavily off a fascinating Italian prince, an equally fascinating French lady and a formidable group of middle-class English people. Yes: there *was* a beauty and there was also a power in the goodness of these naïve and open people, which had not existed for Flaubert and his group. It *is* something different and new which does not fit into the formulas of Europe. What if Lambert Strether *had* missed in Woollett, Massachusetts, many things that he would have enjoyed in Paris: he had brought to Paris something it did not have. And the burden of the book, *William Wetmore Story and His Friends*, which was also written during this time—rather different from that of his early book on Hawthorne—is that American artists might much better stay at home.

And now—in 1904—Henry James revisits America, writes *The American Scene*, returns to it in a novel, *The Ivory Tower*, left unfinished at his death.

In his other unfinished novel, the fantasia called *The Sense of the Past*, he makes a young contemporary American go back into eighteenth-century England. Here the Jamesian ambiguity serves an admirable artistic purpose. Is it the English of the past who are the ghosts or is it the American himself who is a dream?

The Question of Henry James

—will the moment come when *they* will vanish or will he himself cease to exist? And, as before, there is a question of James's own asking at the bottom of the ambiguity: Which is real—America or Europe? It was, however, in the novel, the American who was to remain real. (It is curious to compare *The Sense of the Past* with *A Connecticut Yankee in King Arthur's Court*, with which it really has a good deal in common.)

Yes: in spite of the popular assumption founded on his expatriation, it is America which gets the better of it in Henry James. His warmest tributes to American genius come out of these later years. Though he could not, in *Notes of a Son and Brother*, resist the impulse to remove references to Lincoln as "old Abe" from William James's early letters of the wartime, it contains pages on Lincoln's death of a touching appreciation and pride. "It was vain to say," he writes of Andrew Johnson, of whom he says that the American people felt him unworthy to represent them, "that we had deliberately invoked the 'common' in authority and must drink the wine we had drawn. No countenance, no salience of aspect nor composed symbol, could superficially have referred itself less than Lincoln's mold-smashing mask to any mere matter-of-course type of propriety; but his admirable unrelated head had itself revealed a type—as if by the very fact that what made in it for roughness of kind looked out only less than what made in it for splendid final stamp; in other words for commanding Style." And of the day when the news reached Boston: "I was fairly to go in shame of its being my birthday. These would have been the hours of the streets if none others had been—when the huge general gasp filled them like a great earth-shudder and people's eyes met people's eyes without the vulgarity of speech. Even this was, all so strangely, part of the lift and the swell, as tragedy has but to be of a pure enough strain and a high enough connection to sow with its dark hand the seed of greater life. The collective sense of what had occurred was of a sadness too noble not somehow to inspire, and it was truly in the air that, whatever we had as a nation produced or failed to produce, we could at least gather round this perfection of classic woe." In *The American Scene*, he writes of Concord: "We may smile a little as we 'drag in'

Edmund Wilson

Weimar, but I confess myself, for my part, much more satisfied than not by our happy equivalent, 'in American money,' for Goethe and Schiller. The money is a potful in the second case as in the first, and if Goethe, in the one, represents the gold and Schiller the silver, I find (and quite putting aside any bimetallic prejudice) the same good relation in the other between Emerson and Thoreau. I open Emerson for the same benefit for which I open Goethe, the sense of moving in large intellectual space, and that of the gush, here and there, out of the rock, of the crystalline cupful, in wisdom and poetry, in *Wahrheit* and *Dichtung;* and whatever I open Thoreau for (I needn't take space here for the good reasons) I open him oftener than I open Schiller." Edith Wharton says that he used to read Walt Whitman aloud "in a mood of subdued ecstasy" and with tremendous effect on his hearers.

Henry James's career had been affected by the shift in the national point of view which occurred after the Civil War. It is being shown by Mr. Van Wyck Brooks in his cultural history of New England how the Bostonian of the first part of the century was inspired—as, in our time, the Russians have been—to present the world with a humanity, set free from the caste barriers and poverties of Europe, which should return to the mother country only to plunder her for elements of culture which might contribute to the movement at home; and how, with the triumph of the industrial system, the persons who were occupied with art and thought became gradually ashamed of the United States and tended to take refuge in Europe. Henry James belonged to this second phase, but he had a good deal of the idealism of the first one. It appears in the name of the hero of *The American,* Newman, and in his phrase about Lincoln's "mold-smashing mask"; and, after a period of partial abeyance, when he had been writing largely about Europeans, it cropped up again, as I have shown, and took the field.

But Henry James is a reporter, not a prophet. With less political philosophy even than Flaubert, he can only chronicle the world as it passes, and in his picture the elements are mixed. In the Americans of Henry James's later novels—the Milly Theales, the Lambert Strethers, the Maggie Ververs—he shows us all that

The Question of Henry James

was magnanimous, reviving, and human in the Americans at the beginning of the new century along with all that was frustrated, sterile, excessively refined, depressing—all that they had in common with the Frédéric Moreaus and with the daughters of poor English parsons. There they are with their ideals and their blights. Milly Theale, for example—quite real at the core of the cloudy integument with which James has swathed her about—is one of the best portraits of a rich New Yorker in fiction. It is the great period of the heyday of Sargent; but compare these figures of Henry James's with Sargent's and see with what profounder insight as well as with what superior delicacy James has caught the rich Americans of this race.

VI

And between the first and the second blooming something tragic has happened to these Americans. What has become of Christopher Newman? He is Lambert Strether now: he has been worn down by the factories of Woollett. And these Americans of the later novels—who still bring Europe the American sincerity —what has happened to them to make them so wan? Well, for one thing, they have become very rich, and being rich is a terrible burden: in the process of getting rich, they have starved themselves spiritually at home; and now that they are trying to get something for their money, they find that they have put themselves at the mercy of all the schemers and adventurers of Europe. It seems to me foolish to reproach Henry James for having neglected the industrial background. Like sex, we never get very close to it, but its effects are a part of his picture. James's tone is more often old-maidish than his sense of reality is feeble; and the whole development of American society during his absence is implied in these later books.

Now when he returns—late in the day though it is for him— he reacts strongly and reports vividly what he finds.

The returning New Yorker of *The Jolly Corner* encounters the apparition of himself as he would have been if he had stayed in America: "Rigid and conscious, spectral yet human, a man of his own substance and stature waited there to measure him-

Edmund Wilson

self with his power to dismay." At first the apparition covers its face with its hands; then it advances upon the returned native "as for aggression, and he knew himself give ground. Then harder pressed still, sick with the force of his shock, and falling back as under the hot breath and sensed passion of a life larger than his own, a rage of personality before which his own collapsed, he felt the whole vision turn to darkness," and he fainted.

But at contact with the harsh new America, the old Balzac in James revives. I do not know why more has not been made by James's critics—especially by the critics of the Left, who are so certain that there is nothing in him—of his unfinished novel, *The Ivory Tower.* The work of his all but final period has been "poetic" rather than "realistic"; but now he passes into still a further phase, in which the poetic treatment is applied to what is for James a new kind of realism. The fiction of his latest period is preoccupied in a curious way with the ugly, the poor, and the old, even with—what is unprecedented for James—the grotesque. It is perhaps the reflection of his own old age, his own lack of worldly success, the strange creature that he himself has become. This new vein begins, I think, with *The Papers,* with its fantastically amusing picture of the sordid lives of journalists in London. *Fordham Castle,* in which he said he had attempted to do some justice to the parents of the Daisy Millers, whose children had left them behind, is an excursion into the America of Sinclair Lewis. *The Bench of Desolation*—one of the most beautifully written and wonderfully developed pieces in the whole range of Henry James's work, and, I believe, the last piece of fiction he published—is a sort of poem of loneliness and poverty among the nondescript small shopkeepers and former governesses of an English seaside resort.

And now the revelation of Newport, as it presented itself in the nineteen hundreds—so different from the Newport which he had described years ago in *An International Episode*—stimulates him to something quite new: a kind of nightmare of the American new rich. Here his gusto for the varied forms of life, his interest in social phenomena for their own sake, seems suddenly to wake up from its reveries. The actual appearances of things become suddenly vivid again. In the novels which pre-

The Question of Henry James

ceded *The Ivory Tower,* the carefully selected and charming old-world settings had been steadily fading out; but now, to our amazement, there starts into relief the America of the millionaires, at its crudest, corruptest, and phoniest: the immense summer mansions full of equipment which no one ever seems to have selected or used, the old men of the Rockefeller-Frick generation, landed, with no tastes and no interests, amidst an unlimited magnificence which dwarfs them, the silly or clumsy young people of the second generation with their off-color relationships, their enormous, meaningless parties, their touching longings and resolute strivings for an elegance and cultivation they cannot manage. The apparition in *The Jolly Corner* came upon the Europeanized American "quite as one of those expanding fantastic images projected by the magic lantern of childhood"; and in the same way, for the reader of James, with the opening of *The Ivory Tower,* there emerges the picture of old Abner Gaw sitting and rocking his foot and looking out on the sparkling Atlantic while he waits for his partner to die.

The Ivory Tower is immensely comic, deeply human, and brilliantly observed—and it is poetic in the highest sense, like all these later novels: in the sense that its characters and images, individualized though they are, shine out with the incandescence which shows them as symbols of phases through which the human soul has passed.

The moral of the book—which seems quite plain from the scenario left by James—is also of particular interest. The ivory tower itself, a fine piece of Chinese carving, figures the spiritual isolation, the cultivation of sensations, and the literary activity which are to be made possible for the young American, returned from Europe, who has inherited his uncle's fortune; but it contains, also, the fatal letter in which the vindictive Mr. Gaw has revealed all the swindles and perfidies by which the fortune has been created. So that the young man (he has always had a *little* money) is to come finally to be glad enough to give up the ivory tower with the fortune.

James dropped *The Ivory Tower* when the war broke out in 1914, because it seemed to him too remote from the present. The war seems to have presented itself to him as simply a strug-

[188]

gle between, on the one hand, French and English civilization and, on the other, German barbarism. He had believed in, and had been writing rather vaguely about, the possible salutary effect on human affairs of a sort of international élite such as he tended to depict in his novels; and now he spoke of the past as "the age of the mistake," the time when people had thought that things would be all right. He now became violently nationalistic, or at least violently pro-Ally, and took out citizen's papers in England, because America had not yet gone into the war. It never seems to have occurred to him that in *The Ivory Tower* he had been much closer to contemporary realities than in becoming an English citizen, that the partnership of Betterman and Gaw was a European phenomenon, too—any more than it ever occurred to him that the class antagonisms of *The Princess Casamassima*—his response to the depression of the eighties—must inevitably appear again. But as Hyacinth Robinson died of the class struggle, so Henry James died of the war.

Before he died, the English gave him the Order of Merit. But I do not think that anybody has yet done justice to the genius that, overriding personal deficiencies of a peculiarly disabling kind, finding its bearings in a social situation almost as bewildering as the astronomical one with which the mathematics of relativity deals, surviving the ridicule and indifference of the two peoples whose critic he had made himself, was able to recreate itself to the end and actually to break fresh ground at seventy.

For Henry James *is* a great artist, in spite of everything. His deficiencies are obvious enough. He was certainly rather short on invention; and he tended to hold life at arm's length. Yet when a novelist with a real inventive gift—say Compton Mackenzie—can invent till the cows come home without his inventions' making any lasting impression on us, the things that James *does* invent have so perfect an appropriateness and beauty, even floating though they sometimes are in rather a gray sea of abstract exposition, that they remain in our minds as luminous symbols; and the objects and beings at the end of James's arm, or rather, at the end of his antennae, are grasped with an astonishing firmness, gauged with a marvelous intelligence. His work is incomplete as his experience was; but it is in no respect second-rate, and he can be judged only in the company of the greatest. My argument has not given me an occasion to call attention to the classical equanimity, the classical combination of realism with harmony—I have tried to describe them in writing about Pushkin—which have been so rare in American and in English literature alike and of which James is one of the only examples.

R. P. BLACKMUR

In the Country of the Blue

[1943]

WE are now about to assay the deep bias, the controlling, characteristic tension in the fiction of Henry James as it erupts in those tales where the theme is that of the artist in conflict with society. To erupt is to break out irresistibly from some deep compulsion, whether of disease or disorder, into a major reaction; and that is exactly what happens to James when in the first full maturity of his fifties he began to meditate, to feel borne in upon him, the actual predicament of the artist as a man of integrity in a democratic society. He broke out, he erupted from the very center of his being, and with such violence that to save himself he had need of both that imagination which represents the actual and that which shapes the possible. James made of the theme of the artist a focus for the ultimate theme of human integrity, how it is conceived, how it is destroyed, and how, ideally, it may be regained. For James, imagination was the will of things, and as the will was inescapably moral, so the imagination could not help creating—could not fail rather to re-create—out of the evil of the artist's actual predicament the good of his possible invoked vision. As the artist is only a special case of the man, so his vision is only an emphatic image of the general human vision; that James could make so much of the special case and the emphatic image of the artist comes about because, more than any other novelist of his scope, he was himself completely the artist. By which I mean that he was free to dramatize the artist precisely because he was himself so utterly given up to his profession that he was free of the predicament of the artist the moment he began to write. He felt none of that difficulty about conviction or principle or aim in his work which troubles a lesser writer; both his experience and his values came straight and clear and unquestionable, so much so that he seems to inhabit another world, that other world which has as substance what for us is merely hoped for. James, as an artist, was above all a man of faith. As he said of one of his characters in another connection, he was copious with faith.

But there is a disadvantage in too complete a faith, as well for an artist as for a saint. Complete faith runs to fanaticism or narrowness. The act of faith tends to substitute for understanding of the thing believed in. If your values come to you unquestioned, you risk taking them on principle and of course. Only the steady supplication of doubt, the constant resolution of infirmity, can exercise your values and your principles enough to give them, together, that stretch and scope which is their life. If you dismiss doubt and ignore infirmity, you will restrict the scope that goes with the equivocal and reduce the vitality that goes with richness of texture. So it was with Henry James. His very faith in his powers kept him from using them to their utmost and caused him to emphasize only his chosen, his convicted view. That is why he is not of the very greatest writers, though he is one of the indubitably great artists, and especially in our present focus, the portrait of the artist. That is why, too, as his faith increased he came less and less to make *fictions* of people and more and more to make *fables*, to draw parables, for the ulterior purposes of his faith. He came less and less to tell and more and more merely to say. But—and this is what saves him to us for reading—the habit of the novelist was so pervasive in him that he could no more than breathing help dramatizing his fables or actualizing, to the possible limit of his frame, the story of his parables. Indeed, in his old age, which for him constituted a continuing rebirth, he made of the frame of his fables a new frame for the novel or tale only less than the greatest frames. I refer to *The Ambassadors, The Wings of the Dove, The Golden Bowl*, perhaps to *The Sense of the Past* and *The Ivory Tower*, and certainly to the tales in *The Finer Grain;* for in these works the form of the fable, the point of the parable, are brought to extreme use precisely by being embedded in the

R. P. Blackmur

sensibility of fiction. These take rise, I think, in *The Sacred Fount*, which, not a novel at all but a vast, shadowy, disintegrating parable, disturbing, distressing, distrait, indeed distraught, remains in the degree of its fascination quite ineluctable. It is the nightmare nexus, in James's literary life, between the struggle to portray the integrity of the artist and the struggle to portray, to discover, the integrity of the self.

This is another way of saying that the tales which exhibit the artist occupy an intermediate position in James's work; and we shall see that they look both ways, to the social novels that preceded them and to the fiction of fate that came after them. They look back to the conditions of life in general and forward to the prophecy of life beyond and under, or at any rate in spite of, the mutilating conditions. I think of Isabel Archer, in *The Portrait of a Lady*, how the conditions of life, particularly the conditions of money and marriage and their miring in manners, slowly dawned on her. You feel that if Isabel can only acknowledge the conditions, if she can see for once what life is like, she will be free to go on, where to go on means to meet more and more conditions. We know that in the process of going on she will lose—indeed she has already lost them—the freshness and promise and candor of youth, which are taken as the ordinary expenses laid out for the general look, whether dimmed or sharpened always somehow maimed and marked, of maturity. So for Isabel Archer and most of the early fiction. On the other hand I think of Milly Theale in *The Wings of the Dove*, whom we see actually killed by the conditions of life, acknowledge them how she will, but who yet so transcends them that her image—the image of the lost dead—brings to Kate Croy and Merton Densher, who had betrayed her in life, an unalterable, unutterable knowledge of what life is under its mutilated likeness. Things could, as Kate told Merton at the end, never again be the same between them; all because of the freshness and candor which had not perished but been discovered in the death of Milly Theale, and the unbroken, unbreakable promise of life which merely for *them,* as they had failed Milly, could not be kept but was to hover over them unavailingly ever afterward. Milly had her triumph in death; but in

The Question of Henry James

The Ambassadors, Lambert Strether had his triumph in life, and so Maggie Verver in *The Golden Bowl*, both triumphing precisely over the most mutilating conditions of life that could well have come their way. So again, perhaps with the most beautiful lucidity of all, there is the shabby little bookseller Herbert Dodd in *The Bench of Desolation*, whom we see deprived of the last resource of outward dignity—as a character he is all scar tissue—till he has nothing left but his lonely hours upon his seaside bench of desolation. The bench of desolation is where you sit still with your fate—that of which you cannot be deprived. For Herbert Dodd that bench has these many years turned out to be enough, when the return of the lost love of his youth, who he thought had betrayed him, makes it a bench of triumph as well. The triumph consists for him, as for the others, in the gradual inward mastery of the outward experience, a poetic mastery which makes of the experience conviction.

Between the earlier persons who master life by submitting to its conditions and the later persons who master what lies under the conditions by achieving a conviction of the self—for surely a man's convictions may be said to be the very shape of his self —comes the little, the slightly anomalous race of artists. Why they come between them rather than either as a culmination or a beginning is plain when we look at their characteristic fate. The man who is completely an artist is incompletely a man, though in his art he may envisage man completely. The meaning of the artist in history, that is in life as he lives it, in the conditions under which he works, is like the meaning of history itself. History, as Niebuhr says, is meaningful, but the meaning is not yet. The history of the artist is prophetic, but the meaning of the prophecy cannot now be known. What happens to the artist apart from his meaning, is common enough knowledge. If we look at the fables Henry James offers us, we see at once that all these artists are doomed men, as doomed as the characters in Hemingway, but not as in Hemingway by the coming common death. They are doomed either because they cannot meet the conditions of life imposed upon them by society or because society will have none of them no matter how hard they try.

That, for James, was the drama of the artist, and he put it in the simple white and black terms of the fable and the fairy story. The artist either gave in to the evil and corruption of society, or society refused a living to the good and incorruptible artist. But let us ask why James chose the artist for the living focus of his drama, when it might as well have been the queen or the kitchen maid as in the fairy tales, or the men and women next door who provide us, unadulterated with any self-interest, such excellent views of ourselves. Why, that is, did not James begin with the persons he came to?

We may say that he did not know enough, that he had not matured enough, and perhaps it would be better so to beg the question. But there is a kind of logic which we can apply after the event, which is where logic works best. The artist is *given* as in death struggle with society, as much so as the thief or the murderer but with the advantage of heroism and nobility as a luminous character in the mere murk of the struggle. That every man and woman, and perhaps more so every child, is also engaged in a death struggle with society, or at least with his neighbor's society, is not so clear; you would not think of *yourself* as struggling with society, but the artist and his critics have, I regret to say, vied with each other at every opportunity to see which could say so louder, especially since the spread of literacy and education has multiplied artists of all sorts at the same time that changing institutions took away the function of the artist in society. The artist became thus a natural puppet, ready-made, completely understandable, to represent the great central struggle of man as an individual, which is not often, when you consider the stakes, an understandable struggle at all, and to make a drama of which the novelist has to work from the ground up. It is no wonder then that James should consider the struggle of the artist as one of the great primary themes, especially when you add to the picture that he might incidentally dramatize himself a little—a temptation not beyond the purest artist—and do his trade a good turn.

But the evidence is not limited to the writings of artists and critics. There comes particularly pat to the kind of artist of whom James wrote a passage in De Tocqueville's classic work

The Question of Henry James

on the Republic of the United States of America. It was not quite going to be, he foresaw long before Henry James began writing novels, a model republic of letters. There is a little chapter in the first book of the second part called "The Trade of Literature" from which I extract the following passage: "Democracy not only infuses a taste for letters among the trading classes, but introduces a trading spirit into literature. . . . Among democratic nations, a writer may flatter himself that he will obtain at a cheap rate a meager reputation and a large fortune. For this purpose he need not be admired, it is enough that he is liked. . . . In democratic periods the public frequently treat authors as kings do their courtiers; they enrich and they despise them. . . . Democratic literature is always infested by a tribe of writers who look upon letters as a mere trade; and for some few great authors who adorn it, you may reckon thousands of idea-mongers." The picture is fresh enough for our own day, and we take it with the more authority because it was frankly prophetic on the part of a man more than generously disposed towards democracy. It is a description that James could have made for himself, and which, in fact, he did largely make, both in his life of Hawthorne and in the fiction which we are about to engage. De Tocqueville only reminds us of what James well knew, that an author can expect his readers to know that the race of literary artists is itself composed of good and bad, of very black and very white practitioners; so that the nobility of the good writer will go as granted once it is mentioned, as will the flunkyism of the bad writer. Thus, the author of a fiction about an artist has all the advantages of coarse melodrama without losing any of the advantages of high tragedy. He can merely impute unto his chosen character what virtues or vices he likes without being under any necessity to show them. In fiction, the stated intent of goodness, of high seriousness, is worthless in every realm of life except that of artist; elsewhere the character must be shown as actual, in the artist the stated intention is enough. We shall see that James fully availed himself of this freedom, redeeming himself only by the eloquence of his statement and the lesson of his parable. These, the eloquence and the lesson, will be what we bring away

R. P. Blackmur

with us. For it goes without saying that James was never taken in, in his created characters, by the meretricious, and was always deliberately sold by the high serious. In this respect, as perhaps nowhere else in James, the reader always knows exactly where he is at. What happens to the literary personages will vary with the incident and the conditions recorded; but nothing can happen to their characters once they are stated, for their characters are articulated ready-made as soon after their first appearance as possible, like puppets or like gods as you may choose to think.

This is no accident nor any part of James's idiosyncrasy; it is a limiting condition of the artist as a character in fiction to the extent that he is represented in the role of artist. If he drops the role, anything within the power of the author to represent may happen to him as a person; as artist he is only a shrunken and empty simulacrum of himself in his other roles; he may know the meaning, but he cannot share the motion.

This is one of the lessons that if James's fables are taken literally they best attest; and literally is very near how James meant his lessons to be taken. But we do not need to stick to James. The character of Stephen Dedalus, both in *The Portrait of the Artist as a Young Man* and in *Ulysses,* certainly works of the greatest richness and scope, comes to us very fully as a young man, but as an artist he comes to us only by the eloquence of Joyce's mere statement. The poem he writes and the diary he keeps, the lecture he gives on *Hamlet,* come to us quite independent of the created figure of Stephen. Even the greatest declaration that ends the earlier book, where Stephen resolves that he will "forge in the smithy of his soul the uncreated conscience of his race," must be taken either as a free lyric spoken by an actor, where something else might have done as well, or as an image in which the whole boy shrinks suddenly into an agonized intention that can never be realized in life or act but only in art itself. It is much the same thing with Herr Aschenbach, the old novelist in Thomas Mann's *Death in Venice,* who is never given to us as a novelist except by imputation. The role of artist is indeed called on for other purposes, to give quickly a background against which the reader will find credible and dramatic the image of old Aschenbach, the famous and dignified

The Question of Henry James

novelist, as an outsider, a figure so isolated by his profession of
artist that he fairly aches to corrupt himself, to debase himself,
both as a man and as an artist. It might almost be put that to
the degree that he had become an artist he had ceased existing—
as it were, ceased living—so that the desire for life becomes identified with the temptation to corruption. And so it turns out.
The only possible resumption of life for him is tainted with corruption, with effeminate infatuation, with deliberate indignity
and self-humiliation. But it is too late in the season, the season
of his life and the season in Venice, both of which are struck
down by pestilence. His adored and beautiful Tadzio is taken
away to safety, and Herr Aschenbach resumes his profession, in
the act of dying, by in his delirium re-enacting the *Phaedrus* of
Plato. Aschenbach the artist could have no life except in that
terrible privation of life which is art.

It is only the obverse of the same coin that André Gide shows
us in *The Counterfeiters* where the novelist reaches life only by
a driven and deliberate corruption, a personal disintegration as
great as the formal disintegration of the work of art in which it
it represented. That Mann and Gide show us corruption as the
necessary predilection of the artist, where James and Joyce show
us art—that is, integrity of spirit—as the redemption of life,
is perhaps due to the seeming fact that neither the German nor
the Frenchman have as full and fanatic a conviction of their
profession of artists as that suffered at an equal maximum by
both James and Joyce.

To get back a little nearer to our particular problem of the
portrait of the artist in Henry James—though, indeed, we have
never been far from it—there is another way of expressing the
predicament of the artist as a character in fiction. He comes to
life only as he ceases to be an artist; he comes to life, in a word,
only as he *fails* to be an artist, and he fails when the conditions
of life overcome him at the expense of his art. This becomes a
very pretty problem, indeed, when the novelist reflects that all
this amounts to saying that the actual source of art, the life of
which it is the meaning, is the artist's undoing. Gide solves the
problem, and so does Mann, by disintegrating the art as well as
the life. Joyce, with no greater honesty but with greater moral

[198]

R. P. Blackmur

insight, represents the struggle of the man *in society*, not as an outsider but as one very much at the heart of things, to become an artist. It was not for nothing that Joyce defined the sentimentalist as him who "is unwilling to incur the enormous responsibility for a thing done." Stephen Dedalus is shown to us in the very process of realizing, for the sake of his art, responsibility for every deed of his life. In Joyce, the artist, like God, dies every day. He dies into man and is reborn; the death is necessary to the birth. Henry James had neither the catholicism of Joyce, the bitter protestantism of Gide, nor the Faustian spirit of Mann at his back; he had rather—and only—his unquestioned faith in the adequacy of the free intelligence in life and the freed imagination in art. He had thus less equipment, or at any rate a less articulated philosophy, than the others, and it is perhaps for that reason that he produced his ideal artists who failed only in life and succeeded only in art, and his other artists, equally ideal, who failed in art only because they insisted on success, financial or social success, in life. The realm of the ideal is often nearest to those who have nearest to no philosophy; but so is the realm of the actual, which is the artist's realm, and James may have been nearer right in what he did with his facts than the others.

At least we have James's own abundantly eloquent answer to the charge that he ought never to have exhibited in art creatures who never existed in life. I give part of the answer as he made it in the preface to *The Lesson of the Master*. "What does your contention of non-existent conscious *exposures,* in the midst of all the stupidity and vulgarity and hypocrisy, imply but that we have been, nationally, so to speak, graced with no instance of recorded sensibility fine enough to react against these things? —an admission too distressing. What one would accordingly fain do is to baffle any such calamity, to *create* the record, in default of any other enjoyment of it; to imagine, in a word, the honourable, the producible case. What better example than this of the high and helpful public and, as it were, civic use of the imagination?—a faculty for the possible fine employments of which in the interest of morality my esteem grows every hour that I live. How can one consent to make a picture of the

The Question of Henry James

preponderant futilities and vulgarities and miseries of life without the impulse to exhibit as well from time to time, in its place,
some fine example of the reaction, the opposition or the escape?"

In this passage, and in the whole preface from which it is
taken, I think James reaches the pinnacle of principle to which
he was able to expose the idealism with which he worked; and
I have planted my quotations here in the center of this discussion of the portrait of the artist because they raise—especially
just after our references to the practice of Joyce and Gide and
Mann—considerations of great importance not only to the criticism, the appreciation, of James's fictions, but also to the whole
general theory of fiction itself—if you like to the whole theory
of art. There are several theories of the value of art which are
tenable until you begin to apply them in the interpretation of
particular works of art, when as a rule the value of the art
shrinks at once to nothing and there is *nothing but* moral value
left. No artist and hardly any user of art whose eyes are open
can take the slightest interest in any *nothing but* theory of art's
value. James's theory is very tempting because, if adopted, it
shows how moral value gets into a work of art without leaving
you to shudder for the fate of the art. The artist, he says with
all the rush and eloquence of immediate experience, the artist
creates the moral value out of the same material and by the
same means with which he creates his other values—out of the
actual and by means of imagination. The values are, though distinguishable, inextricable. Some works may show aesthetic values without moral values, and other works very clearly have
no aesthetic values and yet shriek to heaven with their moral
values, but where you have both orders of value as they are created, together, so they must be felt together, at least so long
as the work being enjoyed is enjoyed as art.

Among the consequences which flow from James's statement,
if I understand it right, there are two which deserve emphasis
for the freedom and the privation they impose on the artist. One
has to do with the inclusive nature of moral value in art. As the
experience in art must be somehow of the actual and as the record must be somehow of the imaginative, then the artist is free
to create evil as well as good without risk of police interference.

[200]

R. P. Blackmur

It is not that his vision of evil may overcome his vision of good, but that, if he is to be an artist of any scope, he must create both, and if the emphasis is on the one in a given work it must have the other as its under or supporting side. It is truly the Devil who minds God's business as it is God who gives the Devil something to do. But, and this is the second consequence kept for emphasis from James's statement, to have validity whether moral or aesthetic, whatever the artist *creates* (though not what he merely puts in by the way) must show its source in the actual; for it is otherwise either immoral or vapid, and likely both. If the architecture of even the noblest cathedral were not based on the actual it would fall apart, but without a vision beyond the actual it could never have been built at all. Art, on this view, tends toward the ideal but without ever quite transcending the actual from which it sprang. The ideal, in fact, in this restricted sense of the word, is what the artist creates; but the ideal, to have any significant worth, must approach the actual, with the striking effect which needs every meditation we can give it, that the nearer it approaches the actual the more greatly ideal the creation will seem. There is the force of Dante's ideal hell, that it approaches so close to the actual of this life; and there is the relative weakness of James's tales of the literary life, and despite his plea of moral necessity, that though they spring from hints in the actual world the "super-subtle fry" of his authors do not approach near enough to the actual. The fable is always frailer than the image, however more cogent. Thus, Joyce's Dubliners who translated the initials IHS of *In Hoc Signo* over the cross, as "I Have Suffered," were not blasphemers but better believers for so doing.

The examples are endless; but to our present interest it is the principle that counts, and its relation to the artist, and if we turn to our chosen tales of Henry James we shall find that though as dramas they do not show us very much of the actual, as fables they illuminate the principles by which James was later to anchor his most difficult and precarious ideals safe and firm— poetically valid—in flesh and blood. That is, as these tales occupy an intermediate position in the general development of James as works of art, so they represent for us an intermediate

The Question of Henry James

state of knowledge, that critical and fascinating state when principles fairly itch for action but have not yet run down into the skill of the hand that acts, that in this case writes. As stories they are stories about stories, and the most fascinating kind of stories, those that for both aesthetic and moral reasons can never quite be written. All the moral value is in the possibility not lived up to, and all the aesthetic value is in the possibility not lived down to. It is the same possibility, looking either way, the possibility of the really superior artist triumphing over society by cutting himself off from every aspect of it except the expressive, or the posssibility of this same superior fellow—and I hardly know which version is more tragic—coming to failure and ruin, expressive failure and personal ruin, by hands whose caresses are their most brutalizing blows, the hands of society itself, the society that, in De Tocqueville's phrases, would like an author rather than admire him, or, worse, would enrich and despise him.

The possibilities are indeed wonderful, and furnish half the conversation at literary parties, where the most enriched authors always turn out the most despised, very often justly. James does not deal with the literary party, whether because the institution had not grown much in his day or because it was open only to satire, which was not his purpose. He deals rather with the English house party and the English dinner party where there is a reputable author present for demolition. The effect is not too different, and affords the advantages of an outwardly more decorous set of conventions and even for a welcome shift of scenes from lawn to church, dinner table to parlor, or parlor to smoking room, smoking room to bedroom; which taken together, as even a novice at fiction should know, makes the problem of moving people from place to place and so of setting up new relations or modifying old ones, relatively easy. So it is that all but one of the fables we are dealing with make use of the machinery of entertainment for the mechanics of the plot. That is, the artifices that in actual society do most to prevent communication and obscure situations, James uses to promote intimacy and to clarify situations. He mastered the means which because of his life—in one London year he dined out three hun-

R. P. Blackmur

dred times—were almost alone at his disposal; the lesson of which may be that it explains why so many of James's people are never able to meet each other openly and yet contrive to put everything between them that is necessary.

That is exactly the situation in *The Figure in the Carpet* where I think we may put it that we know what the puzzle is precisely to the extent we realize it is insoluble, like the breath of life. The narrator who is himself a writer and nameless (the narrators of all these tales are writers and most of them are nameless) reviews the latest novel of Hugh Vereker in a magazine called the *Middle,* and shortly afterwards attends a house party where Vereker is a guest, as is his book, both unopened by any of the company, though both are the principal subjects of attention. Someone shows Vereker the review and Vereker says it is very bad; he has not realized the reviewer is present. When he does so, he apologizes to the narrator but insists that, nevertheless, like everybody else, he has missed the Figure in the Carpet: the general intention, the string to his pearls, the passion of his passion. The narrator tries his best to make up, both by reading Vereker's works and by tackling him personally. On his failure he passes the puzzle along to his friend George Corvick, who shares the problem with his fiancée. They in their turn grow futile and frenzied—so frenzied that their marriage comes to hang upon their success. Corvick goes off to Bombay as a correspondent, and while there wires: Eureka. The narrator and Corvick's fiancée, Gwendolyn Erme, try to guess what it must be. Corvick stops off on Vereker at Rapallo during his return journey, and writes that Vereker has verified his discovery. Gwendolyn marries George on condition that he reveal his secret; he dies on his honeymoon before writing it down. Gwen refuses to tell the narrator what it is, because, says she, it is her life. Vereker dies. Then Gwen, who has remarried to Drayton Deane, a critic, herself dies on the birth of a second child. After a decent but excruciated interval—for in James decency most of all is subject to excruciation—the narrator does his best to discover from Deane what the secret of Vereker's work had been. But Gwendolyn had never told him; and the figure in the carpet is safe. Nobody knows or can know what it can be. What

The Question of Henry James

then was the puzzle? It may be that there was none, or none except to those who wrote—or read—for the passion of the passion; which was certainly not how the narrator, nor any of his friends, either wrote or read. A frenzied curiosity is not passion. Or it may be that the figure in the carpet is necessarily ineluctable. Perhaps it only ought to be there; that much, acuteness can discover. In his prefatory remarks, James does nothing to help; but says only that "the question that accordingly comes up, the issue of the affair, can be but whether the very secret of perception hasn't been lost. That is the situation, and *The Figure in the Carpet* exhibits a small group of well-meaning persons engaged in a test." We can only note that well-meaning persons are notoriously unperceptive, and add that the secret of perception in readers comes very near the secret of creation in artists.

The Figure in the Carpet is perhaps a tea-time and tepid-whisky fable, for it is over these beverages that it largely occurs; and so represents, I think, no more than at most can be made out of obsessed gossip. James may have meant more for it—his preface suggests that he did—but it would seem actually, as written, to mean no more than that there is a figure in the carpet if you can imagine it for yourself; it is not there to discover. It is rather like Kafka, *manqué*, the exasperation of the mystery without the presence of the mystery, or a troubled conscience without any evidence of guilt.

Rather similar but carried further, further for actuality, by the very conventionality of its fantasy—its *glaring* incredibility—is the fable of *The Private Life*. Here again the narrator is a writer unnamed, this time on vacation in the Alps in a house full of people connected with the arts. Among the guests are Clare Vawdrey, a writer of genius but a second-rate man; Lord Mellfont, a magnificent public figure but nothing much when not in public; and Blanche Adney, a great actress, for whom Vawdrey is writing a play, and who is quite friendly with the narrator. The second-rateness of Vawdrey and the magnificent public presence of Mellfont gradually become suspect to Blanche and the narrator. Pursuing their curiosity, the narrator sneaks into Vawdrey's room in the evening, while Vawdrey is outside talking to Blanche; there the narrator discovered Vawdrey's other self writing industriously in the dark. Later, by plan, Blanche gets her chance, and while the narrator keeps Vawdrey outside herself makes the acquaintance of the other or "ghost" self and falls in love with him. Meantime, the narrator finds the outer self even duller than he had thought: "the world," he reflects, "was vulgar and stupid, and the real man would have been a fool to come out for it when he could gossip and dine by deputy." Lord Mellfont, on the other hand, must be himself an apparition, called into being by a public relation only; by himself he must be nothing, literally nothing. Blanche and the narrator go looking for him on that assumption, and of necessity he appears in front of them; if they had not looked for him, he would have been unable to materialize. "He was all public and had no corresponding private life, just as Clare Vawdrey was all private and had no corresponding public." Of this little piece what does one say but that the ghost story is the most plausible form of the fairy tale; it makes psychological penetration ominous because not verifiable. Who would care to verify a ghost, especially two ghosts who have the unity only of opposites? Life, the actuality, lies somewhere between; and it is a relief to think that your dull man of genius keeps a brilliant ghost in his workroom, just as it is a malicious delight to figure that your brilliant public man is utterly resourceless without a public.

The Private Life is a fantastic statement, so far as it has a serious side, of the inviolable privacy of the man of genius. *The Death of the Lion* makes a plea for the protection of that privacy, and for much more, on the ground that if you successfully violate it your genius, if he have no deputy self to gossip and dine, perishes from exposure. The narrator is again a young, detached writer and journalist with a strong sense of allegiance to the great, is sent to write up Neil Paraday at the moment he achieves, at the age of fifty, after a long illness, with his new book, the public success of being made a subject of a leader in the *Empire*. An interviewer for thirty-seven syndicated papers arrives just after Paraday has read the narrator the manuscript plan—a plan finished and perfect in itself—of his next and greatest book. The narrator takes over the interviewer, and goes on to take over as much protective custody of Paraday as possible. But Paraday, with his success, is nevertheless taken up by the unreading, by those who hate literature in the guise of adoring writers, especially by a Mrs. Wimbush who has the fortune of a great brewery. Paraday a little excuses his not throwing Mrs. Wimbush out of doors on the ground that he can get material for his writing out of her. The narrator, however, has a single success in keeping off an American girl with an autograph album to fill, but who really loves Paraday's work, understands that reading is greater than personality, and agrees to seek the author, as the narrator tells her to, "in his works even as God in Nature." Neil Paraday had been made, as the narrator says, a contemporary. "That was what had happened: the poor man was to be squeezed into his horrible age. I felt as if he had been overtaken on the crest of the hill and brought back to the city. A little more and he would have dipped down the short cut to posterity and escaped." To be a contemporary was to be a lion and lions of the contemporary necessarily die soon. Thus Paraday soon *wants* to become ill again; he knew what was happening to him, but he could not help surrendering to it. "He filled his lungs, for the most part, with the comedy of his queer fate: the tragedy was in the spectacles through which I chose to look. He was conscious of inconvenience, and above all of a great renouncement; but how could he have heard a mere dirge in the bells of his accession?"

What happens is inevitable from the title and from what has already been said. Paraday is seduced into going to a house party at Mrs. Wimbush's country place which is called Prestidge—a surface quality obtained, if you remember your etymology, by sleight of hand. There is to be a great foreign princess there, and many others, all to hear him read his precious manuscript plan. He falls sick and, dying, instructs the narrator to print it as his last work, small but perfect. However, Mrs. Wimbush has lent it to a guest who in turn has lent it to another, and so on, none of them by any chance reading it; so that it is lost. Before our Lion actually dies he has become a burden, for the next two in Mrs. Wimbush's series of Lions come before he is out of the way; and it is in the identity of the new beasts that

R. P. Blackmur

we see the true estimation in which Mrs. Wimbush—in which society—holds literature. The new beasts are two popular successes, Guy Walsingham, who is a woman, and Dora Forbes, who is a man with red mustaches. Their publishers think it necessary that they take opposite sexes in their pen names. But the narrator says rather that they are writers of some third sex: the success sex, no doubt, which can alone cope with the assaults of an adulating society.

Here we see the figure of a great writer preyed upon; the Lion is brought down by the brutality of a society which could have no use for him except as quarry. In *The Next Time* we have the contrary fable, that of the writer who struggles desperately to make society his prey, but fails because he cannot help remaining the harmless, the isolated monarch of his extreme, imaginative, ardent self. Society, seen as his prey, has no trouble at all in keeping out of his way. Ray Limbert's only successful step was the initial step of a "bad" marriage to a good wife, who has a mother and bears children who require support. He has a sister-in-law who is a successful popular novelist, where he himself is incontestably a great writer. He gave the narrator (again a literary man) "one of the rarest emotions of the literary life, the sense of an activity in which I could critically rest." However, it was necessary for him to earn his living, and after failing at journalism, the narrator gets him the post of editor with a year's contract at complete liberty. As an editor, Ray Limbert resolves to contribute serially a deliberately bad novel in the hope of achieving success, and requires of his friends that they do not read the installments for shame. His difficulty there was that he was one of those "people who can't be vulgar for trying." He loses his post as editor, partly because of the authors whom he had printed but mostly because of his own novel, which so far from being popular or obvious was "charming with all his charm and powerful with all his power: it was an unscrupulous, an unsparing, a shameless merciless masterpiece. . . . The perversity of the effort, even though heroic, had been frustrated by the purity of the gift." As the narrator finished his reading he looked out the window for a sight of the summer dawn, his eyes "compassionately and admiringly filled. The

[207]

eastern sky, over the London housetops, had a wonderful tragic crimson. That was the colour of his magnificent mistake." It was a mistake which Ray Limbert—by the terms of the fable—repeated, always believing that the next time he would do the trick. All the narrator could say was "that genius was a fatal disturber or that the unhappy man had no effectual *flair*. When he went abroad to gather garlic he came home with heliotrope." Finally he forgot "the next time." "He had merely waked up one morning again in the country of the blue and had stayed there with a good conscience and a great idea," and died, writing.

"In the country of the blue" is a very lonely place to be, for it is very nearly empty except for the self, and is gained only by something like a religious retreat, by an approximation of birth or death or birth-in-death. James tried for it in fiction I think but once, in *The Great Good Place*, here mentioned but in passing, where there is an adumbration rather than an account given of the retreat of the author George Doane, made for the recovery of genius, "which he had been in danger of losing"; he had returned to himself after eight hours to find his room "disencumbered, different, twice as large. It was all right." Yet there was some constant recourse for James to the country of the blue; it was where he would have had his projected great authors live, and it was where, as we shall see he reported, he sometimes lived himself.

But before we look at that sight, let us look at the tale which of all that James wrote best prepares us for it, *The Lesson of the Master*. This is probably the finest, surely the clearest, most brilliant, and most eloquent of all James's pleading fables of the literary life. It has greater scope than the others, itself rings with greatness, and is more nearly dramatic in character, more nearly joins the issue of the ideal and the actual. Unlike the other tales in our present list it is related in the third person from the point of view of the most implicated person in it, Paul Overt. The relations between that distinguished young talent and the master, Henry St. George, who has for years done less than his best work, are exhibited in terms of Marian Fancourt, of an interest and an intelligence in the arts hardly less than

R. P. Blackmur

her beauty, as a nexus for the conflict of loyalties between the master and the disciple. All three meet for the first time on a country week end at Summersoft. Both men are taken with Marian Fancourt. Overt respects St. George vastly, and when St. George tells him that he is good and must be better, referring to his own inadequacy, he responds by a kind of preliminary submission. In London Overt falls in love with Marian, St. George more or less making way for him. For each the two others are the poles of attraction. Overt visits St. George in his study after a party, and for most of thirteen pages St. George exhorts him magnificently to give up everything, marriage, money, children, social position—all the things to which St. George himself had succumbed—for the sake of his art. Overt takes the master pretty much at his word and goes abroad for two years writing his best thing yet under great privation of all personal life. While he is abroad St. George's wife dies, and Overt returns to find St. George and Marian on the verge of marriage, and so feels brutally cheated. It turns out that St. George has married Marian partly to save Overt from succumbing to the false gods, to save him from having everything but the great thing.

The great thing is "The sense of having done the best—the sense which is the real life of the artist and the absence of which is his death, of having drawn from his intellectual instrument the finest music that nature had hidden in it, of having played it as it should be played." When Overt complains that he is not to be allowed the common passions and affections of men, St. George answers that art is passion enough. When the whole ascetic position—for it is no less than ascetic in that it draws the artist as mostly not a man—Overt sums it up for him by crying that it leaves the artist condemned to be "a mere disfranchised monk" who "can produce his effect only by giving up personal happiness. What an arraignment of art!" And St. George takes him up: "Ah you don't imagine that I'm defending art? 'Arraignment'—I should think so! Happy the societies in which it hasn't made its appearance, for from the moment it comes they have a consuming ache, they have an uncurable corruption, in their breast. Most assuredly is the artist in a false position! But

The Question of Henry James

I thought we were taking him for granted." It was when Overt found Marian married to St. George that he realized *what* he had been taking for granted. One *hardly* knows whether society or the artist is worse flayed here; but one knows, and there is only the need one feels for a grace note in James's concluding remark that "the Master was essentially right and that Nature had dedicated him to intellectual, not to personal passion."

The portrait of the artist in Henry James is now almost complete: the man fully an artist is the man, short of the saint, most wholly deprived. This is the picture natural to the man still in revolt, to the man who still identifies the central struggle of life in society as the mere struggle of that aspect of his life of which he makes his profession, and who has not yet realized, but is on the verge of doing so, that all the professions possible in life are mutually inclusive. One's own profession is but the looking glass and the image of the others; and the artist is he who being by nature best fitted to see the image clear is damned only if he does not. If he sees, his vision disappears in his work, which is the country of the blue. That is why the only possible portrait to paint of the artist will be a portrait of him as a failure. Otherwise there will be only the portrait of the man. That is why James portrayed the artist chiefly during his intermediate dubious period, and why in his full maturity, like St. George, but in a different richer sense, took the artist for granted and portrayed men and women bent, not on a privation but a fullness of being.

There remains still to record only James's portrait of himself as the artist in the man mature, and for that there are two passages to quote, of which one is from a letter written at the age of seventy to Henry Adams urging him to cultivate the interest of his consciousness. "You see I still, in presence of life (or of what you deny to be such,) have reactions—as many as possible—and the book I sent you is proof of them. It's, I suppose, because I am that queer monster, the artist, an obstinate finality, an inexhaustible sensibility. Hence the reactions—appearances, memories, many things, go on playing upon it with consequences that I note and 'enjoy' (grim word!) noting. It all takes doing—and I *do*. I believe I shall do yet again—it is still an act of life."

That is the man in life as artist. The other passage, with which we end this chapter, is taken from some penciled notes written some time in his last years on a New Year's Eve, near midnight, during a time of inspiration. Lubbock prints the whole of the notes in the introduction to his edition of the *Letters,* saying that "There is no moment of all his days in which it is now possible to approach him more clearly." I quote only the last paragraph. The shape, the life, the being of a novel having shown itself clear, the exaltation is so great that James is left once again with just the story of a story to tell, this time of himself.

Thus just these first little wavings of the oh so tremulously passionate little old wand (now!) make for me, I feel, a sort of promise of richness and beauty and variety; a sort of portent of the happy presence of the elements. The good days of last August and even my broken September and my better October come back to me with their gage of divine possibilities, and I welcome these to my arms, I press them with unutterable tenderness. I seem to emerge from these recent bad days—the fruit of blind accident—and the prospect clears and flushes, and my poor blest old Genius pats me so admirably and lovingly on the back that I turn, I screw round, and bend my lips to passionately, in my gratitude, kiss its hands.

The feeling in this passage is not uncommon; most of us have been terrified at its counterpart; but the ability to surrender to the expression of it is rare, and is what brought James himself, for the moment of expression, into the blue.

MORTON D. ZABEL

The Poetics of Henry James

[1935]

A PURPOSE and an achievement like Henry James's are lost on no department of writing, not even one with which he has as little practical concern as poetry. The latest revival of interest in him, having now warranted the first collection of his critical prefaces to his own books under the title *The Art of the Novel,* must include the attention of contemporary poets. What he did to prepare the day for them in England and America, and what, indirectly, he saw their problem to be, is an important part of our literary intelligence. His prefaces are the document in which it is most comprehensively stated; Mr. Blackmur's account of their definitions and doctrines is an excellent foreword to what will in time doubtless be recognized as an authentic poetics not only for novelists but for other literary craftsmen in the twentieth century. It has already been recognized as such in several quarters since James's death in 1917. The memorial issue of the *Little Review* (August, 1918) was an early testimony; Pound's program notes to the novels printed there now reappear in his latest collection of essays, *Make It New,* and establish the connection with modern poetry which was already apparent in Eliot's early verse; the studies of F. M. Ford, Pelham Edgar, J. W. Beach, and Percy Lubbock have lent the scrutiny of more formal analysis; and the *Hound and Horn* last April offered a critical retrospect of thirteen aspects of James's art and age.

In a time when most literary forms tend to become absorbed into that loose and amorphous species called the "novel," James's principles must have at least the negative value of telling what

Morton D. Zabel

the novel is not: what is inappropriate, unspecific, or unnatural to it, and how its special character and function must be maintained, thus keeping poets from reckless entry on its preserves and consequent damage to their own. But he has a more positive value for them. He saw, from the vantage point of a lifetime's discipline and responsibility, the disintegrating and cheapening tendencies at work in the entire body of literature; he was able by the clairvoyance of a resolute artist's unflinching intelligence to see that these tendencies, at the beginning of this century, were entering on their most productive and ruinous phase. At an advanced age he sat down to write his prefaces as

a sort of plea for Criticism, for Discrimination, for Appreciation on other than infantile lines—as against the so almost universal Anglo-Saxon absence of these things; which tends so, in our general trade, it seems to me, to break the heart. . . . They ought, collected together, none the less, to form a sort of comprehensive manual or *vademecum* for aspirants in our arduous profession.

They were to stand, in other words, as a warning against license and as a guide through the deceptive privileges of a free age for authorship. That guidance touches on the contemporary poetic problem at four important points: the motives of technique, the nature of artistic intelligence, the duty of self-determination, and the character of modernity. All of them have been paramount in literature during the past half-century, made so by the decline of romantic principles and the resistance of creative integrity to the confusion which those principles induced. And it is worth noting that the corrective which James formulated for his branch of literature, fiction, was, when he wrote the prefaces in 1907-1909, fully as imperative among poets as among the generation of novelists from whom he now towers as an exemplar and standard.

That generation, in England and America between 1880 and the war, was the enthusiastic inheritor of naturalism. The zest for experience had not yet been curbed by the terrors or the surfeit of realism; the feast of detail had not yet been restricted by the cautions of selective taste and form. France, the country of James's spiritual affinity and apprenticeship, had furnished

The Question of Henry James

both—the discipline of fact in Zola and the Goncourts, the rigor of design in Flaubert. England had to wait several decades for a similar correction. When Pater, Moore, Gissing, and Butler appeared, their value was disregarded or denounced, and in America the day for a Henry Adams or Stephen Crane had not yet been prepared. The new generation of storytellers were chiefly products of a higher journalism—Wells, Bennett, Galsworthy, Dreiser—rescued for periods by the finer conscience of their material but descending too readily to tract-writing or the manufacture of best sellers. James viewed this hazardous interval in the novel with distress; his opinions may still be read in *Notes on Novelists*. He saw twentieth-century novelists as declining from a great tradition, as standing in a precarious position where they no longer commanded the vigor of that tradition's early novelty, but still too immature in critical acumen to find in true perception or formal maturity the antidote that might rescue them from the "sickness of popularity." He was aware that this interval had bred certain masters; his praise of Conrad shows that he saw how a dangerous transition might be bridged. But he was also aware that between the deterioration of romantic sentiment (in Stevenson) and of realism (in Reade, Wells, and Walpole), there survived one certain mediator—the proving discipline of technique. He was particularly aware of this because he himself had been rescued by such an austerity, patiently mastered through forty years of work. He, in his earlier generation, had been obliged to pass from the exuberant fertility of pioneer experiences (in *Roderick Hudson, Confidence, The American*) to the gradual mastery of a critical authority which would allow him to control not only the abundant novelties of the American scene but the larger prospects of a European heritage. For him the age of discovery was past, but the age of values had just begun. The copious omniscience which had descended from Dickens, Melville, and Tolstoy, and in poetry from Hugo, Whitman, and Swinburne, disclosed to him its perils as well as its privileges. For novelists wise enough to care, his career as an artist from 1875 to 1910 provided the best possible example of how this danger might be resisted. From that resistance he derived the increasingly refined and subtilized style

Morton D. Zabel

which has been, for most readers, James's chief claim to distinction. The poets of English-speaking countries had no similar model of discipline; they had to turn to France. The age that was dominated by Whitman was one of inventive fertility and exploration, but not of discrimination; James's influence in the field of fiction anticipates by a quarter-century the efforts toward limitation and concretion which have been paramount in poetic theory and writing since the war.

But James's famous stylistic subtlety and refinement have more to justify them than their aim to perfect the instrument of language. They are indissociable from his conception of the artist's intelligence. The omniscience to which modern writers lay claim was to him not a matter of scope but of insight, not of expansion but of penetration. In this he directly opposes the disciples of Whitman. His effort to perfect his technique was not only, as Mrs. Wharton has said, an attempt to lift the novel out of its infantile delight in block-building to an adult concern for structure and manipulation; it was his way of showing what the creative intelligence is and should be, and the objects to which it should be applied. As Mr. Blackmur says:

James had in his style and perhaps in the life which it reflected an idiosyncrasy so powerful, so overweening, that to many it seemed a stultifying vice, or at least an inexcusable heresy. . . . He enjoyed an excess of intelligence and he suffered, both in life and art, from an excessive effort to communicate it, to represent it in all its fullness. His style grew elaborate in the degree that he rendered shades and refinements of meaning and feeling not usually rendered at all. . . . His intention and all his labor was to represent dramatically intelligence at its most difficult, its most lucid, its most beautiful point. This is the sum of his idiosyncrasy.

In other words, it ceased to be an idiosyncrasy and became a test of character and strength, a realization in the most profound way of what an artist's special function in life is.

One might, with optimism, say that if James had been a poet instead of a novelist his consummate sense of this artistic responsibility would not have been considered mere idiosyncrasy; the poet's duty is not only "to charge language with the maxi-

The Question of Henry James

mum degree of meaning" but to extract that meaning from the essential heart of the experience around and within him. But the fate of the poets who have tried, in any age, to do this has never been an easy one. In his early book on *French Poets and Novelists* James saw their ordeal in the nineteenth century and anticipated it in the twentieth. He was able to criticize Baudelaire without overlooking the fact that Baudelaire furnished a new morality and purpose to poets in an age that promised to confound and bewilder them by the fecundity and complexity of its literary resources.

For James the salvation from such confusion lay precisely in that conquest of identity which he made the adventure of his focal heroes and heroines—Milly Theale, Maggie Verver, Lambert Strether. These people, living lives of emotional or social conformity, embody the modern sensibility surrounded by the external equipment of modern sophistication; they comprehend at once the splendors of tradition, the weight of inherited instinct and decorum, and the license of current liberalism. From this confusion of privileges each has to retreat, through ordeal and agony, to the final authority of selfhood. When that is attained, in triumph or in tragedy, the truth of life is at last disclosed. Their problem, in different terms, is that of the modern poets who have written, out of lives of purer feeling or intellect, such poems as *Sunday Morning, The Man Who Died Twice, The Waste Land, Hugh Selwyn Moberley,* and *The Tower*—the rescue of personality from an excess of sophistication, erudition, self-indulgence, and privilege. The antagonism of these forces is James's definition of the modern problem; it closely resembles Valéry's, though it differs widely in the solution he offers. He saw this predicament as an antagonism of intelligent selfhood against the depersonalized scientific comprehension of all things in their "unprejudiced identities." The labyrinth, for the writer, permits only one safe exploration—that guided by a man's complete and realized personality, to which all data of experience must attach to gain meaning. Such meaning it is the artist's special duty to interpret and express, and James defined the poet as the artist who must express it with the highest authority.

Morton D. Zabel

The "taste" of the poet [a blessed comprehensive name for many of the things deepest in us] is, at bottom and so far as the poet in him prevails over everything else, his active sense of life: in accordance with which truth to keep one's hand on it is to hold the silver clue to the whole labyrinth of his consciousness. . . . The seer and speaker under the descent of the god is the "poet," whatever his form, and he ceases to be one only when his form, whatever else it may nominally or superficially or vulgarly be, is unworthy of the god: in which event, we promptly submit, he isn't worth talking of at all.

Poets have seldom been honored, in any age, by as high a duty and as certain a dignity as this.

F. O. MATTHIESSEN

The Ambassadors

[1944]

THE AMBASSADORS, the first of James's three crowning works to be completed, has proved by far his most popular book with the critics. In this they have followed his lead, since he announced in the preface that it was "frankly, quite the best, 'all round,' " of all his productions. He wrote it with gusto, declaring to Howells as he felt his way into its composition in the summer of 1900, that it was "human, dramatic, international, exquisitely 'pure,' exquisitely everything. . . . My genius, I may even say, absolutely thrives." Such fresh confidence carried into the texture of the book. After the strained virtuosity of *The Awkward Age* and *The Sacred Fount*, James expanded into a theme that was both opulent and robust. He expressed the mood that had been phrased by Longfellow's brother-in-law, Tom Appleton: "All good Americans, when they die, go to Paris." Appleton was talking of the era directly after the Civil War, the era James had recorded in *The American*. But the mood was to persist, and for the next postwar period, for the generation of the 1920's, Paris was still the same "huge iridescent" jewel it was for Strether, the symbol of liberation from every starved, inadequate background into life.

What caused James's preference for the book was not its theme, but its roundness of structure. On the same grounds of " 'architectural' competence" his second favorite was *The Portrait of a Lady*. In *The Ambassadors* we have a fine instance of the experienced artist taking an external convention, and, instead of letting it act as a handicap, turning it to his own signal advantage. James had always been uneasy—as well he might

[218]

F. O. Matthiessen

have been!—with his age's demand for serialized fiction. But here for once he felt a great stimulus to his ingenuity, and he laid out his novel organically in twelve books, each of which could serve for a month's installment. His subject was well fitted to such treatment, since it consisted in Strether's gradual initiation into a world of new values, and a series of small climaxes could therefore best articulate this hero's successive discoveries. It is interesting to note also the suspense that James creates by the device of the delayed introduction of the chief characters in Strether's drama.

The opening book at Chester, where Strether, arriving from Liverpool to meet his friend Waymarsh, encounters first Maria Gostrey, is really a prologue that strikes the theme of Europe—the Europe of old houses and crooked streets which was also being stamped upon American imaginations by James's contemporary, Whistler. The second book begins in London, and though Strether is already started on his eager growth through fresh impressions, how far he still has to go is indicated by Maria's remark that the theater which he takes "for—comparatively divine" is "impossible, if you really want to know." During this conversation Chad Newsome's name is first casually introduced, and then followed by expertly swift exposition of the situation which Strether has come out to rectify. But we don't see Chad himself for some time yet. Strether must have his initial taste of Paris, that "vast bright Babylon." As he stands in the Boulevard Malesherbes looking up at the balcony of Chad's apartment, he recognizes in a flash, in the essence of Jamesian revelation, that the life which goes on in such balanced and measured surroundings cannot possibly be the crude dissipation that Woollett, Massachusetts, believes. His initiation has reached its crucial stage.

Only at the end of this third book does Chad himself appear, with a dramatic entrance into the back of Maria's and Strether's box at the Comédie. In a neat instance of how he could meet the devices of the serial, James has him sit there through the darkness of the act, with Strether intensely conscious of his presence; and brings the two of them face to face in conversation not until after the play, at the beginning of book four. In that book Strether tactfully feels his way into friendship with Chad; and in the next he is introduced to Madame de Vionnet. It is significant that the declaration for life which was the seed of this novel flowers into its full form, as spoken by Strether to little Bilham, immediately after this introduction. The next two books concentrate on Strether's developing relations with Madame de Vionnet, from his first call on her to his boldly flouting Woollett and taking her out to lunch. Before the end of this book, a little more than halfway through the novel, his position and Chad's are reversed: Chad says he is willing to go home and it is Strether who now urges him to stay.

Such conduct brings its swift retribution, with the arrival, in book eight, of the new ambassador, Mrs. Newsome's formidable daughter, Sarah Pocock, who has been sent to take over the duties of the wavering Strether. The portrait of the Pococks —Sarah, Jim, and Mamie—is one of James's triumphs in light-handed satire, in the manner he had mastered in *Daisy Miller* and had developed further in that lesser-known but delightful *jeu d'esprit*, *The Reverberator*. With the Pococks the cast is finally complete, and it is an astonishing tribute to James's skill that the most intensely realized presence in the novel is that of Mrs. Newsome, who never appears at all and yet looms massively like "some particularly large iceberg in a cool blue northern sea."

The critical point in book nine is the announcement that Madame de Vionnet's daughter is to be married, which leaves Strether, blind until now to the actual situation, with the growing awareness that it must be Madame de Vionnet herself to whom Chad is somehow bound. The tenth book moves rapidly to Sarah's being outraged at what she regards as Strether's treachery to her mother, and to her ultimatum that her entourage is leaving Paris. The eleventh book rises to the most effective climax of all, Strether's glimpse of Chad and Madame de Vionnet together on the river, and his long-delayed perception of their real relationship. What is left for the concluding book is his final interview with Madame de Vionnet, which James was inclined to regard as the novel's "most beautiful and interesting" scene. Then, after a last talk with Chad, Strether faces

F. O. Matthiessen

with Maria what the whole experience has come to mean for him.

What most concerned James in this structure was also his principal contribution to the art of the novel, his development in Strether of a center of consciousness. What Strether *sees* is the entire content, and James thus perfected a device both for framing and for interpreting experience. All art must give the effect of putting a frame around its subject, in the sense that it must select a significant design, and, by concentrating upon it, thus empower us to share in the essence without being distracted by irrelevant details. James's device serves greatly to reinforce such concentration, since if every detail must be observed and analyzed by Strether, we obtain a heightened singleness of vision. We obtain both "the large unity" and "the grace of intensity" which James held to be the final criteria for a novel. His contribution here has been fully assessed by critics, and has been assimilated in varying degrees by many subsequent novelists. Indeed, some have gone so far as to declare *The Ambassadors* the most skillfully planned novel ever written. The chief reminder we need now is that there is a vast difference between James's method and that of the novels of "the stream of consciousness." That phrase was used by William James in his *The Principles of Psychology*, but in his brother's novels there is none of the welling up of the darkly subconscious life that has characterized the novel since Freud. James's novels are strictly novels of intelligence rather than of full consciousness; and in commenting on the focus of attention that he had achieved through Strether, he warned against "the terrible *fluidity* of self-revelation."

What James saw in Strether was what made him want to write the novel, as his long notebook entry of 1895 had elaborated. The idea that had come to him first was that of "an elderly man who hasn't lived, hasn't at all, in the sense of sensations, passions, impulses, pleasures. . . . He has never really enjoyed—he has lived only for duty and conscience . . . lived for effort, for surrender, abstention, sacrifice." James had begun at once to imagine the possibilities. He shied away at first from having the revelation come to his hero in Paris, on the grounds

The Question of Henry James

of being too expected and banal. He wasn't absolutely certain that the man should be American: "he might be an Englishman." But as James went on to conceive the putative histories of men who had not lived, his hero's background became unmistakable: "I can't make him a novelist—too like W. D. H. and too generally *invraisemblable*. But I want him 'intellectual,' I want him fine, clever, literary almost: it deepens the irony, the tragedy. A clergyman is too obvious and *usé* and otherwise impossible. A journalist, a lawyer—these men *would* in a manner have 'lived,' through their contact with life, with the complications and turpitudes and general vitality of mankind. A doctor—an artist too. A mere man of business—he's possible; but not of the intellectual grain that I mean. The Editor of a Magazine—that would come nearest: not at all of a newspaper. A Professor in a college would imply some knowledge of the lives of the young—though there might be a tragic effect in his seeing at the last that he hasn't even suspected what these lives might contain. They have passed by him—he had passed them by."

The austerity and aloofness of the still unnamed Strether have by now determined him as unquestionably a New Englander. One aspect of his situation that James projected in his notebook outline but did not use in the book was that his hero's blindness to passion should have caused him in the past to have misunderstood and so to have sacrificed some wild son or younger brother. But now all the sources of emotion, all the "influences and appeals" he had not reckoned with are to be brought home to him. James hit directly upon the situation he was to use, that of his hero's having come to Europe to bring back some young man whose family are anxious. "The idea of the tale," as he summed it up, was to consist then in "the revolution that takes place in the poor man" as he ranges himself unexpectedly *"du côté du jeune homme."* James has already conceived what sacrifice that will mean for his hero, that he will lose "the strenuous widow," whom he was to have married, "and all the advantages attaching to her." "It is too late, too late *now* for *him* to live—but what stirs in him with a dumb passion of desire, of I don't know what, is the sense that he may

F. O. Matthiessen

have a little supersensual hour in the vicarious freedom of another." The signal omission from this outline is any mention of Madame de Vionnet. The transformation of that phrase, "of I don't know what," into the richest source of Strether's awakening is one token of how much James's final themes accrued by the years in which he let his imagination play over them before bringing them to completion.

The challenge to *live*, in its short initial form, had dwelt solely on the elderly man's warning—James stipulated his age as fifty-five—against the repetition of his mistake. James's immense elaboration of this challenge tells how much it meant to him. As Strether delivers it in Gloriani's garden, it becomes in fact the quintessential expression of a dominant theme that runs throughout James's work. A whole succession of his heroes and heroines had been possessed with the same desire. Roderick Hudson's thirst for experience had been so violent that it had hurled him to destruction; but for Christopher Newman, who had retired from business in early middle life, and for Isabel Archer, just on the threshold of her twenties, there had seemed every possibility for the abundance Strether had missed. All these characters were Americans for whom the symbol of abundance had been Europe, but a similar eagerness for liberation was to seize upon some of James's European heroes—notably Hyacinth Robinson (of *The Princess Casamassima*), who was finally crushed by the class divisions that had kept him from his desire, and Nick Dormer (of *The Tragic Muse*), who had turned his back on a political career to live more intensely in the practice of art. Such is the recurrent pattern of James's novels, and the same theme could be followed through any number of his short stories, from the frustrated aspirations of Clement Searle, "the passionate pilgrim" (1871), down to the tragedy of the spiritual emptiness of John Marcher, in *The Beast in the Jungle* (1903), whose lot it was to have been the man "to whom nothing whatever was to happen."

Strether introduces into his version of this declaration for life a highly complex image, which serves to reveal his Puritan heritage. It is the image of life as a tin mold, be it plain or fluted or embossed, into which the "helpless jelly" of one's conscious-

[223]

The Question of Henry James

ness is poured by "the great cook." In this way Strether symbolizes the illusion of free will: the form of the individual consciousness has been predetermined and limited, not, to be sure, by the Puritans' God, but by every force in the individual's background and environment. Yet Strether insists that we make the most of life by enjoying our illusion, that we should act as though we were free. James had already shown his concern with such a philosophical theme in *The Portrait of a Lady*. Isabel Archer, a daughter of the transcendental enlightenment, was confident that the world lay all before her, that she could make whatever fine choice she liked. James knew how wrong she was in that belief, and demonstrated that her every act was determined by her innocence, the willful eagerness, the generous but romantic blindness to evil that she had derived from her nineteenth-century American conditioning.

James himself did not have the heritage of American Puritanism. He spoke of his not being a New Englander "as a danger after all escaped." He remarked also, "Boston is absolutely nothing to me—I don't even dislike it." But to understand all the overtones with which he charged the imperative *live*, we must remember that his grandfather was an Irish Presbyterian. Against that background James's father was in revolt. Yet even as he responded to Emerson's rejection of the old restrictions, he found that philosopher dangerously limited by his refusal to reckon with Calvinism "as a fact at all" in his sublime superiority to evil. Most of Henry James Senior's own declarations, as he ripened into his version of Swedenborgianism, were on the side of optimism and expansion. In that he proved himself a child of his age, but the strong residue of his concern with the nature of evil was to be transmitted to his sons, though ultimately more to the brooding novelist than to the hopeful philosopher.

Yet Strether's declaration, except for its qualifying of free will, continues, essentially, the transcendental mood of liberation. What had proved so heartening to Emerson's contemporaries was his insistence that life for Americans no longer needed to be starved. The most intense expression of that conviction, perhaps the most intense single passage in American writing, is

F. O. Matthiessen

Thoreau's development of a theme extraordinarily like Strether's. When Thoreau declared why he went to the woods, he, too, revealed the depth of the New England dread that a man might die without ever having lived. But Thoreau's will was in dynamic response to the challenge, and he expressed his desire "to suck out all the marrow of life" in a series of physical images, the energy of which was quite beyond Strether—or James.

The relative attenuation of Strether's desire, its passive rather than active scope, is one of the most striking consequences of James's own peculiar conditioning. No experimental child of the nineteenth century, not even John Stuart Mill, was brought up more deliberately on a theory. That theory, as James described it in *Notes of a Son and Brother,* sprang from his father's profound aversion to the narrow, competitive drives of American life. What he wanted for his sons was the greatest possible range of spiritual experience—"spiritual," as Henry noted, was his father's "most living" word—before they should be limited by the dictates of a career. In fact, as Henry was humorously aware, his father carried his dread of their being circumscribed to such lengths as to deplore their decision upon any career at all, and continued in the hope that they were instead "just to *be* something, something unconnected with specific doing, something free and uncommitted. . . ."

Such a theory could have resulted in utter dispersion in a group with less passion for ideas than the James family possessed. But as it affected both the older boys, it induced a slow but richer ripening. It may well have caused some of William's early nervous tensions, as he struggled to find himself by turning from painting to experimental science to medicine, and only finally to psychology and philosophy. But it meant that when he finally wrote his first book, at the age of forty-seven, in the same year as Henry's *The Tragic Muse,* he produced a masterpiece, *The Principles of Psychology.* Henry's tensions were less apparent but extremely acute, and the more glimpses we catch of them, the more we perceive why a declaration like Strether's spoke so much for himself as well. On the verge of manhood, the injury to his back that kept him from participating in the Civil War made him feel that his was the peculiar case of having

The Question of Henry James

to live inwardly at a time of "immense and prolonged outwardness." For many years thereafter his health continued to be so
precarious that he was afraid he might never be able to bring his
expression of life to the fullness for which he longed, an anxiety
which found its way into such a story of an artist's frustration
as *The Madonna of the Future.* As he came through to middle
age, he began to find stability, and though in his "summing up"
he could recall that his twenties had been "a time of suffering so
keen that that fact might seem to pin its dark colours to the
whole period," nevertheless the dominant strain in his memories
was quite other. He could feel at last the satisfaction of having
"wanted to do very much what I have done, and success, if I
may say so, now stretches back a tender hand to its younger
brother, desire."

But he was still to have many hours of his old anxiety, of
feeling merely on the verge of completion. And though, unlike
Strether, he had not been shut out from the opportunity for impressions of life, still he was to come back again and again to a
central dilemma. He made his most complete declaration of it
shortly after he had started to work for the stage. His advice
to himself should be put beside Strether's advice to Bilham:
"The upshot of all such reflections is that I have only to let myself *go.* So I have said to myself all my life—so I said to myself
in the far-off days of my fermenting and passionate youth. Yet
I have never fully done it. The taste of it—of the need of it—
rolls over me at times with commanding force: it seems the formula of my salvation, of what remains to me of a future. I am
in full possession of accumulated resources—I have only to use
them, to insist, to persist, to do something more,—to do much
more,—than I *have* done. The way to do it—to affirm one's self
sur la fin—is to strike as many notes, deep, full, and rapid, as
one can. All life is—at my age, with all one's artistic soul the
record of it—in one's pocket, as it were. Go on, my boy, and
strike hard; have a rich and long St. Martin's Summer. Try
everything, do everything, render everything—be an artist, be
distinguished to the last."

Another decade was to elapse before he was able to let himself
go to his full extent, and to say finally the most that he had to

[226]

F. O. Matthiessen

say. His St. Martin's summer really began with *The Ambassadors*. It is notable that the two New England minds of his own generation with whom he had most enjoyed friendship during his Boston years were to come to equally late flowering. Henry Adams was not to write his *Mont-Saint-Michel and Chartres* until he was past sixty-five and his *Education* until he was almost seventy. Wendell Holmes was to arrive at his full stature only after he reached the Supreme Court, at sixty-one, in the same year as *The Ambassadors* appeared. These other late harvests, along with those of the James brothers, are evidence against the current belief that American talents always burn themselves out after an early promise. They may indicate, too, that the older New England strain could come to valuable expression, in the period of New England's cultural decline, only if it had the stamina to survive its arid surroundings and so mature at last the rich juices for which Adams in particular felt himself parched.

What Strether awakened to in Paris was not unlike the aesthetic experience that Adams came finally to know only as he discovered the beauty of the cathedrals. Strether keeps emphasizing the importance of seeing, and we know that James himself lived in large measure by his eyes. He developed very early the feeling that intense life concentrated itself into scenes of which he was the absorbed spectator. This was to mean that of the two types into which Yeats divides artists, those who, like Blake, celebrate their own immediate share in the energy that "is eternal delight," and those who, like Keats, give us a poignant sense of being separated from what they present, James belonged to the latter. He described his own early romantic longing for "otherness" in terms very close to those Yeats was to use for Keats:

> I see a schoolboy when I think of him,
> With face and nose pressed to a sweet-shop window. . . .

James said that in his childhood "to *be* other, other almost anyhow, seemed as good as the probable taste of the bright compound wistfully watched in the confectioner's window, unattainable, impossible. . . ." His account, too, of the kind of

[227]

delight he took in his first "pedestrian gaping" along Broadway delineates even more sharply the type to which he belonged. For at this very same time, in the early 1850's, an incipient American poet had also been drinking in the sights of this same street. But Whitman was to make his poetry out of passionate identification with everything he saw, not out of detachment. James, on the other hand, came to believe that "the only form of riot or revel" his temperament would ever know would be that "of the visiting mind," and that he could attain the longed for "otherness" of the world outside himself only by imaginative projection which, by framing his vision, could give it permanence.

What Strether sees is what James saw, the Europe of the tourist. But James conceived of seeing in a multiple sense, as an act of the inward even more than of the outward eye. An interesting chapter of cultural history could be written about the nineteenth century's stress on sight. When Emerson declared that "the age is ocular," and delighted in the fact that the poet is the seer, he was overwhelmingly concerned with the spiritual and not the material vision. But concern with the external world came to mark every phase of the century's increasing closeness of observation, whether in such scientific achievements as the lenses for the telescope and the microscope, or in the painters' new experiments with light, or in the determination of the photographers and the realistic novelists to record every specific surface detail. Matthew Arnold was to note that "curiosity" had a good sense in French, but unfortunately only a bad one in English. James, an early convert to Arnold's culture, set himself to prove the value of the furthest reaches of curiosity. The distance that he had traveled from Emerson may be measured by the fact that though both knew their chief subject matter to be consciousness, the mind's awareness of its processes, for Emerson that awareness reaffirmed primarily the moral laws. James was also a moralist, but aesthetic experience was primary for him, since ἀισθητικός meant perceptive. He had turned that double-edged word "seer" back to this world. As he said in the preface to *The Ambassadors*, "art deals with what we see, it must first contribute full-handed that ingredient; it

F. O. Matthiessen

plucks its material, otherwise expressed, in the garden of life—
which material elsewhere grown is stale and uneatable." But
what distinguished him from French naturalists and English
aesthetes alike was that he never forgot the further kind of seeing, the transcendent passage to the world behind appearance
and beyond the senses.

Emerson had exulted that the eye was "the best of painters,"
but his poetry and prose were both woefully lacking in plastic
quality. James deliberately cultivated the skills of the painter.
The first form he had experimented with as a small boy was
what he called in his reminiscences "dramatic, accompanied by
pictorial composition," short scenes each followed by its illustration. At the time when William was working in Hunt's
studio, Henry at seventeen had shown his own shy curiosity in
sketching. And although he soon realized that he had no talent,
and turned to fiction, "it was to feel, with reassurance, that the
picture was still in essence one's aim." He was to continue to
train his eye by means of his long series of "portraits of places,"
wherein he followed the lead of Gautier and other Frenchmen
who were bringing literature closer to the art of the Impressionists. He was finally to arrive at the explicit statement that
he wanted such a story as *The Coxon Fund* to be "an Impression—as one of Sargent's pictures is an impression."

The perfected instance of his belief that the novelist should
"catch the colour of life" is the way he initiates both Strether
and the reader into Paris. His accuracy of presentation is such
that he can really suggest the quality of Chad's existence
through the very look of his house, "its cold fair grey, warmed
and polished a little by life." James makes such a magnificently
functional use of his architectural details that his hero is persuaded—and thousands of his countrymen have had the same
yearning belief—that the life which goes on behind those win-
dows and that balcony must also be characterized by tact and
taste, by "the fine relation of part to part and space to space."
And when Strether throws to the winds all scruples as to what
Mrs. Newsome would think, and invites Madame de Vionnet
to lunch, James presents us with a fully achieved canvas: "How
could he wish it to be lucid for others, for any one, that he, for

[229]

the hour, saw reasons enough in the mere way the bright clean ordered water-side life came in at the open window?—the mere way Madame de Vionnet, opposite him over their intensely white table-linen, their *omelette aux tomates,* their bottle of straw-colored Chablis, thanked him for everything almost with the smile of a child, while her grey eyes moved in and out of their talk, back to the quarter of the warm spring air, in which early summer had already begun to throb, and then back again to his face and their human questions."

Here he has come to the essence, not of Sargent's effects but of Renoir's, in the wonderful sense of open air; in the sensuous relish of all the surfaces, with exactly the right central spot of color in that *omelette aux tomates;* in the exquisite play of light around his figures. And when James added a further accent, it made for the very kind of charm by which the Impressionists declared their art a release from stuffy manners as well as from stale techniques: Madame de Vionnet "was a woman who, between courses, could be graceful with her elbows on the table. It was a posture unknown to Mrs. Newsome. . . ."

James's cities, unlike Balzac's or Joyce's, focus on the inviting vistas presented to the well-to-do visitor. The very air of Strether's Paris has the taste "of something mixed with art, something that presented nature as a white-capped master-chef." But James was not ignorant of what he called "the huge collective life" going on beyond his charmed circle; and at the end, when Strether is meditating on Madame de Vionnet's suffering, he thinks too of the vast suffering Paris has witnessed, and senses in the streets their long ineradicable "smell of revolution, the smell of the public temper—or perhaps simply the smell of blood." Yet such omens are black shadows looming only at the very edge of James's pictures. What he chose to frame, specially selected though it is, takes on an intensity to the degree that he could realize the multiple kinds of seeing in which he had striven to perfect himself, and could demonstrate that he had mastered "the art of reflection" in both senses of that phrase—both as a projector of the luminous surfaces of life, and as an interpreter of their significance. Perhaps the most brilliant instance of this double skill in all James's work is the

F. O. Matthiessen

recognition scene on the river, a scene which reveals also his extraordinary awareness of how art frames experience. He took great delight in adapting plastic devices for a highly developed, wholly unexpected illustration of this aesthetic process. When Strether decides on a day in the country, what leads him there is his far-off memory "of a certain small Lambinet that had charmed him, long years before, at a Boston dealer's." It is interesting to recall that this nearly forgotten painter of scenes along the Seine was of the era of Rousseau and Daubigny, all of whom James noted as having been first shown to him in the early days by Hunt.

On one plane, Strether's being drawn by art to nature to verify an old impression, shows the curious reversal of order in the modern sensibility. On another plane, as he dwells on how much a canvas, not expensive but far beyond his purse, had meant to him in the Tremont Street gallery, we have a sharp contrast between Strether's New England actuality and his long smothered French ideal. But James doesn't leave it at that. Strether's entire day progresses as though he had "not once overstepped the oblong gilt frame." The whole scene was there, the clustered houses and the poplars and the willows: "it was Tremont Street, it was France, it was Lambinet." In the late afternoon, as he sits at a village café overlooking a reach of the river, his landscape takes on a further interest. It becomes a Landscape with Figures, as a boat appears around the bend, a man rowing, a lady with a pink parasol. There, in an instant, was "the lie in the charming affair." The skill with which James has held our eyes within his frame has so heightened the significance of every slight detail that such a recognition scene leaps out with the force of the strongest drama.

What Strether has seen comes to him as a great shock, but it does not cause him to waver in his judgment of how much Chad has improved. What he is anxious about now is whether Chad is really worthy of what Madame de Vionnet has given him, and there are plenty of undeveloped hints at the close that he is not, that he is already restive, that he will not be happy permanently without the business world, and that he may even soon be turning to a younger woman. What then finally is the

The Question of Henry James

positive content of Strether's challenge to Bilham? As far as that young painter is concerned, the possibilities seem very slight. His eye has taken in so much of the beautiful surface of Paris that his productive power has faltered before it; and though he is happy with his vision, his is certainly a mild version of the doctrine of being rather than of doing.

What then of Strether himself, what has he gained from his initiation? Waymarsh warned him at the outset that he was "a very attractive man," and Maria Gostrey says that he owes more to women than any man she ever saw. Yet when he encounters Gloriani, Strether is acutely conscious of his own "rather grey interior." He expresses his sense of the Italian sculptor's vitality through an image of the sexual jungle: he both admires and envies "the glossy male tiger, magnificently marked." How far James himself had advanced in his penetration into character may be instanced by his different handling of this same Gloriani in *Roderick Hudson* nearly thirty years before. There the worldly sculptor had been somewhat cheap in his sophistication as he played the role of a Mephistopheles to Roderick's Faust. But now James suggests an unfathomable depth of "human expertness" in his eyes, an enormous fund of "terrible" energy behind his smile.

It is revelatory of the careful pattern that James worked out in *The Ambassadors* to note the sequence of events in this crucial scene in Gloriani's garden. As he first takes in the beauty of his surroundings in the heart of the Faubourg Saint-Germain, Strether reflects to Bilham: "You've all of you here so much visual sense that you've somehow all 'run' to it. There are moments when it strikes one that you haven't any other." Almost at once thereafter Strether is presented to Madame de Vionnet, and when she moves on after a few moments' conversation, he faces Bilham with his declaration for life. This, in turn, he follows with his expressed envy of Gloriani. None of these connections are made explicit, a sign that James's way of creating Madame de Vionnet's charm is to render it more pervasive in its operation than anything he says about it. Before the close of this scene he remarks that Strether is the kind of man who receives "an amount of experience out of any proportion to his adven-

[232]

F. O. Matthiessen

tures." That, we recall, is what James also rejoiced over in his preface, that in Strether he had had his full chance "to 'do' a man of imagination."

But what does Strether finally make of his experience? The issue at the close shows how rigorously James believed that an author should hold to his structure. He had posited his hero's sense that it was too late for him to live; and had reinforced this with Strether's New England scrupulosity that in siding with Chad his conscience could be clear, since there was to be "nothing in it for himself." And no matter how bewilderingly iridescent he finds the jewel-image of Paris, since "what seemed all surface one moment seemed all depth the next," Strether never loses his moral sense. James seems to have taken his own special pleasure in avoiding the banal by not making Paris the usual scene of seduction but instead the center of an ethical drama. Another aspect of the structure—and its most artificial —is the role of *ficelle* conceived for Maria Gostrey. She exists only as a confidante for Strether, only as a means of letting him comment on his experience. Consequently, as James himself noted, she had a "false connexion" with the plot which he had to bend his ingenuity to make appear as a real one. But his device of having her fall in love with Strether and hope wistfully to marry him does not achieve such reality.

It serves rather to exaggerate the negative content of Strether's renunciation. He has come at last, as he says, to *see* Mrs. Newsome, and we know by now how much is involved in that word. But he leaves Paris and Maria to go back to no prospect of life at all. We are confronted here with what will strike us much more forcibly in *The Golden Bowl,* the contrast in James between imputed and actual values. The burden of *The Ambassadors* is that Strether has awakened to a wholly new sense of life. Yet he does nothing at all to fulfill that sense. Therefore, fond as James is of him, we cannot help feeling his relative emptiness. At times, even, as when James describes how "he went to Rouen with a little handbag and inordinately spent the night," it is forced upon us that, despite James's humorous awareness of the inadequacy of his hero's adventures, neither Strether nor his creator escape a certain soft fussiness.

The Question of Henry James

What gives this novel the stamina to survive the dated flavor of Strether's liberation is the quality that James admired most in Turgenev, the ability to endow some of his characters with such vitality that they seem to take the plot into their own hands, or rather, to continue to live beyond its exigencies. The center of that vitality here is the character not reckoned with in James's initial outline. For what pervades the final passages is Strether's unacknowledged love for Madame de Vionnet. James has succeeded in making her so attractive that, quite apart from the rigid requirement of his structure, there can really be no question of Strether's caring deeply for any other woman. The means that James used to evoke her whole way of life is a supreme instance of how he went about to give concrete embodiment to his values. Just as he devoted the greatest care to the surroundings for Strether's declaration and explicitly drew on his own memories of the garden behind the house where Madame Récamier had died, so he created Madame de Vionnet entirely in terms of and inseparable from old Paris. Every distinction in her manner is related to Strether's impression of her house, where each chair and cabinet suggests "some glory, some prosperity of the First Empire, some Napoleonic glamour, some dim lustre of the great legend." In his "summing up" James had attempted to convey why the great English houses had grown to mean so much to him. It was primarily their "accumulations of expression": "on the soil over which so much has passed, and out of which so much has come," they "rose before me like a series of visions. . . . I thought of stories, of drama, of all the life of the past—of things one can hardly speak of; speak of, I mean at the time. It is art that speaks of those things; and the idea makes me adore her more and more."

That gives us insight into why James, to a greater degree than any other American artist, was a spokesman for the imagination as a conserving force. He believed that art is the great conserver, since it alone can give permanence to the more perishable order of society. Yet, despite the usual view of him, James dwelt very little in the past. His impressions and his reading were preponderantly, almost oppressively, contemporary. His one living taproot to the past was through his appreciation of such an exquisite product of tradition as Madame de Vionnet. Yet, as he created her, she was the very essence of the aesthetic sensibility of his own day. Strether can hardly find enough comparisons for her splendor. Her head is like that on "an old precious medal of the Renaissance." She is "a goddess still partly engaged in a morning cloud," or "a sea-nymph waist-high in the summer surge." She is so "various and multifold" that he hardly needs to mention Cleopatra. And though Mona Lisa is not mentioned, James is evoking something very like Pater's spell. Although James's moral residues are considerably different from Pater's, both Strether and James could have subscribed to much of Pater's famous exhortations for fullness of life, particularly to the sentence which urges that one's passions should yield "this fruit of a quickened, multiplied consciousness."

But Madame de Vionnet is more human than Pater's evocation. On the last night that Strether sees her, she seems older, "visibly less exempt from the touch of time." And though she is still "the finest and subtlest creature" he has ever met, she is, even as Shakespeare's Cleopatra, troubled like "a maid servant crying for her young man." In an image which enables him to fuse the qualities with which he especially wants to endow her, James makes Strether think that her dress of "simplest coolest white" is so old-fashioned "that Madame Roland must on the scaffold have worn something like it." Madame de Vionnet's end is also to be tragic. She has learned from life that no real happiness comes from taking: "the only safe thing is to give." Such a nature is far too good for Chad, and she realizes now that "the only certainty" for the future is that she will be "the loser in the end." Her positive suffering and loss are far more affecting than Strether's tenuous renunciation.

STEPHEN SPENDER

The Golden Bowl

[1936]

THE GOLDEN BOWL is extremely simplified, because there
are only four main characters and two subsidiary choric
figures, and no one else is of the slightest importance. The
key to the situation is the fact that there are, in effect, before
the action begins, two original groupings. Maggie is the companion of her father, Mr. Verver, and they live together in
their relationship always gaily referred to as their marriage.
Meanwhile, unknown to them, their two future *sposi*—as they
are always called—Amerigo, the prince, and Charlotte, an adventurous, moneyless, "wonderful" friend of Maggie, are having their little affair. The leading choric character, Mrs. Assingham, now steps in and breaks up the grouping from *AB,
CD*—Maggie, Mr. Verver; the prince, Charlotte; into *AC, BD*.
The prince marries Maggie. Maggie is now deeply conscious of
the loneliness of her father, and her father is also conscious
that her concern for him may not be best for her marriage.
Meanwhile, Charlotte returns from America, and, just before
the wedding, she walks through Mayfair with the prince, where,
in a curio shop, they look at the golden bowl with a flaw in it,
which they discuss, but decide not to buy, for Maggie's wedding present. After the marriage, Charlotte stays with the
Ververs, and then Mr. Verver takes her to Brighton, and pro-
poses to her. They marry, and soon after the marriage, the
prince and Charlotte start living together. Thus, after a transition, in which the figures are *AC, BD*, we return to the original
order *AB, CD*. The dramatic climax of the book is Maggie's
passionate fight to restore the order of the marriages, which she

Stephen Spender

at last succeeds in doing. Thus the book falls into this sort of pattern:—

Spectators	AB		CD	
	The Golden Bowl			
The major and Fanny	AC		BD	The major and Fanny
Assingham	AB		CD	Assingham
	The Golden Bowl			
	AC		BD	

This symmetry symbolizes the social order.

The golden bowl with its flaw represents, of course, the flaw in the order of their lives.

The moral problem in the book is extremely important. It is not merely a struggle between the injured and duped father and child and the strident, aristocratic, sensual lovers, who are living on the money of the weaker couple, which would resemble the situation of *The Wings of the Dove*. There is a far deeper conflict, between the two kinds of marriage, the spiritual and the platonic. Maggie will not abandon her father: the injury done to the *sposi* is that the marriages have been arranged— Maggie's in part, Mr. Verver's entirely—simply in order to improve the relationship of the father and daughter. Mrs. Assingham, who arranges the first marriage, knows that in providing his daughter with a prince, she is also providing Mr. Verver with an invaluable "piece" for his collection. Moreover, the father and daughter agree that their life is too closed in, too selfish, that they see too little of the world, that they are altogether lacking in free air and large experience, and Maggie's marriage presents an excellent way out.

Both marriages having been made, the father and daughter continue to see a good deal of each other, so it follows that stepmother and son-in-law are also thrown together. Moreover, the platonic relationship of the daughter and father not only competes with the relationship of Charlotte and Amerigo; it also affects a third concurrent relationship, which is the sexual life of each party with his or her marriage partner. The platonicism of the father and daughter evidently creeps into their marriages. Charlotte suffers most from this, because her husband is in any case an old man; and although the suggestion that he is wonderfully young is bravely kept up—it becomes part of the system of the book—he cannot have a child. Maggie has a child—the Principino—but she does not satisfy her pleasure-loving Italian husband. He is politely but infinitely bored by the Ververs. Finally, Maggie is passionately and deeply in love with the prince: like Cordelia, she recognizes that her love for her husband is deeper even than that for her father; to that extent the marriage is not in the least a marriage of convenience.

Thus, the moral problem much more decisively demands an answer in this than in any other book of James. Maggie is not in the position of Milly or Strether, who have only to live according to their lights, and then to lose everything. In James's other books he has convinced us that a part of life, of the *real* life of a human being, as apart from the performance of an automaton, is the power to choose to die. The question James has not yet answered is whether it is possible in the modern world **to cho**ose to live: and Maggie triumphantly answers it for him.

Her answer takes her far beyond the aesthetics of behavior, although, like all James's characters, she is deeply concerned with these. She lives and saves the situation by the force of her patience, her generosity, and her love. Twice she affirms a faith that is also her policy. Once to Mrs. Assingham, who, being the original matchmaker, unifies the sense of moral responsibility which weighs on all the characters.

"Maggie thoughtfully shook her head. 'No; I'm not terrible, and you don't think me so. I do strike you as surprising, no doubt—but surprisingly mild. Because—don't you see?—I *am* mild. I can bear anything.'

" 'Oh, "bear"!' Mrs. Assingham fluted.

" 'For love,' said the Princess.

"Fanny hesitated. 'Of your father?'

" 'For love,' Maggie repeated.

"It kept her friend watching. 'Of your husband?'

" 'For love,' Maggie said again."

Once more, at the end of the book, Maggie reaffirms her declaration, this time to her father, when in their most wonder-

Stephen Spender

ful confabulation the father and daughter, without ever betraying their loyalty to their marriages, or revealing to each other their knowledge of the intrigue between Charlotte and the prince, reveal only, indeed, their anxious tenderness for each other, their unshaken belief in each other, and that their understanding went deeper than anything which they need say.

"My idea is this, that when you only love a little you're naturally not jealous—or are only jealous also a little, so that it doesn't matter. But when you love in a deeper and intenser way, then you are, in the same proportion, jealous; your jealousy has intensity and, no doubt, ferocity. When, however, you love in the most abysmal and unutterable way of all—why, then you're beyond everything, and nothing can pull you down."

The scene of *The Golden Bowl* is the most ambitious James ever attempted, and the first half of the book, allotted to the prince, does really little more than construct the vast stage on which his drama is enacted. That stage is set in England, but upon it meet America and Italy. Italy is represented by Amerigo, so that his ancestry recalls the greatness and the crimes of the Empire. America, with all its wealth and all its innocence, is Adam Verver and his daughter.

Set against this great historical and geographical tradition, there is the strangely insulated, shut-off life of the actors. The two married couples, on this immense stage, in their admired and plausible surroundings, are yet living a life which is grotesquely at odds with their happy setting of envied appearances, and unsuited to the standards of the tradition to which they are trying to conform. They are perpetually at the edge of something quite sordid: of the divorce court, the reported evidence of servants, and love letters printed in the news. The struggle of the Ververs is a struggle to make the picture fit the frame; they are constantly struggling to make their lives worthy of their dead surroundings.

They are handicapped in this endeavor by two psychological difficulties. The first is that the Ververs are absorbed in their own private life, whereas the people they marry are, in a modern, almost a journalistic sense, suited to the public life. The Ververs are a lovable, cozy pair of very simple, very clever people who are immensely rich. It is emphasized throughout the book that everything about them is, by mere contrast with their huge setting, very small. Their virtues are a human understanding which does not extend beyond the individuals immediately around them, an immense personal tenderness, and a love which hardly reaches further than each other and the pair whom they marry. The word "small" is constantly associated with Maggie, and it is she who in one of her moments of greatest exaltation realizes that her father was "simply a great and deep and high little man, and that to love him with tenderness was not to be distinguished, a whit, from loving him with pride." One remembers him always, with his dim smile, his quiet, very youthful manner, in the unassuming little scene; gazing at a "piece" in his collection, or wandering vaguely about his garden. On the other hand, everything about Charlotte and the prince is on the grand scale. As Maggie says when she recommends Charlotte to her father, "I may be as good, but I'm not so great— and that's what we're talking about. She has a great imagination. She has, in every way, a great attitude. She has above all a great conscience."

Secondly, Charlotte, being so great, consistently underestimates Maggie's intelligence. It is, then, this failure of Charlotte's own intelligence which produces the crack in their situation which requires so much understanding and courage to repair. In James's world, a failure of intelligence—that is to say, of intelligence in life—may amount to a moral failing. But Maggie's behavior shows that it does not follow that intelligence alone is morality: for it is Maggie's love that saves the marriages.

What most lives in one's memory of *The Golden Bowl* is the pattern of monologue contrasted with certain unforgettable scenes. Especially a few of the scenes, such as the ironic scene in which the prince and Charlotte meet on their vow to care for his wife and her husband.

" 'It's sacred,' he said at last.

" 'It's sacred,' she breathed back to him. They vowed it, gave it out and took it in, drawn, by their intensity, more closely together. Then of a sudden, through this tightened circle, as at the issue of a narrow strait into the sea beyond, everything

broke up, broke down, gave way, melted and mingled. Their
lips sought their lips, their pressure their response and their response their pressure; with a violence that had sighed itself the
next moment to the longest and deepest of stillnesses they passionately sealed their pledge."

Again, there is the scene in the carriage, where Maggie tries
to protest to her husband, and when she detects how he uses his
sensuality to silence her: "He put his arm round her and drew
her close—indulged in the demonstration, the long, firm embrace by his single arm, the infinite pressure of her whole person
to his own, that such opportunities had so often suggested and
prescribed."

But the most extraordinary scenes of all are those with Charlotte at the end of the book. They follow on that very remarkable climax when Mrs. Assingham deliberately throws down
and smashes the golden bowl, which Maggie has accidentally
bought from the shop in Mayfair: and bought with it, too, the
knowledge that Charlotte and her husband were deeply intimate
before her marriage. The prince comes into the room, and just
because he is let off having to explain, he learns all the more
clearly that Maggie knows, has always known, and also that
she does not require any explanation. This is the first step in his
conversion to Maggie, and he marks it by *not* telling Charlotte
that Maggie knows: thus Charlotte is in the dark, and Maggie
and the prince are together, as it were, in the light of Maggie's
generosity. The ground is thus elaborately prepared for the description of that terrible evening when Charlotte, "the splendid
shining supple creature was out of the cage, was at large." James
is at his most prodigious in the description of the meeting of the
two women, and of the high spirit with which Maggie tells her
wonderful lie, denying that Charlotte has done her any injury,
and thus keeping her compact of silence with the prince. "They
were keeping together thus, he and she, close, close together—
whereas Charlotte, though rising there radiantly before her, was
really off in some darkness of space that would steep her in solitude and harass her with care." But the scene ends with Charlotte's triumph, for the nature of Maggie's victory is precisely
in letting Charlotte enjoy her own value, which is greatly to

triumph. On this occasion the triumph is in the form of a public embrace: "But there was something different also, something for which, while her cheek received the prodigious kiss, she had her opportunity—the sight of the others, who, having risen from their cards to join the absent members of their party, had reached the open door at the end of the room and stopped short, evidently, in presence of the demonstration that awaited them."

This scene, as though it demands an encore, is followed by a parallel scene in the daytime, when Maggie goes out into the garden on the excuse of taking Charlotte a book which she had forgotten. Here again the patient and loving resolve of Mr. Verver, who has now played his part in deciding that he and Maggie must separate and that he must go with his wife to America, is made part of Charlotte's indignant triumph.

These scenes, in their vast, resonant setting, and extending into variations in Maggie's thought, have the air of those *surréaliste* paintings in which one islanded, accurate object, perhaps a house, or a fragment of ruined stone wall, is seen against an empty background which seems perhaps to be the whole sea, or the whole sky, or the whole of space.

For the monologues dip into an abyss where they become part of the unconscious mind of Europe. They are written in a language in which one loses oneself among imagery which is poetry, but which has not the rhythm or the diction of a writer who is completely a poet. The particular effects in *The Golden Bowl* fail; but the total effect of the book is as striking as the third movement—the "Heiliger Dankgesang"—of Beethoven's *Quartet in A Minor*, Opus 130. In that movement, the drawn-out, religious harmonies are contrasted with the two islands of feverish dramatic ecstasy, which they enclose, like an endless, calm sea.

Throughout *The Golden Bowl* the descriptive passages deliberately suggest vast spaces opening out into mystery and vagueness. "This love of music, unlike his other loves, owned to vagueness, but, while, on his comparatively shaded sofa, and smoking, smoking, always smoking, in the great Fawns drawing-room as everywhere, the cigars of his youth, rank with associations—while, I say, he so listened to Charlotte's piano, where the score was never absent, but, between the lighted candles, the picture distinct, the vagueness spread itself about him like some boundless carpet, a surface delightfully soft to the pressure of his interest." Here Mr. Verver is set like a little island against his sea of vagueness.

It is from this deliberately conjured atmosphere that there arise, as from the depths, the dream images of the unconscious. Too often these images, not being ordered by metric, almost overwhelm the reader, swamping all other associations, and making him forget the story. "She might fairly, as she watched them, have missed it as a lost thing: have yearned for it, for the straight vindictive view, the rights of resentment, the rages of jealousy, the protests of passion, as for something she had been cheated of not least: a range of feelings which for many women would have meant so much, but which for *her* husband's wife, for *her* father's daughter, figured nothing nearer to experience than a wild eastern caravan, looming into view with crude colours in the sun, fierce pipes in the air, high spears against the sky, all a thrill, a natural joy to mingle with, but turning off short before it reached her and plunging into other defiles." Before we have fully recovered, in the same paragraph, Maggie has another vision: one which, in the story, is of far greater significance than the first, because of the light in which it presents Charlotte: "She saw at all events why horror itself had almost failed her; the horror that, foreshadowed in advance, would, by her thought, have made everything that was unaccustomed in her cry out with pain; the horror of finding evil seated, at all its ease, where she had dreamed only of good; the horror of the thing hideously *behind*, behind so much trusted, so much pretended, nobleness, cleverness, tenderness."

It is the feeling of horror, of foreboding before some calamity, that never fails, and that sometimes produces a poetry so pure and so dreadfully true of our whole situation, that it reaches far beyond the "small despair" of the Ververs. One such passage occurs in the scene between Maggie and Fanny Assingham, just after Maggie has bought the golden bowl. Fanny conceals what she knows from Maggie, for to relax the tension in Maggie's spirit would be the signal for her to collapse and despair: what she knows about her husband she has to learn through her own suffering, so that she learns also the way out. "Though ignorant still of what she *had* definitely met, Fanny yearned, within, over her spirit; and so, no word about it said, passed, through mere pitying eyes, a vow to walk ahead and, at cross roads, with a lantern for the darkness and wavings away for unadvised traffic, look out for alarms."

It is such passages in James, which in their use of imagery derived from everyday life, predict the best in modern poetry. But the feeling of a horror that is entirely modern, is emphasized even more strongly, in the passages which describe the mental suffering of Maggie. When Maggie first tries to explain her position to Mrs. Assingham, she says: "If I'm jealous—don't you see?—I'm tormented, and all the more if I'm helpless. And if I'm both helpless *and* tormented I stuff my pocket-handkerchief into my mouth, I keep it there, for the most part, night and day, so as not to be heard too indecently moaning."

Nor is this account of her torture any mere figure of speech. In her great scene with Charlotte, when Charlotte had triumphed, we are told: "Oh, the 'advantage,' it was perfectly enough, in truth, with Mrs. Verver; for what was Maggie's own sense but that of having been thrown over on her back, with her neck, from the first, half broken and her helpless face staring up?" Maggie suffocates, she has for ever the sense of "the beast at her throat."

Nor is it only Maggie who endures these horrors. They pursue Charlotte, and one of the really terrifying moments is the description of Charlotte's lecture to some visitors on her husband's collection.

". . . 'The largest of these three pieces has the rare peculiarity that the garlands, looped round it, which, as you see, are the finest possible *vieux Saxe*. . . .'

"So the high voice quavered, aiming truly at effects far over the heads of gaping neighbours. . . . Maggie meanwhile, at the window, knew the strangest thing to be happening: she had turned suddenly to crying, or was at least on the point of it—the lighted square before her all blurred and dim. The high voice went on; its quaver was doubtless for conscious ears only,

Stephen Spender

but there were verily thirty seconds during which it sounded,
for our young woman, like the shriek of a soul in pain."

The horror then pursues the prince: he has his own agonized
way of sitting in his room and reading the newspapers, *Figaro*
and the *Times*.

When one considers these examples, one begins to feel certain
that beneath the stylistic surface, the portentous snobbery, the
golden display of James's work, there lurk forms of violence
and chaos. His technical mastery has the perfection of frightful
balance and frightful tension: beneath the stretched-out com-
positions there are abysses of despair and disbelief: *Ulysses* and
The Waste Land.

What after all do these images of suffocation, of broken
necks, of wailing suggest but a collection of photographs of the
dead and wounded during the Great War? We remember his
phrase, made in 1915: "to have to take it all now for what the
treacherous years were all the while really making for and
meaning, is too tragic for any words."

W. H. AUDEN

At the Grave of Henry James
[1943]

THE snow, less intransigeant than their marble,
Has left the defence of whiteness to these tombs;
      For all the pools at my feet
Accommodate blue now, and echo such clouds as occur
To the sky, and whatever bird or mourner the passing
      Moment remarks they repeat

While the rocks, named after singular spaces
Within which images wandered once that caused
      All to tremble and offend,
Stand here in an innocent stillness, each marking the spot
Where one more series of errors lost its uniqueness
      And novelty came to an end.

To whose real advantage were such transactions
When worlds of reflection were exchanged for trees?
      What living occasion can
Be just to the absent? O noon but reflects on itself,
And the small taciturn stone that is the only witness
      To a great and talkative man

Has no more judgment than my ignorant shadow
Of odious comparisons or distant clocks
      Which challenge and interfere
With the heart's instantaneous reading of time, time that is
A warm enigma no longer in you for whom I
      Surrender my private cheer.

[246]

W. H. Auden

Startling the awkward footsteps of my apprehension,
The flushed assault of your recognition is
    The *donnée* of this doubtful hour:
O stern proconsul of intractable provinces,
O poet of the difficult, dear addicted artist,
    Assent to my soil and flower.

As I stand awake on our solar fabric,
That primary machine, the earth, which gendarmes, banks,
    And aspirin pre-suppose,
On which the clumsy and sad may all sit down, and any who
        will
Say their a-ha to the beautiful, the common locus
    Of the master and the rose.

Our theatre, scaffold, and erotic city
Where all the infirm species are partners in the act
    Of encroachment bodies crave,
Though solitude in death is *de rigueur* for their flesh
And the self-denying hermit flies as it approaches
    Like the carnivore to a cave.

That its plural numbers may unite in meaning,
Its vulgar tongues unravel the knotted mass
    Of the improperly conjunct,
Open my eyes now to its hinted significant forms,
Sharpen my ears to detect amid its brilliant uproar
    The low thud of the defunct.

O dwell, ironic at my living centre,
Half ancestor, half child; because the actual self
    Round whom time revolves so fast
Is so afraid of what its motions might possibly do
That the actor is never there when his really important
    Acts happen. Only the past

Is present, no one about but the dead as,
Equipped with a few inherited odds and ends,
    One after another we are

The Question of Henry James

Fired into life to seek that unseen target where all
Our equivocal judgments are judged and resolved in
    One whole Alas or Hurrah.

And only the unborn remark the disaster
When, though it makes no difference to the pretty airs
    The bird of Appetite sings,
And Amour Propre is his usual amusing self,
Out from the jungle of an undistinguished moment
    The flexible shadow springs.

Now more than ever, when torches and snare-drum
Excite the squat women of the saurian brain
    Till a milling mob of fears
Breaks in insultingly on anywhere, when in our dreams
Pigs play on the organs and the blue sky runs shrieking
    As the Crack of Doom appears,

Are the good ghosts needed with the white magic
Of their subtle loves. War has no ambiguities
    Like a marriage; the result
Required of its *affaire fatale* is simple and sad,
The physical removal of all human objects
    That conceal the Difficult.

Then remember me that I may remember
The test we have to learn to shudder for is not
    An historical event,
That neither the low democracy of a nightmare nor
An army's primitive tidiness may deceive me
    About our predicament.

That catastrophic situation which neither
Victory nor defeat can annul; to be
    Deaf yet determined to sing,
To be lame and blind yet burning for the Great Good Place,
To be radically corrupt yet mournfully attracted
    By the Real Distinguished Thing.

[248]

W. H. Auden

And shall I not specially bless you as, vexed with
My little inferior questions, today I stand
    Beside the bed where you rest
Who opened such passionate arms to your *Bon* when It ran
Towards you with its overwhelming reasons pleading
    All beautifully in Its breast?

O with what innocence your hand submitted
To these formal rules that help a child to play,
    While your heart, fastidious as
A delicate nun, remained true to the rare noblesse
Of your lucid gift and, for its own sake, ignored the
    Resentful muttering Mass

Whose ruminant hatred of all which cannot
Be simplified or stolen is still at large;
    No death can assuage its lust
To vilify the landscape of Distinction and see
The heart of the Personal brought to a systolic standstill,
    The Tall to diminished dust.

Preserve me, Master, from its vague incitement;
Yours be the disciplinary image that holds
    Me back from agreeable wrong
And the clutch of eddying muddle, lest Proportion shed
The alpine chill of her shrugging editorial shoulder
    On my loose impromptu song.

Suggest; so may I segregate my disorder
Into districts of prospective value: approve;
    Lightly, lightly, then, may I dance
Over the frontier of the obvious and fumble no more
In the old limp pocket of the minor exhibition,
    Nor riot with irrelevance.

And no longer shoe geese or water stakes, but
Bolt in my day my grain of truth to the barn
    Where tribulations may leap

The Question of Henry James

With their long-lost brothers at last in the festival
Of which not one has a dissenting image, and the
    Flushed immediacy sleep.

Into this city from the shining lowlands
Blows a wind that whispers of uncovered skulls
    And fresh ruins under the moon,
Of hopes that will not survive the *secousse* of this spring
Of blood and flames, of the terror that walks by night and
    The sickness that strikes at noon.

All will be judged. Masters of nuance and scruple,
Pray for me and for all writers living or dead;
    Because there are many whose works
Are in better taste than their lives; because there is no end
To the vanity of our calling: make intercession
    For the treason of all clerks.

Because the darkness is never so distant,
And there is never much time for the arrogant
    Spirit to flutter its wings,
Or the broken bone to rejoice, or the cruel to cry
For Him whose property is always to have mercy, the author
    And giver of all good things.

ANDRÉ GIDE

Henry James

(From an unsent letter to Charles Du Bos)

[AMERICAN PUBLICATION, 1930]

HE lets only just enough steam escape to run his engine ahead, from page to page: and I do not believe that economy, that reserve, has ever sagaciously been carried further. The proportion remains perfect between the propulsive force and the drawing out of the narrative. No wonder, since nothing really alive nourishes him, and James only extracts from his brain what he knows to be there, and what his intelligence alone has put there. The interest is never in the outpouring, but is solely in the conduit. His work is like that of the spider, who ceaselessly widens her web by hanging new threads from one chosen support to another. Doubtless I shall praise him for taking his stand always on the same data of a problem. The skillfully made network spun out by his intelligence captivates only the intelligence: the intelligence of the reader, the intelligence of the heroes of his books. The latter seem never to exist except in the functioning of their intellects, they are only winged busts; all the weight of the flesh is absent, and all the shaggy, tangled undergrowth, all the wild darkness. . . .

Another thing: these characters never live except in relation to each other, in the functioning of these relations: they are desperately mundane; I mean by this that there is nothing of the divine in them, and that intelligence always explains what makes them act or vibrate. I do not feel so much that the author is snobbish as *profane:* yes, profane, incurably so. To tell the truth, he does not interest me at all; or rather, it is his *métier* that interests me, his *métier* only, the prodigious virtuosity. But here also, there would be a great deal to say, and say again: this need of delineating everything, this conscience even, this scruple against leaving anything in the shadow, this minuteness of information, all this fatigues me, wears me out; his narratives are without color, without flavor; I hardly ever feel behind his figures, which are lighted from every side, that cone of unexplorable shadow where the suffering soul lies hidden, but his characters have no need of shelter—they have no souls. And I have not succeeded in persuading myself that this patience, this meticulousness . . . no, that is not great art; his strokes are too fine; he is afraid of the robust touches; he proceeds through subtleties.

And, again, this distresses me: he dominates his narrative from too great a height; he does not commit himself to it, nor compromise himself; it is as if he himself had perhaps nothing to confess to us. I notice incidentally that a character never interests me so greatly as when it is created—like Eve—from the very flesh of the author; when it is not so much observed as invented—and there indeed is the secret of the profoundest "analysts." I think of Dostoevski, of Stendhal, and am most grateful to M— who remarked in the September issue of the *Nouvelle Revue Française* that Stendhal as an observer was rather mediocre, and that he drew from himself the best in his work. Not that these authors are exactly portrayed in any one of their characters, but nearly every one of their characters (I am thinking now especially of Dostoevski's) is, properly speaking, only the projection of an anguish, personal, private. Dostoevski himself lives diffused in all of his heroes, and yet without ever concentrating himself in a single one. So it is that James, in himself, is not interesting; he is only intelligent; he has no mystery in him, no secret; no Figure in the Carpet. At the most, he does at moments hoodwink us, as happens with the author hero of that specious narrative. Yes, this is exactly what distresses me—and what distresses me also in Meredith—to feel the author dominate, glide above the conflict that he invents, pull from too great a height the wires that make the actors move. (It seems to me that the value of Fielding, of Defoe, of Dickens, of

André Gide

George Eliot, of Hardy, comes from the fact that they never believe themselves, never show themselves, superior.)

Never do I feel that James is "in" with any one of them—and I am most certainly grateful to him for being impartial: but Dostoevski, for example, finds a way of being impartial and committing himself at the same time to the most contrary, the most contradictory characters, who make him enter the heart of life, and us after him. Yes, it is just that; the secret of the great novelist is not in the domination of situations, but rather in the multiplicity of his intimate connivances. Undoubtedly, these novels of James are marvels of composition; but one might say as well that the qualities of his narratives are always, are never anything but, the qualities of composition. We can marvel at the delicacy, at the subtlety of the gear wheels, but all his characters are like the figures of a clock, and the story is finished when they have struck the curfew; of themselves they return to the clockcase and to the night of our forgetting.

It goes without saying, nevertheless, that I am aware of all the importance of H. James; but I believe him more important for England than for France. England has never sinned up to the present by too much good cooking; James is a master cook. But, as for me, I like precisely those great, untrimmed chunks that Fielding or Defoe serves us, barely cooked, but keeping all the "blood-taste" of the meat. So much dressing and distinction, I am satiated with it in advance; he surpasses us in our own faults.

JACQUES BARZUN

Henry James, Melodramatist

[1943]

IN a casual essay entitled "Books and You," Mr. Somerset Maugham, while scorning James's work as trivial and superficial, is nevertheless forced to admit that it somehow "keeps the reader going from page to page." The opinion that James's novels deal only with the amenities of high life is, of course, not new and unhappily not confined to those who, like Mr. Maugham, would be content to dismiss James as a "social twitterer." Even for some of James's admirers, the pleasure he affords is in direct proportion to the elegance of his atmosphere and the rarefaction of his meaning. These readers are never so sure of his artistry as when he entrusts to a lordling some stammering speech, heavy with adverbs and precious with colloquialisms, which together suggest one of Ollendorff's conversation manuals. Whether scornful or admiring, this attitude toward James only proves how often critical generalities are based not on what is plainly there to be generalized about, but solely on what is strange or striking. For the high life, the fine-spun surface, the Old Pretender style, would not by themselves account for the truth which Mr. Maugham grants but does not explain: we still ask what it is that keeps the reader going.

The first step towards a right answer is to recognize that James does not deal with etiquette detached from deep feeling; that his characters are not exclusively, or even mainly, drawn from a class which is beyond the reach of gross circumstance or vulgar appetites. On the contrary, most of his novels and tales deal with middling people pursuing the two simplest objects of human concern—love and money. When I say "sim-

[254]

Jacques Barzun

plest," I mean, of course, that abstractly considered they are elemental and have kept their primacy in life and literature ever since the war that was fought for "Helen and all her wealth." It is true that James's mind is engrossed by the complexities and refinements to which passion and greed give rise in a world of elaborate laws and subtle modes of communication. But even in the course of inventing and unmasking the numberless disguises which these basic passions can assume, James holds to a simple view of their meaning. In acting out their feelings, people turn out either good or evil—a moral attitude which, taken with James's addiction to violent plots, leads me to say that he is a writer of melodrama.

No doubt the word needs to be enlarged upon in order to convey the sense I intend. We generally think of melodrama as a form of stage play which flourished "in the nineties"—we are no longer quite sure of the century—and which had to do with mothers and mortgages, destitution and drink. The villain was a deliberate evildoer, identifiable by his clothes, coloring, and intonation, and providentially created to bring out the finest exertions on the part of the hero. In short, melodrama, even at its crudest, depicts the endless battle of God and Satan. For although the villain in these conventional pieces usually came to grief before the final curtain, it was clear in retrospect that his aims were precisely the same as the hero's: he wanted the girl and the money. The difference which marked him off as evil was evidently a matter of style. He was not fastidious enough in the means he employed to gratify his otherwise natural desires. Hence, if we disregard the particular symbols current in the 1890's to move the ordinary audiences, and consider only the beliefs leading to the use of those symbols, the essence of melodrama appears as a deep conviction that certain deformed expressions of human feeling are evil and that this evil is positive and must be resisted.

This definition would, of course, put many great works of the past, hitherto called tragedies, into the class of melodrama. Much of Shakespeare and Euripides is melodrama in this sense. If it is asked why we need to reclassify or relabel these works, the answer is that criticism ought to bring together under one name

[255]

those fictions that record man's horror in the face of evil. Tragedy is not a sufficiently wide name, for it traditionally implies a *heroic* fall under the blow of a *fated* evil. What do we make of the plays, and of the even more numerous novels and tales, which lack a magnanimous hero as well as a sense of overriding fate? Tragedy can only be a subclass under melodrama—the highest—just as the plays of the nineties were the lowest and cheapest.

Considered from the point of view of substance, the difference between them is that tragedy respects the limits I have named; considered from the point of view of artistic pleasure, the only difference between them is one of skill. In cheap melodrama, the words, symbols, and plots are hackneyed. They are loosely put together to bring out an automatic response. In the highest tragedy these artistic elements satisfy more exacting demands by their uniqueness and close articulation: they make poetry. In between the two groups stands the bulk of modern prose fiction, from Richardson to Balzac—"aesthetic melodrama," if you will—and it is to this class that James's work belongs.

In this nomenclature, melodrama is distinguished by its feeling and intention from the parallel and contrasting category of comedy. Comedy, likewise, has its common and rare forms, ranging as it does from burlesque and farce to the "high" or serious comedies of Molière and Shakespeare. All storytelling falls into one or the other of these two great realms, and there is, I think, some virtue in being aware of their mutual exclusiveness. I have long puzzled over the undoubted fact that relatively few persons are admirers of both Henry James and Meredith. Superficially, it should seem as if the same kind of social, intellectual, and even verbal art were displayed by the two men. But deep down they are antithetical. Meredith takes the comic point of view, not only in his own special sense, but also in the sense I contrast here with melodrama. He creates no superstitious dread of man's passions. He believes in faults, errors, follies, but not in terrifying evil. Sir Willoughby Patterne may be egotistical enough to make his intended bride run away, for the prospect of a lifetime at his side is of a grim monotony; but

Sir Willoughby is, so to speak, a recognized, life-size menace; he is under social control. There is nothing dark or inhuman about him, nor indeed about any of Meredith's villains, except perhaps Richard Feverel's father. They cause deep unhappiness —as in Diana's life or Beauchamp's career—but this yields tragi-comedy, not melodrama.

Compare Diana's or Clara Middleton's sense of being caged with Isabel Archer's state of soul after she has married Osmond: the panic fear, the mystery of the horror, are entirely absent from Meredith's treatment and overwhelmingly present in James. Perhaps the point needs illustration and refining rather than amplification. If we extract what might be called the prose meaning of *The Golden Bowl* or *The Wings of the Dove*, that is, if we make a synopsis of their plots, what do we find? Both novels revolve about the possession of human beings or of money for the love of either or both. Accordingly, we find two stage moralities—the one, a story of supreme goodness over-coming surreptitious evil; the other, a story of greed allied to weakness destroying pure affection. The last speech in *The Wings of the Dove* is even in a usual sense a melodramatic speech:

" 'As we were?'

" 'As we were.'

"But she turned to the door and her headshake was now the end. 'We shall never be again as we were!' "

It is perfectly true that Charlotte Stant and Kate Croy are not villainesses according to the crude pattern of the green-eyed siren, but this is the difference of texture and surface and skill that I spoke of as establishing gradations in melodrama. James obviously works in a spirit and in a social milieu that exclude stagy expression; sometimes they even exclude direct expression of any kind. The ramification of self-contained thought seeking to convey a hint or to redirect its own passion is what deceives Mr. Maugham and delights the professional Jamesian. But neither should remain blind to the fire and force beneath the surface. There is only one kiss in *The Golden Bowl*, but it is as fully expressive and adulterous as would be a juridical ac-count of the lovers' every assignation. Melodrama does not re-

The Question of Henry James

quire a set form of words or choices of instances. Aeschylus and Shakespeare find other words for Clytemnestra and Gertrude rebuking their sons than "How can you treat your poor mother so?" Yet that is surely what the two women are feeling; or rather, like James's characters, they are feeling this common core of emotion *plus* the fringes of other feelings that belong to themselves alone and give rise to the precise words they use. To the ear trained to catch the nuances of a subdued rhetoric, the impact is no less great; it is, in fact, reinforced by the minute particulars, by the complete personification of the more general melodramatic truth that is being portrayed.

Recall how often, especially in his short stories, James wants simply to administer a moral shock: "Look! It is not as you think!" Then observe how often this shocking effect is achieved either by carefully maintained mystery—by hinting everything and thus drawing on the reader's own supply of "melodramatic truth"; or more simply still by making much of little, raising expectancy by defeating it. *In the Cage* is an instance of the former; *The Pension Beaurepas,* of the latter. In every sense but that of vulgar expression, the insoluble mystery of *In the Cage* is pure melodrama, even to the use of the devices of thrillers: telegrams, rendezvous, the "papers" concealing a "dark secret" —is it adultery, theft, abortion?—we never know, for we see the events through the simple, engaging young woman in the cage, emblem of the lower classes watching "the quality" misbehave, half-tempted herself and yet "naturally good."

In *The Pension Beaurepas* we could, by forcing the note, discover a tract against selfish, spendthrift American women. But there is no forcing of the note. The story is an accumulation of trifles, a series of apparently aimless observations, which lead us to that sudden revulsion of disgust at the mother and daughter of "poor Mr. Ruck," one of James's Cinderella-fathers. It is only at the end of the story that the narrator says of him: "I'm afraid he's not at all well." The daughter is at that moment buying herself a diamond cross, and the mother replies, "Well, I must say I wish he'd improve."

The wickedness of being cold, of deliberately sacrificing others to one's lusts, of taking advantage of another through legal or

Jacques Barzun

social or emotional privilege, obsesses James. *Washington Square* is an unparalleled example, in which Dr. Sloper's remark to his daughter, "You will do what you like," is as terrifying as the crack of a whip. And its force is derived from the essentially melodramatic situation of a motherless daughter victimized by a subservient aunt and a selfish father—a being for whom the melodramatic epithet of "fiend in human form" is no longer sayable but still just.

The paradox of James's way with melodramtic material is that he seems to conceive with all the exaggeration necessary for "straight" effects and then to submerge the felt enormity under a flood of details relevant to be sure, and illuminating as well, but above all lifelike in their haphazard discovery and disconnected sequence. At times the dimming effect of detail is purposely left incomplete, and soft and harsh are given us side by side, as it were to show us that the beast is not in the jungle but in the drawing room. Take for instance the opening of *The Bench of Desolation,* which has to do with a breach of promise. "She had practically, he believed, conveyed the intimation"—so far this is Jamesian haze but now comes, without a break, the Jamesian directness—"the horrid, brutal, vulgar menace in their last dreadful conversation. . . ." This juxtaposition of effects is repeated a few lines below: "There was no question of not understanding—the ugly, the awful words ruthlessly formed by her lips. . . ." And finally, after another cushion of comment comes her "I'll sue, unless. . . ."

At other times, the horror is less certain. We feel it but know neither where to find it, nor how to confound the evildoers. Like "poor Mr. Ruck," Greville Fane, the woman novelist who has brought up her two children by dint of writing salable trash, becomes the pitiable victim of their insolent contempt, and yet we can hardly give a name to their crime. All we can do is to say with James that "they go too far." For James is free enough from the preconceptions of uniformity in wickedness to recognize that the commonest social form of human evil is not the palpable villain but the shady character. His gallery illustrating the type is very rich, from Madame Merle and the young Bostonian aboard the S.S. *Patagonia* to the satanic fam-

[259]

The Question of Henry James

ilies in which Newman, the American, and the English tutor of
The Pupil find themselves. Again in these more shaded performances, the management of the plot is by mystery or the
accumulation of trivialities—little lies, easygoing indifference
to small duties, failures to act or respond in time. Time is important, for under the laws of society as well as under those of
melodrama, technicalities are the very abettors of evil.

It is simply because life in society makes multitudinous occasions for pain that James's studies report evil as nearly always
triumphant. The possible complications of life—and none are
impossible—translate themselves into plots for stories, in which
it is remarkable with what disregard of their intelligence or
merit the guileless are undone. Lovers—on whom James lavishes
his manly tenderness—are separated by money or the lack of it;
by misunderstanding or excessive insight; by secrets or revela-
tions; by pride or humility. Free will makes the wrong choice in
either case simply because it is will. It seemed so to James from
the very beginning, as is recorded in one of his earliest tales, the
Civil War story of thwarted love called *Poor Richard*. Death
alone makes life under such conditions bearable, and this may
be why even when he works in his most delicate impressionist
manner, James is not afraid of crashing cymbals for the denoue-
ment. Daisy Miller dies; the girl on the S.S. *Patagonia* jumps
overboard; the Pupil wastes away; Valentin de Bellegarde is
killed in a duel; the unappreciated author catches cold and is
buried from the house of the Lion huntress who has forgotten
him; the girl who betrayed herself by a proposal dies of shame.
Strictly considered, all these deaths are unnecessary, implausible;
but they are indispensable as a relief from and as sanctions for
James's moral judgment, which is that the world is too full of
desires and not sufficiently full of people in whom desire is purified by grace.

Two works of James's, which deserve to be better known
than they are, throw a decisive light on his belief in the ubiquity
of evil. I refer to *The Other House* and *The Reprobate*, both
originally intended for the stage. The circumstances surround-
ing the writing of *The Other House* in its present form account
for its relative obscurity. Persuaded by Clement Shorter to

Jacques Barzun

write a "popular" serial for the *Illustrated London News,* James took a three-act play which he had on hand and by the addition of a few introductory pages turned the violent drama of jealousy and murder into a novel unique among his works for speed, style, and force. It was not popular in any sense, certainly not popular with the readers of the *Illustrated London News.* On this point it is not hard to believe the egregious Mr. Shorter, who privately printed his correspondence with James and his views of the transaction. For *The Other House* has the same tenseness and mystery as *The Turn of the Screw* but without any escape for our apprehensions through the loophole of the supernatural. We know from the start that we face the diabolical and the real in one embodiment, and it is only on a second reading that we perceive how this fusion is achieved: James has systemically translated love, fear, hatred, suspicion, envy, and the premeditation of crime into bodily gesture. The novel betrays its stage origin by the visible motion and the sharp detonating speech of its characters; yet, except in a few passages, all the symbols are original, constituting a new and direct melodramatic idiom unlike anything else in fiction—James's included. But although the plot is simple, the characters are not; and one guesses that what must chiefly have bewildered the readers of the "serial" was the mixture of charm and ferocity, brains and blindness, bestowed by the author on "good" and "bad" alike, despite the distinction that he maintains between them to the end.

Because of unpleasant dealings with his editor—Shorter tried to bully James into attending "Omar Khayyam dinners" without ever satisfactorily explaining what or why they were—James contracted a permanent dislike for the novel and excluded it from the New York Edition. But its significance remains as the one full-length story of earthly horror and violence, couched in his most naked manner, in which he faces steadily from beginning to end the unmixed evil that always and in every shape haunted him.

The Reprobate, a three-act play published by James in 1895 but never acted until after his death, is unique among his works for the contrary reason that it represents the comic view of the doer of evil. It is the only one of James's four "Theatricals" which does not contain a downright malicious character. In *The Reprobate* all the dramatis personae are jokes; not the sardonic jokes whom James knows how to keep half descriptive, half damnatory,[1] but thoroughly laughable jokes. Paul Doubleday, the reprobate whom everybody puts into Coventry for his depravities—smoking, drinking, reading novels, and talking to pretty women—is at once charming, innocent, and fatuous. He is "saved" by the heroine, who does not vanquish his vices but confirms them by her approval. She is the ludicrous counterpart of Maggie Verver. Indeed, the play, which Shaw in 1919 found well worth seeing on the stage, is not merely comic or even light, but farcical. Paul Doubleday is treated by his guardians as if his passions were not youthful but infantile. And in the end, it is the adults who seem most childish, least competent to deal with life. What we are shown is the nature of evil as it is seen from the planet Mars, with the consequences brushed aside and the pain forgotten. How James sustains this fantastic atmosphere while keeping alive the excitement of a twice-triangular plot is a test of his skill in verbal modulation—a tour de force which, as might have been expected, deceived certain critics into saying that here again James meant well but was obscure.

To instance *The Reprobate* and *The Other House* as sidelights upon James's melodramatic intent is to raise the question of his attitude towards drama in general. James felt—and said— that he was basically and always a dramatist. He was twice lured into writing for the stage not simply for its rewards in money but because he sought the intensified effect of the play form— the short, sharp conflict which must be made plain as it progresses and which must nonetheless be kept half-hidden to hold the feelings of wonder or horror in suspense. On these topics, both before and after his failure with the London managers and

[1] A whole essay should be written on James as humorist, but I suspect it would show that his humor, inexhaustible though it is, remains predominantly sardonic, just short of bitter. A characteristic example can be found in the opening pages of *Nona Vincent* describing a great man of business, large, heavy, powerful: "He admired his wife . . . and liked her to have other tastes than his, as that seemed to give a greater acreage to their life."

Jacques Barzun

the London audience, James wrote much, in his letters as well as in his stories and prefaces. And this concern left a significant mark on all his later work. The observance of the "point of view'" which he made into a dogma for the novelist, the building up of his novels and tales by scenes, the division of his characters into actors and narrators—all imply an adaptation of stage effects to printed fiction. Even the expansion of dialogue into something gigantic, searching, omniscient, does not contradict this tendency; Jamesian dialogue only expresses the conflict of wills more precisely than the crude, traditional words associated with stock situations. The proof of this effectiveness is that such a reader as Mr. Maugham, even while he complains of James's "involuted style," feels himself pulled along by the strong current beneath.

Besides, in all the fiction of the later years, James made use of physical images and of vulgar colloquialisms for the special purpose of maintaining the intensity of his scenes at the requisite pitch. Only think how often his dialogue is buttressed by endless variants of the one metaphor: "she gave it to him full in the face"—"he braced himself to meet it"—and so down to the very nearly "pulp" level of "she let him have it." And action follows metaphor. How many readers, if asked to identify this bit of fiction, would give James as its author:

"Listen to me before you go. I will give you a life's devotion," the young man pleaded. He barred her way.

"I shall never think of you—let me go!" she cried with passion.

This propensity toward violence, and even more this sense that violence is to be found even in casual utterance and gesture is, of course, by now good Freudian analysis. The "civilized" being, if he is also human, can always be caught off guard, and the conflicts that interest a dramatist are nothing but a succession of these moments. It is not necessary to add that James's "psychology" was not a doctrine learned and applied; it came out of his temperament and self-education. His readers have perhaps not sufficiently noticed how native to his character is the love of exaggeration. His reported speech is always a magnification of feeling—"'COME!'" Henry James cried,

The Question of Henry James

raising his hands to Heaven. " 'I would walk across London with bare feet on the snow to meet George Santayana. At what time? One thirty! I will come. At one thirty I shall inevitably, inexorably make my appearance!' " This was no isolated outburst. Most anecdotes of his apprehensions or predicaments, like his comments upon the feelings of his fictional heroes, are filled with "big," "dreadful," "hideous" or conversely, with "beautifully," "so admirably," "all too wonderfully."

Endowed with the exquisiteness of a Lilliputian, his senses yield Brobdingnagian images. Occasionally one of these will rise to the height of genius, as when he greeted the recital of a friend's morning activities with the exclamation, "What a princely expenditure of time!" But it also accounts for the appearance of pusillanimity for which he has been rather too easily ridiculed. He has been called snob and weakling because he seemed afraid of doing the wrong thing and of not having enough money; and his brother William has been shown off in contrast as a man who courageously breasted every adverse tide. This is true of William, and Henry's apprehensions no doubt make rather unsatisfactory biographical matter. Yet I think the sense of threatening evil was not at bottom very different in the two brothers. William was a Manichean whose courage, though real, was born of deep inner uncertainty—an irrepressible doubt which in its philosophic guise made him the critic of all dogmatic and optimistic certainties: nothing for him was ever finally won or held safe.

Henry, one feels, shared the same conviction, but was too intent on expressing it in fiction to devise a fighting strategy for his own personal use. This in itself was a form of courage. He spoke his fears and, unlike some of his deeply mistaken devotees, never wished life secure. "Life," he said, "is far more interesting than its regularization," and he thought so well of it that he had the strength, at the age of seventy-two, to go, Whitman-like, among the wounded of the World War and reanimate their wish to live. One desperately mutilated man, it is recorded, he brought back when everyone else had failed.

This feat alone should help to correct the overwritten portrait which we owe to Edith Wharton and her kind, of a helpless, complicated, timorous great man. A better image—if we must put a pinch of derision into our mixture—is that of James coping with fire at Lamb House in Rye. His own account is symbolic of the Manichean fight; he personifies the burning rafter: "We put him out, we made him stop, with soaked sponges—and then the relief: even while gazing at the hacked and smashed and disfigured floors." James goes to bed, well pleased with his heroism, but the fire breaks out again, the professionals come and act, fortunately "without too much zeal," and after a sleepless night James signs himself to his correspondent "your startled but re-quieted and fully insured H.J."

To describe what personal influences played upon and shaped his sense of ever-present evil would be a study in itself. *A Small Boy and Others,* which gives us, like William's earlier letters, glimpses of a retiring, impressionable youth overwhelmed by exceedingly bright and articulate relatives; the four years of war, experienced from afar but at the formative close of adolescence; the death of the fair cousin, the peculiar, patent ugliness of the American catch as catch can, comparable to the more concealed cutthroat rivalries of literary Paris—these things among others seen by James before his thirtieth year must have corroborated his sense of the rawness of human passion and concentrated his mind on the problem: How to keep passion natural and yet extinguish its harvest of evil.

For James is no ascetic, no admirer of tepid feeling, systematic constraint, or dilettante refinements. He pillories Gilbert Osmond for being such a dilettante and makes us love Isabel Archer for her moral spontaneity. We are made to share the zest with which she wants to taste life and even admire Caspar Goodwood for the robustness of his desires, which embrace equally the possession of Isabel and of worldly goods. M. A. de Wolfe Howe has also told us how on one occasion James passed judgment on the brownstone fronts of Boston by exclaiming, "Do you feel that Marlborough Street is—precisely—*passionate?*"

This acceptance of life *quand même,* or even because of encompassing evil, James held to from the first. In a review of Dickens's *Our Mutual Friend,* written when he was twenty-two, James complains that "the friction of two *men,* of two char-

acters, of two passions, produces stronger sparks than Wray-
burn's boyish repartees and Headstone's melodramatic commonplaces." The review as a whole is less a balanced judgment on
Dickens's masterpiece than a program for James's future fiction.
The keynote, from the partial point of view I have adopted in
these pages, is, of course, "melodramatic commonplaces." Finding new artistic forms to kindle into life by means of the sparks
that conflicting passions strike was to be James's problem, and
having succeeded in making them is his title to greatness.

In so doing he was not only expressing his own personal
awareness of the vast dominions of human evil but performing
a task assigned to him by the literature of the nineteenth century. He must criticize the melodrama that had become commonplace—in Dickens, in Balzac, in George Sand, in Victor
Hugo. But contrary to a usual belief, James was not turning
his back on their view of life, on their "exaggeration," on their
"romanticism." James was not a "realist" in the meaning that
Flaubert gave to the term: realism had been the first reaction to
nineteenth-century romanticism. James came a full generation
after Flaubert, whose artistic passion he admired more than
its "realistic" product, for the product was bitter and, in the
end, life denying. Rather James went back, over the realists'
heads, to the romanticists whom he wished to purge and reno-
vate. His published criticism of that earlier generation is fundamentally sympathetic; and his opinion remarkably appreciative
when it has to deal with a neoromantic calling himself a naturalist in the person of Zola, and even with a pastiche-romantic in
the person of Robert Louis Stevenson. James's allegiance in fact
never swerved from the master of them all, Balzac, in whom
melodrama can be found at its most conscious, forthright, and
moralistic; put there for the double purpose of nerving men to
face life and of keeping the reader going.

WILLIAM TROY

The Altar of Henry James

[1943]

THIS is, perhaps, an unfortunate title; it does not refer, for example, to the increasing number of people who have been throwing themselves at the feet of Henry James in the last few years. At least a half-dozen full-length studies of his work are in preparation; not all of his books are easily available on the market; his reputation is higher than at any moment in his own lifetime. It is clear enough that to the present generation he means something more than to the generation of Van Wyck Brooks and Lewis Mumford or to the addled and intolerant generation of the thirties. Also clear is that what he means is something different. To say what this something is in every case is, of course, impossible. What this article undertakes is to suggest that if he makes such a great appeal to so many of us today it must be because there lies at the center of his work something that corresponds to our deepest contemporary needs and hopes. It raises the question of what was James's *own* altar—or, if one prefers, the particular object of piety to which he was able to devote himself at the end.

All this is to strike the religious note; and, indeed, since we have no better word for the kind of passionate and responsible sense of human things that James possessed, he must be accounted a religious man. In this he simply followed his astonishing father, who ached out a lifetime trying to reconcile a heritage of respectability and good sense with a taste for Swedenborgian mysticism. Nor was he essentially unlike his brother William, whose too sudden plunge into the darker cellars of the personality, during the period of his breakdown, frightened him

[267]

into a loud and quasi-religious philosophy of optimism. All the Jameses were religious. The important thing about Henry is that he was an artist; that is, he had to work in a concrete medium and in a more or less fixed craft which did not permit him the consolations of shaking his head over Brook Farm experiments or becoming the Socrates of the Chautauquas. It meant that he could not evade the really great questions because these questions were stubbornly imbedded in the very materials of his craft—the lived and observed human situation.

For us it means that if we are to look for what is essential in James we are not likely to find it on the surface of his writing. (This is probably what T. S. Eliot means by the remark, "James had a mind so pure that no idea could violate it.") As in any authentic artist, the "meaning" in James is contained in the total arrangement and order of his symbols, and in the novel everything—people, events, and settings—are capable of being invested with symbolic value. In only a few novelists like Turgenev, Joyce, and the Mann of *Death in Venice* are meaning and literal statement so indivisible; the great works of the last period, *The Ambassadors* and *The Golden Bowl,* are put together, if not like a vastly exfoliated lyric, like one of the final plays of Shakespeare. And to approach them in the manner of Spurgeon or Knight on Shakespeare is almost certainly to uncover conflicts of feeling that are more often than not belied by the overt urbanity of style. It is also to raise the question of how much is conscious, how much unconscious, in any artist's work—in James's case, the often noted element of ambiguity. Is it merely an accident, for example, that in an early work like *The Portrait of a Lady* all the great climaxes in Isabel Archer's career—from her refusal of the English lord to her final flight from Caspar Goodwood—are made to occur in a garden? If an accident, it was a fortunate one, for the garden-symbol provides a wonderful point of concentration for the widest possible number of associations—the recollection especially of the famous garden in which one of Isabel's ancestresses was also confronted with the fruit of the tree of the knowledge of good and evil. It enables us to arrive at the formula, nowhere explicit in the book, that the real trouble with Isabel is that she is someone

William Troy

who will have none of the bitter fruit and runs from the garden in panic. And it might lead us to an even wider formula regarding James's own attitude toward these matters at this point in his development.

For the symbolic approach to James, besides lifting the mystery of individual works, makes possible a more organic study of his whole growth and achievement than the usual chronological division of his career into three periods. If the garden-symbol began as an accident, for example, it persists with remarkable frequency; and it is submitted to a series of drastic modifications. In *The Portrait of a Lady* it is clearly ambivalent. On the one hand, it is all that rich if uncertain promise of beautiful fulfillment that life is opening up to Isabel—wealth, marriage, Europe. On the other, it is the dwelling place of the unknown terror that is actually in herself—the terror of experience which at the end she rationalizes in terms of moral obligation. If the novel ends with such manifest ambiguity it is because James himself has not yet resolved certain issues in his mind and temperament. In the novels and tales of the nineties, the so-called "middle period," the symbol is first split wide asunder into its two aspects, then one of them is made to dominate. When the governess in *The Turn of the Screw* begins her afternoon walk in the garden everything is calm and radiant and peaceful. It is with the force of a shock, she tells us, that it suddenly becomes transformed for her into a scene of desolation and death. Once again we know that this is a case of projection; the garden is all that alarming and unsuspected side of her nature which she cannot accept because she believes it to be evil. Nor do we feel that James accepts it; evil, working in the guise of zeal, is triumphant; and the story adds up to another terrifying treatment of the Othello motif, the infinite amount of mischief done in the world, in the name of goodness, by self-blinded innocence. Even more terrifying perhaps in its nightmarish cancellation of all normal motives is *The Other House,* in which nearly all the action occurs in a garden. James did not include this in the New York Edition; it is the one altogether evil book that he ever wrote. But it sounds the depths of what must have been in his life a period of the most torturous metaphysical panic and moral despair. Without such a sojourn in the abyss as it represents he would never have attained to the full-bodied affirmation of the last and greatest period. Like Strether, in *The Ambassadors*, he wins through, by a long and difficult "process of vision," to an acceptance of human life as it is lived—qualified, of course, by a revalidation of the naïvely grasped moral certitudes of his youth. It is in Gloriani's garden that Strether makes the celebrated speech with the refrain, "Live, live while you can!" But life now is to be lived always with the wary knowledge of the shadows lurking ever in the dark corners of the garden.

To point out that the full import of James is to be derived only from some such weighing of his major symbols is not to deny that throughout his work he does let drop explicit judgments and opinions on important matters, although never like Tolstoy or Proust to the temporary abnegation of his role. It so happens that in one of the final stories of the middle period— not one of the best known or most admired—he has given us what may be taken as something like a testament of belief. *The Altar of the Dead* is unique in the James canon, fluttering on the edge of a morbid emotionalism and sustained only by a marvelous tonality of style. It is also a masterpiece of its kind in English—the long short story or *novella*. But for our purpose it is significant because it is the only one of James's works in which a character is made to come face to face with the problem of religion.

Its hero, one of those sensitive middle-aged gentlemen whom James apologizes for writing about in the nineties, shocked by the callousness of a friend who remarries too soon after his first wife's death, dedicates himself to keeping up the memory of his dead friends. "What came to pass was that an altar, such as was after all within everybody's compass, lighted with perpetual candles and dedicated to these secret rites, reared itself in his spiritual spaces. He had wondered of old, in some embarrassment, whether he had a religion; being very sure, and not a little content, that he hadn't at all events the religion some of the people he had known wanted him to have. Gradually this question was straightened out for him—it became clear to him that

William Troy

the religion instilled by his earliest consciousness had been simply
the religion of the Dead." Difficulties begin when quite by accident he enters a church and is tempted to light real candles before the real altar of a religion in which he does not believe. For
he soon acquires a companion in mourning—a woman given to
the same rites for a dead friend. In time it turns out that this
friend, who had actually been her ruin, is also the one man
among his friends whom the hero cannot commemorate because
of some betrayal in the past. This coincidence threatens their
relationship; they can no longer pay tribute at the same altar.
A resolution is managed only when the hero realizes that the
true "religion of the Dead" requires that we remember even
our enemies—just because they were once part of ourselves and
helped make us what we are.

What does James intend by this strange and tenuous parable,
which he himself refers to as a "conceit"? It is, as he tells us
in a preface, an instance of the "exasperated piety" of the Londoner of his time: "an instance of some such practiced communion was a foredoomed consequence of life, year after year,
amid the densest and most materialized aggregation of men on
earth, the society most wedded by all its conditions to the immediate and finite." It is a commentary on the pathetic desolation of the individual in our society—a desolation shared by
both the living and the dead. Toward the dead it expressed the
same kind of sympathy that we find in Baudelaire's

> Les morts, les pauvres morts, ont de grandes douleurs,
> Et quand Octobre souffle, émondeur des vieux arbres,
> Son vent mélancolique à l'entour de leurs marbres,
> Certe, ils doivent trouver les vivants bien ingrats.

And in its emphasis on the still potent influence that the dead
can exercise on the living it recalls Joyce's fine story, *The Dead*.
As to the living, or the living-dead, it explains their desolation
as the absence of any ritual by which some principle of continuity in human experience may be recognized and observed. For
it is continuity that it represented as the basis of everything—
of personality, friendship, morality, and civilization itself.
Without some sense of it the individual is no more than a mo-

ment in time and a speck in space; he has nothing by means of which he can define his own identity.

What James tells us, finally, is that we exist only by virtue of the existence of others, living and dead, with whom we have ever had relations. The individual, in the language of modern physics, is only an "event," to be defined in terms of a given field of forces. These relations or forces bring with them certain obligations, and the greatest of these is the formal act of commemoration. It is not morbidity that prompts James to write: "The sense of the state of the dead is but part of the sense of the state of the living; and, congruously with that, life is cheated to almost the same degree of the finest homage (precisely this our possible friendships and intimacies) that we fain would render it." We pay respect to the dead because they enhance the state of the living, and the dead is, of course, a metaphor for the whole tradition of civilized humanity of which we are a part and in terms of which we must ultimately be measured. This sense of the continuum between past and present, between all who share the memory of a common experience, is now known to be at the base of every religion in the world. For James it is a very real religion, although wholly without any theological cast. Or, if we prefer, he emerges as one of our great humanists, the greatest perhaps, because his humanism was grounded in such a rich tragic experience. And, in that case, his altar—what would it be but the sometimes splendid and exultant, sometimes mangled and ignoble, body of humanity stretched out in imagination in time and space? At a moment when loss of continuity is our gravest threat, when personality is everywhere at a discount, when all consequent values dissolve in the general terror, it is probably no great wonder that more and more people are turning to Henry James.

PHILIP RAHV

Attitudes Toward Henry James

[1943]

HENRY JAMES is at once the most and least appreciated figure in American writing. His authority as a novelist of unique quality and as an archetypal American has grown immeasurably in the years since his death, and in some literary circles his name has of late been turned into the password of a cult. But at the same time he is still regarded, in those circles that exert the major influence on popular education and intelligence, with the coldness and even derision that he encountered in the most depressed period of his career, when his public deserted him and he found himself almost alone.

To illustrate the extent to which he is even now misunderstood, let me cite the opening gambit of the section on James in *The College Book of American Literature,* a text currently used in many schools. "It is not certain that Henry James really belongs to American literature, for he was critical of America and admired Europe." The attitude so automatically expressed by the editors of this academic volume obviously borders on caricature. The responsibility for it, however, must be laid at the door of all those critics and historians who, in response to a deep, anti-intellectual compulsion or at the service of some blindly nationalistic or social creed, are not content merely to say no to the claims made in James's behalf but must ever try to despoil him utterly. The strategy is simple: James was nothing but a self-deluded, expatriate snob, a concoctor of elegant if intricate trifles, a fugitive from "reality," etc., etc. Professor Pattee, a run-of-the-mill historian of American writing, permits himself the remark that James's novels "really accomplish nothing."

The Question of Henry James

Ludwig Lewisohn is likewise repelled by the novels—"cathedrals of frosted glass" he calls them; in his opinion only the shorter narratives are worth reading.[1] In his *Main Currents in American Thought* Parrington gives two pages to James as against eleven to James Branch Cabell, and he has the further temerity (and/or innocence) to round out his two pages by comparing James— much to his disadvantage, of course—to Sherwood Anderson. And Van Wyck Brooks does all he can, in *New England: Indian Summer*, to promote once more the notoriously low estimate of the later James to which he committed himself in *The Pilgrimage*. Brooks may well believe that the Jamesian attachment is to be counted among the fixed ideas of our native "coterie writers" —and plainly the best cure for a fixed idea is to stamp on it.

This depreciation of James is prepared for by some of the leading assumptions of our culture. The attitude of Parrington, for example, is formed by the Populist spirit of the West and its open-air poetics, whereas that of Brooks is at bottom formed by the moralism of New England—a moralism to which he has reverted, even though in practice he applies it in a more or less impressionistic and sentimental manner, with all the vehemence of a penitent atoning for his backsliding in the past. And the difference between such typical attitudes is mainly this: that while Parrington—like Whitman and Mark Twain before him —rejects James entirely, Brooks at least recognizes the value and fidelity to life of his earlier novels. Yet if James can be named, in T. S. Eliot's phrase, "a positive continuator of the New England genius," then surely Brooks must be aware of it as well as any of us; for he is nothing if not a pious servitor of this genius; after all, he, too, is a paleface. But still he scoffs at the more complex and, so to speak, ultimate James. And this Brooks does essentially for the same reasons, I think, that the Boston public of the 1870's scoffed at the works he now admits into his canon. We know that when the first of James's books appeared in America, they were actively disliked in Boston: Mrs. Fields (the wife of the publisher) relates that they were thought "self-conscious, artificial and shallow." A like animus is now betrayed

[1] But Lewisohn, who exhibits this truncated taste for James in *Expression in America*, is neither a nationalist nor a sociological critic.

Philip Rahv

in Brooks's judgment of such novels as *The Spoils of Poynton*, *The Wings of the Dove*, and *The Golden Bowl*:

> Magnificent pretensions, petty performances!—the fruits of an irresponsible imagination, of a deranged sense of values, of a mind working in a void, uncorrected by any clear consciousness of human cause and effect (*The Pilgrimage of Henry James*).
> There was scarcely enough substance in these great ghosts of novels. . . . What concerned him now was form, almost regardless of content, the problems of calculation and construction. . . . His American characters might be nobler, but, if the old world was corrupt, its glamor outweighed its corruption in his mind . . . so that he later pictured people, actually base, as eminent, noble and great (*New England: Indian Summer*).

What are such extreme statements if not critical rationalizations of the original Boston prejudice? Brooks begins by magnifying the distinctions between James's early and late manner into an absolute contradiction, and ends by invoking the charge of degeneracy. But the fact is that the changes in James's work mark no such gap as Brooks supposes but are altogether implicit in the quality of his vision, flowing from the combined release and elaboration of his basic tendency. Moreover, these changes, far from justifying the charge of degeneracy, define for a good many of his readers the one salient example in our literature of a novelist who, not exhausted by his initial assertion of power, learned how to nourish his gifts and grow to full maturity. To me he is the only really fine American writer of the nineteenth century who can truly be said to have mastered that "principle of growth," to the failure of which in our creative life Brooks has himself repeatedly called attention in his earlier preachments.

For what is to be admired in a late narrative like *The Wings of the Dove* is James's capacity to lift the nuclear theme of his first period—the theme of the American innocent's penetration into the "rich and deep and dark" hive of Europe—to a level of conscious experience and aesthetic possession not previously attained. James orders his world with consummate awareness in this narrative, applying successfully his favorite rule of an "exquisite economy" in composition. There are brilliant scenes in it of London and Venice, and strongly contrasted symbols of social glamor and decay; it is invigorated, too, by an unflagging realism in the plotting of act and motive and by the large movement of the characters. No literary standpoint that allows for the dismissal of this creation as a "petty performance" can possibly be valid. Is its heroine, Milly Theale, a character without reality? She remains in our mind, writes Edmund Wilson, "as a personality independent of the novel, the kind of personality, deeply felt, invested with poetic beauty and unmistakably individualized, which only the creators of the first rank can give life to."

James suffers from a certain one-sidedness, to be sure. This tends to throw off balance such readers as are unable to see it for what it is—the price he paid, given the circumstances of his career, for being faithful to his own genius. For James could continue to develop and sustain his "appeal to a high refinement and a handsome wholeness of effect" only through intensively exploiting his very limitations, through submitting himself to a process of creative yet cruel self-exaggeration. The strain shows in the stylization of his language, a stylization so rich that it turns into an intellectual quality of rare value, but which at times is apt to become overwrought and drop into unconscious parody. It is further shown in his obsessive refinement —a veritable delirium of refinement—which again serves at times to remove us from the actuality of the represented experience. This should be related to his all-too-persistent attempts, as Yvor Winters has observed, to make the sheer *tone* of speech and behavior "carry vastly more significance than is proper to it." It is true that, for instance, in novels like *The Sense of the Past* and *The Awkward Age*, he pushes his feelings for nuances and discriminations to an unworkable extreme. But such distortions, inflated into awful vices by his detractors, are of the kind which in one form or another not only James but most of the considerable modern artists are forced to cultivate as a means of coping with the negative environment that confines them. To regard such distortions as the traits of a willful coterie is utterly naïve. They are the traits, rather, of an art which, if it is to survive at all in a society inimical to all interests that are

Philip Rahv

pure, gratuitous, and without cash value, has no other recourse save constantly to "refine its singularities" and expose itself more and more to the ravages of an unmitigated individualism.

But in all this I do not mean to imply that I agree with those enthusiasts who see no moral defects whatsoever in James. From the viewpoint of social criticism, there is a good deal of justice in Ferner Nuhn's mordant analysis of *The Golden Bowl*. Nuhn shows up one such defect in James's close identification with Adam and Maggie Verner's upper-class American illusions and self-righteousness. (One is persuaded of this view by the evidence of the tone and the inner manipulation of the scale of value, for here too the author makes the story "tell itself.") Nuhn fails to bring out, however, the enormous assets with which this novel is otherwise endowed. There is a use of symbols in it and a scenic and dramatic power scarcely equaled, to my mind, anywhere in American prose. Furthermore, whatever one may think of the millionaire self-indulgence of the Ververs, this is a far cry from the charge that his long exile put James into such a bad state that he could no longer distinguish between the noble and the base. This sort of charge is answered once and for all, it seems to me, by Stephen Spender in his study, *The Destructive Element*:

> The morality of the heroes and heroines [in the last great novels] is to "suffer generously." What they have to suffer from is being more intelligent than the other characters. Also, there are no villains. It is important to emphasize this, because in these really savage novels the behavior of some of the characters is exposed in its most brutal form. But the wickedness of the characters lies primarily in their situation. Once the situation is provided, the actors cannot act otherwise. Their only compensation is that by the use of their intelligence, by their ability to understand, to love and to suffer, they may to some extent atone for the evil which is simply the evil of the modern world.

As against the sundry moralizers and nationalists who belittle James, there are the cultists who go to the other extreme in presenting him as a kind of culture hero, an ideal master whose perfection of form is equaled by his moral insight and stanch allegiance to "tradition." This image is, no doubt, of consolatory value to some high-minded literary men. It contributes, how-

The Question of Henry James

ever, to the misunderstanding of James, in that it is so impeccable, one might say transcendent, that it all but eliminates the contradictions in him—and in modern literature, which bristles with anxieties and ideas of isolation, it is above all the creativity, the depth and quality of the contradictions that a writer unites within himself, that gives us the truest measure of his achievement. And this is not primarily a matter of the solutions, if any, provided by the writer—for it is hardly the writer's business to stand in for the scientist or philosopher—but of his force and integrity in reproducing these contradictions as felt experience. Very few of us would be able to appreciate Dostoevski, for instance, if we first had to accept his answer to the problem of the Christian man, or Proust if we first had to accept his answer to the problem of the artist. We appreciate these novelists because they employ imaginative means that convince us of the reality of their problems, which are not *necessarily* ours.

T. S. Eliot was surely right in saying that the soil of James's origin imparted a "flavor" that was "precisely improved and given its chance, not worked off" by his living in Europe. Now James differs radically in his contradictions from European novelists—that is why readers lacking a background in American or at least Anglo-Saxon culture make so little of him. And the chief contradiction is that his work represents a positive and ardent search for "experience" and simultaneously a withdrawal from it, or rather, a dread of approaching it in its natural state. Breaking sharply with the then still dominant American morality of abstention, he pictures "experience" as the "real taste of life," as a longed-for "presence" at once "vast, vague, and dazzling—an irradiation of light from objects undefined, mixed with the atmosphere of Paris and Venice." Nevertheless, to prove truly acceptable, it must first be Americanized as it were, that is to say, penetrated by the new-world conscience and cleansed of its taint of "evil." This tension between the impulse to plunge into "experience" and the impulse to renounce it is the chief source of the internal yet astonishingly abundant Jamesian emotion; and because the tension is not always adequately resolved, we sometimes get that effect, so well described by Glenway Wescott, of "embarrassed passion and hinted meaning in excess of the narrated facts; the psychic content is too great for its container of elegantly forged happenings; it all overflows and slops about and is magnificently wasted." On this side of James we touch upon his relationship to Hawthorne, whose characters, likewise tempted by "experience," are held back by the fear of sin. And Hawthorne's ancestral idea of sin survives in James, though in a secularized form. It has entered the sensibility and been translated into a revulsion, an exasperated feeling, almost morbid in its sensitiveness, against any conceivable crudity of scene or crudity of conduct. (The trouble with American life, he wrote, is not that it is "ugly"—the ugly can be strange and grotesque—but that it is "plain"; "even nature, in the western world, has the peculiarity of seeming rather crude and immature.") Any failure of discrimination is sin, whereas virtue is a compound of intelligence, moral delicacy, and the sense of the past.

And Hawthorne's remembrance of the religious mythology of New England and his fanciful concern with it is replaced in James—and this too is a kind of transmutation—by the remembrance and fanciful concern with history. It was for the sake of Europe's historical "opulence" that he left his native land. Yet this idea is also managed by him in a contradictory fashion, and for this reason W. C. Brownell was able to say that he showed no real interest in the "course of history." Now, as a critic, Brownell had no eye for James's historical picture of the American experience in Europe; but it is true that on the whole James's sense of history is restricted by the point of view of the "passionate pilgrim" who comes to enrich his personality. Thus there is produced the Jamesian conception of history as a static yet irreproachable standard, a beautiful display, a treasured background, whose function is at once to adorn and lend perspective to his well-nigh metaphysical probing of personal relations, of the private life. There never was a writer so immersed in personal relations, and his consistency in this respect implies an antihistorical attitude. This helps to explain the peculiarities of his consciousness, which is intellectual yet at the same time indifferent to general ideas, deeply comprehensive yet unattached to any open philosophical motive.

The Question of Henry James

These contradictions in James—and there are others besides those I have mentioned—are chiefly to be accounted for in terms of his situation as an American writer who experienced his nationality and the social class to which he belonged at once as an ordeal and as an inspiration. His characteristic themes all express this doubleness. The "great world" is corrupt, yet it represents an irresistible goal. Innocence points to all the wanted things one has been deprived of, yet it is profound in its good faith and not to be tampered with without loss. History and culture are the supreme ideal, but why not make of them a strictly private possession? Europe is romance and reality and civilization, but the spirit resides in America. James never faltered in the maze of these contraries; he knew how to take hold of them creatively and weave them into the web of his art. And the secret of their combination is the secret of his irony and of his humor.

LYON N. RICHARDSON

Bibliography

THIS TABLE of biographical and critical studies is reprinted from *American Writers Series: Henry James*—Representative Selections, with Introduction, Bibliography, and Notes by Lyon N. Richardson, Copyright 1941, by American Book Company.

ARVIN, NEWTON. "Henry James and the Almighty Dollar," *Hound & Horn*, VII, 434-43 (April-May, 1934).

BAKER, ERNEST A. *The History of the English Novel*. London: 1938, IX, 243-287.

BEACH, JOSEPH WARREN. "Henry James," in *The Cambridge History of American Literature*. New York: c.1921, III, 96-108; IV, 671-75.

BEACH, JOSEPH WARREN. *The Method of Henry James*. New Haven: 1918; also London: 1918. (Original, elaborate, invaluable study of technique.)

BEACH, JOSEPH WARREN. "The Novel from James to Joyce," *Nation*, CXXXII, 634-36 (June 10, 1931).

BEACH, JOSEPH WARREN. "Subjective Drama: James," "Point of View: James," "Point of View: James and Others," "Point of View: James, Stendhal," in *The Twentieth Century Novel: Studies in Technique*. New York: c.1932, pp. 177-92, 193-203, 204-17, 218-28.

BEER, THOMAS. "The Princess Far Away," *Saturday Review of Literature*, I, 701-02, 707 (April 25, 1925).

BENNETT, ARNOLD. "Henry James," in *Books and Persons: Being Comments on a Past Epoch: 1908-1911*. New York: c.1917, pp. 263-66.

BENNETT, ARNOLD. "Henry James," in *Things That Have Interested Me*. First series. New York: 1921, pp. 323-32.

[281]

Bibliography

Bennett, Arnold. "Two Reputations," in *Savour of Life: Essays in Gusto*. New York: 1928, pp. 117-21.

Benson, Arthur Christopher. "Henry James," *Cornhill Magazine*, n.s. XL, 511-19 (April, 1916). (Enlightening and authoritative remarks by a friend of many years.)

Benson, Arthur Christopher. "Henry James," in *Memories and Friends*. New York: 1924, pp. 214-28.

Benson, Arthur Christopher. "Lamb House, Rye," in *Rambles and Reflections*. New York: 1926, pp. 29-37; also London: 1926. (Intimate glimpses of James at work.)

Bethurum, Dorothy. "Morality and Henry James," *Sewanee Review*, XXXI, 324-30 (July, 1923).

Bicknell, Percy F. "Mr. James's Memories of Boyhood," *Dial*, LIV, 372-74 (May 1, 1913).

Blackmur, Richard P. "Introduction," to *The Art of the Novel: Critical Prefaces, by Henry James*. New York and London: 1934, pp. vii-xxxix. (Collection and organization of ideas which James had expressed in star-scattered fashion throughout his Prefaces.)

Blackmur, Richard P. "The Critical Prefaces," *Hound & Horn*, VII, 444-77 (April-May, 1934).

Bogan, Louise. "Henry James on a Revolutionary Theme," *Nation*, CXLVI, 471-74 (April 23, 1938).

Bosanquet, Theodora. "Henry James," *Fortnightly Review*, n.s. CI, 995-1009 (June, 1917); *Living Age*, CCXCIV, 346-57 (August 11, 1917); *Bookman* (New York), XLV, 571-81 (August, 1917).

Bosanquet, Theodora. *Henry James at Work*. London: 1924. (The author was James's stenographer through a period of years; her remarks are highly informative.)

Bosanquet, Theodora. "The Record of Henry James," *Yale Review*, n.s. X, 143-56 (October, 1920).

Boughton, Alice. "A Note by His Photographer," *Hound & Horn*, VII, 478-79 (April-May, 1934).

Bowen, Edwin W. "Henry James, the Realist: An Appreciation," *Methodist Review*, CI (Fifth series, XXXIV), 410-19 (May, 1918).

Boyd, Ernest Augustus. "Henry James," in *Literary Blasphemies*. New York and London: 1927, pp. 213-26.

Bradford, Gamaliel. "Henry James," in *American Portraits: 1875-1900*. New York: 1922, pp. 171-96.

Bradford, Gamaliel. "Portrait of Henry James," *North American Review*, CCXIII, 211-24 (February, 1921).

Bibliography

BRAGDON, CLAUDE. "The Figure in Mr. James's Carpet," *Critic*, XLIV, 146-50 (February, 1904).

BRAGDON, CLAUDE. "A Master of Shades," *Critic*, XLVI, 20-22 (January, 1905).

BREWSTER, DOROTHY, and BURRELL, ANGUS. "Paris and the Puritan," in *Dead Reckonings in Fiction*. New York: 1924, pp. 19-41.

BROOKS, SYDNEY. "Henry James at Home," *Harper's Weekly*, XLVIII, 1548-49 (October 8, 1904).

BROOKS, VAN WYCK. "Henry James: An International Episode," *Dial*, LXXV, 225-38 (September, 1923).

BROOKS, VAN WYCK. "Henry James as a Reviewer," in *Sketches in Criticism*. New York: c.1932, pp. 190-96.

BROOKS, VAN WYCK. "Henry James of Boston," *Saturday Review of Literature*, XXII, 3-4 (July 13, 1940).

BROOKS, VAN WYCK. "Henry James: The American Scene," *Dial*, LXXV, 29-42 (July, 1923).

BROOKS, VAN WYCK. "Henry James: The First Phase," *Dial*, LXXIV, 433-50 (May, 1923).

BROOKS, VAN WYCK. *The Pilgrimage of Henry James*. New York: 1925. (Development of the man-without-a-country psychological explanation of the nature of James.)

BROWN, IVOR. "*The Tragic Muse*—Adapted by Hubert Griffith from the novel of Henry James," *Saturday Review*, CXLVI, 14 (July 7, 1928).

BROWNELL, WILLIAM CRARY. "Henry James," in *American Prose Masters: Cooper—Hawthorne—Emerson—Poe—Lowell—Henry James*. New York: 1909, pp. 339-400.

BROWNELL, WILLIAM CRARY. "Henry James," *Atlantic Monthly*, XCV, 496-519 (April, 1905).

BROWNELL, WILLIAM CRARY. "James's *Portrait of a Lady*," *Nation*, XXXIV, 102-03 (February 2, 1882).

BUCHANAN, ROBERT. "The Modern Young Man as Critic," *Universal Review*, III, 355-59 (March, 1889).

BURRELL, JOHN ANGUS. "Henry James: A Rhapsody of Youth," *Dial*, LXIII, 260-62 (September 27, 1917).

BURTON, RICHARD. "Björnson, Daudet, James: A Study in the Literary Time-Spirit," in *Literary Likings*. Boston: 1898, pp. 107-09, 122-28.

BYNNER, WITTER. "A Word or Two with Henry James," *Critic*, XLVI, 146-48 (February, 1905).

CAIRNS, WILLIAM B. "Character-Portrayal in the Work of Henry

Bibliography

James," *University of Wisconsin Studies in Language and Literature,* no. 2. Madison, Wisconsin: 1918, pp. 314-22.

CAIRNS, WILLIAM B. "Meditations of a Jacobite," *Dial,* LX, 313-16 (March 30, 1916).

CANBY, HENRY SEIDEL. "Henry James," in *Definitions: Essays in Contemporary Criticism.* First series. New York: c.1922, pp. 278-81.

CANBY, HENRY SEIDEL. "Henry James," *Harper's Weekly,* LXII, 291 (March 25, 1916).

CANTWELL, ROBERT. "A Little Reality," *Hound & Horn,* VII, 494-505 (April-May, 1934).

CANTWELL, ROBERT. "The Return of Henry James," *New Republic,* LXXXI, 119-21 (December 12, 1934).

CARY, ELISABETH LUTHER. "Henry James," *Scribner's Magazine,* XXXVI, 394-400 (October, 1904).

CARY, ELISABETH LUTHER. *The Novels of Henry James: A Study.* With a Bibliography by Frederick A. King. New York and London: 1905.

CESTRE, CHARLES. "La France dans l'œuvre de Henry James," *Revue Anglo-Américaine,* X, 1-13, 112-22 (October, 1932).

CHAIGNON LA ROSE, PIERRE DE, ed. *Notes and Reviews by Henry James.* Cambridge, Mass.: 1921. (Collection of twenty-five early reviews appearing during the years 1864-66.)

CHISLETT, WILLIAM, JR. "Henry James: His Range and Accomplishments," in *Moderns and Near-Moderns: Essays on Henry James, Stockton, Shaw, and Others.* New York: 1928, pp. 11-66.

CLARK, A. F. BRUCE. "Henry James," *University Magazine* (Montreal), XVIII, 45-68 (February, 1919).

COLBY, FRANK MOORE. "In Darkest James," in *Imaginary Obligations.* New York: 1904, pp. 321-35. Same, in *Essays of the Past and Present,* compiled by Warner Taylor. New York: c. 1927, pp. 405-12.

COLBY, FRANK MOORE. "The Queerness of Henry James," *Bookman* (New York), XV, 396-97 (June, 1902).

COLLINS, NORMAN. "Henry James," in *The Facts of Fiction.* London: 1932, pp. 228-36; also New York: c.1933.

CONRAD, JOSEPH. "Henry James: An Appreciation," *North American Review,* CLXXX, 102-08 (January, 1905); CCIII, 585-91 (April, 1916); also in *Notes on Life and Letters.* New York: 1921, pp. 11-19.

COOPER, FREDERICK TABER. " 'The American Scene,' " *North American Review,* CLXXXV, 214-18 (May 17, 1907).

Bibliography

CORNELIUS, ROBERTA D. "The Clearness of Henry James," *Sewanee Review*, XXVII, 1-8 (January, 1919).

CROLY, HERBERT. "Henry James and His Countrymen," *Lamp*, XXVIII, 47-53 (February, 1904).

CROSS, WILBUR LUCIUS. "Henry James and Impressionism," in *The Development of the English Novel*. New York: 1899, pp. 263-68.

DARGAN, E. PRESTON. "Henry James the Builder," *New Republic*, VII, 171-74 (June 17, 1916).

DAVRAY, HENRY D. "Un déraciné Anglo-Américain: Henry James, d'après sa correspondance," *Mercure de France*, CXLVI, 68-84 (February 15, 1921).

DE LA MARE, WALTER. "Henry James," *Living Age*, CCLXXXIX, 122-25 (April 8, 1916).

DE MILLE, GEORGE E. "Henry James," in *Literary Criticism in America: A Preliminary Survey*. New York: 1931, pp. 158-81.

DRAPER, MURIEL. "I Meet Henry James," *Harper's Magazine*, CLVI, 416-21 (March, 1928); also in *Music at Midnight*, New York: 1929, pp. 87-96.

DUNBAR, OLIVIA HOWARD. "Henry James as a Lecturer," *Critic*, XLVII, 24-25 (July, 1905).

DWIGHT, H. G. "Henry James—'in His Own Country,'" *Putnam's Monthly*, II, 164-70 (May, 1907); 433-42 (July, 1907).

EDEL, LÉON. "The Exile of Henry James," *University of Toronto Quarterly*, II, 520-32 (July, 1933).

EDEL, LÉON. *Henry James: Les années dramatiques*. Paris: 1931.

EDEL, LÉON. "A Note on the Translations of H. James in France," *Revue Anglo-Américaine*, VII, 539-40 (August, 1930).

EDEL, LÉON. *The Prefaces of Henry James*. Paris: 1931.

EDGAR, PELHAM. "The Art of Henry James," *National Review*, LXXXIII, 730-39 (July, 1924).

EDGAR, PELHAM. "Henry James and His Method," *Proceedings and Transactions of the Royal Society of Canada*, Series III; XII, Section II, 225-40 (December, 1918, March, 1919).

EDGAR, PELHAM. *Henry James: Man and Author*. London: 1927; also New York: 1927. (Standard descriptive and critical biography.)

EDGAR, PELHAM. "Henry James, the Essential Novelist," *Queen's Quarterly*, XXXIX, 181-92 (May, 1932).

EDGAR, PELHAM. "The Letters of Henry James," *Queen's Quarterly*, XXVIII, 283-87 (January, 1921).

EDGAR, PELHAM. "Three Novels of Henry James," *Dalhousie Review*, IV, 467-75 (January, 1925).

Bibliography

EGAN, MAURICE FRANCIS. "The Revelation of an Artist in Literature," *Catholic World*, CXI, 289-300 (June, 1920).

ELTON, OLIVER. "The Novels of Mr. Henry James," *Living Age*, CCXL, 1-14 (January 2, 1904); also in *Modern Studies*. London: 1907, pp. 245-84; also New York: 1907.

FAWCETT, EDGAR. "Henry James's Novels," *Princeton Review*, N.S. XIV, 68-86 (July, 1884).

FERGUSSON, FRANCIS. "The Drama in *The Golden Bowl*," *Hound & Horn*, VII, 407-13 (April-May, 1934).

FIELDING, H. M. "Henry James, the Lion," *Reader*, V, 364-67 (February, 1905).

FOLLETT, HELEN THOMAS, and FOLLETT, WILSON. "Henry James," *Atlantic Monthly*, CXVII, 801-11 (June, 1916).

FOLLETT, HELEN THOMAS, and FOLLETT, WILSON. "Henry James," in *Some Modern Novelists: Appreciations and Estimates*. New York: 1918, pp. 75-98.

FOLLETT, WILSON. "Henry James's Portrait of Henry James," *New York Times Book Review*, pp. 2, 16 (August 23, 1936). (Offers the thesis that *The Sacred Fount* illustrates James's distinction between life and literature.)

FOLLETT, WILSON. "The Simplicity of Henry James," *American Review*, I, 315-25 (May-June, 1923).

FORBES, ELIZABETH LIVERMORE. "Dramatic Lustrum: A Study of the Effect of Henry James's Theatrical Experience on His Later Novels," *New England Quarterly*, XI, 108-20 (March, 1938).

FORD, FORD MADOX.—See also HUEFFER, FORD MADOX.

FORD, FORD MADOX. "Henry James: the Master," in *Portraits from Life*. New York: 1937, pp. 1-20; also in *American Mercury*, XXXVI, 315-27 (November, 1935).

FORD, FORD MADOX. "Three Americans and a Pole," *Scribner's Magazine*, XC, 379-86 (October, 1931). (As a personal friend of James, Ford's anecdotes and comments are interesting.)

FORD, FORD MADOX. "Techniques," *Southern Review*, I, 20-35 (1935-36).

FRANCE, WILMER CAVE. "Henry James as a Lecturer," *Bookman* (New York), XXI, 71-72 (March, 1905).

FREEMAN, JOHN. "Henry James," in *The Moderns: Essays in Literary Criticism*. New York: 1917, pp. 219-41; also London: 1916.

FULLERTON, MORTON. "The Art of Henry James," *Quarterly Review*

Bibliography

(London), CCXII, 393-408 (April, 1910); *Living Age*, CCLXV, 643-52 (June 11, 1910).

GARLAND, HAMLIN. "Henry James at Rye," in *Roadside Meetings*. New York: 1930, pp. 454-65. (Detailed account of Garland's visit at Rye.)

GARLAND, HAMLIN. "Roadside Meetings of a Literary Nomad; Lover of America" (Sections LXXVII-LXXX), *Bookman* (New York), LXXI, 427-32 (July, 1930).

GIDE, ANDRÉ. "Henry James," *Yale Review*, XIX, 641-43 (March, 1930).

GILL, W. A. "Henry James and His Double," *Atlantic Monthly*, C, 458-66 (October, 1907); *Fortnightly Review*, N.S. LXXXVI, 689-700 (October, 1909).

GILMAN, LAWRENCE. "Henry James in Reverie," *North American Review*, CCVII, 130-35 (January, 1918).

GOSSE, EDMUND. "Henry James," *London Mercury*, I, 673-84 (April, 1920), II, 29-41 (May, 1920). (Mr. Gosse was a good friend of James; his articles are trustworthy and based on first-hand knowledge.)

GOSSE, EDMUND. "Henry James," *Scribner's Magazine*, LXVII, 422-30, 548-57 (April-May, 1920).

GOSSE, EDMUND. "Henry James," in *Aspects and Impressions*. New York: 1922, pp. 17-53; also London: 1922.

GRATTAN, CLINTON HARTLEY. "The Calm within the Cyclone," *Nation*, CXXXIV, 201-03 (February 17, 1932).

GRATTAN, CLINTON HARTLEY. "Henry James," in *The Three Jameses: A Family of Minds*. New York: 1932, pp. 208-357. (Indispensable.)

GREENE, GRAHAM. "Henry James," in *The English Novelists*, Derek Verschoyle, ed. London: 1936, pp. 215-28.

GREENE, GRAHAM. "Henry James—An Aspect," in *Contemporary Essays*, Sylva Norman, ed. London: 1933, pp. 65-75.

GREGORY, ALYSE. "A Superb Brief," in *American Criticism: 1926*, William A. Drake, ed. New York: c.1926, pp. 95-100.

GRETTON, M. STURGE. "Mr. Henry James and His Prefaces," *Contemporary Review*, CI, 69-78 (January, 1912); *Living Age*, CCLXXII, 287-95 (February 3, 1912).

GUEDALLA, PHILIP. "The Crowner's Quest," *New Statesman*, XII, 421-22 (February 15, 1919).

HACKETT, FRANCIS. "Henry James," and "A Stylist on Tour," in *Horizons: A Book of Criticism*. New York: 1918, pp. 74-82, 268-

Bibliography

73. "A Stylist on Tour" appeared previously, *New Republic*, II, 320-21 (May 1, 1915).

HALE, EDWARD E. "Henry James," *Dial*, LX, 259-62 (March 16, 1916).

HALE, EDWARD E. "The Impressionism of Henry James," *Faculty Papers of Union College*, II, 3-17 (January, 1931).

HAMILTON, CLAYTON. "Disengaged," *Forum*, XLI, 342-43 (April, 1909).

HAPGOOD, NORMAN. "Henry James," *Bachelor of Arts*, III, 477-88 (October, 1896).

HAPGOOD, NORMAN. "Henry James," in *Literary Statesmen and Others: Essays on Men Seen from a Distance*. Chicago: 1897, pp. 193-208.

HARKINS, E. F. "Henry James," in *Famous Authors (Men)*. Boston: c.1901, pp. 91-105.

HARLAND, HENRY. "Mr. Henry James," *Academy*, LV, 339-40 (November 26, 1898).

HARRIS, JOEL CHANDLER. "Provinciality in Literature—a Defence of Boston," in *Joel Chandler Harris: Editor and Essayist: Miscellaneous Literary, Political, and Social Writings*, Julia Collier Harris, ed. Chapel Hill, N. C.: 1931, pp. 186-91.

HARTWICK, HARRY. "Caviar to the General," in *The Foreground of American Fiction*. New York: c.1934, pp. 341-68.

HARVITT, HÉLÈNE. "How Henry James Revised *Roderick Hudson*: A Study in Style," *Publications of the Modern Language Association*, XXXIX, 203-27 (March, 1924).

HAVENS, RAYMOND D. "The Revision of *Roderick Hudson*," *Publications of the Modern Language Association*, XL, 433-34 (June, 1925).

HAYS, H. R. "Henry James, the Satirist," *Hound & Horn*, VII, 514-22 (April-May, 1934).

HELLMAN, GEORGE S. "Stevenson and Henry James, The Rare Friendship Between Two Famous Stylists," *Century*, N.S. LXXXIX, 336-45 (January, 1926).

HERRICK, ROBERT. "Henry James," in *American Writers on American Fiction*, J. C. Macy, ed. New York: c.1931, pp. 298-316.

HERRICK, ROBERT. "Tolstoi and Henry James," *Yale Review*, N.S. XII, 181-86 (October, 1922).

HERRICK, ROBERT. "A Visit to Henry James," in *The Manly Anniversary Studies in Language and Literature*. Chicago: 1923, pp. 229-42; *Yale Review*, N.S. XII, 724-41 (July, 1923), N.S. XIII, 206-08

Bibliography

(October, 1923). (Contains important references to the changes in James's style when he began dictation.)

HICKS, GRANVILLE. "Fugitives," in *The Great Tradition: An Interpretation of American Literature Since the Civil War*. New York: 1933, pp. 100, 105-24.

HIGGINSON, T. W. "Henry James, Jr.," in *Short Studies of American Authors*. Boston: 1880, pp. 51-60. Originally in *The Literary World*, X, 383-84 (November 22, 1879). (One of the best early contemporary evaluations.)

HIND, CHARLES LEWIS. "Henry James," in *Authors and I*. New York: 1921, pp. 161-65.

HOLLIDAY, ROBERT CORTES. "Henry James, Himself," in *Walking-Stick Papers*. New York: c.1918, pp. 121-29.

HOWELLS, WILLIAM DEAN. "Editor's Study," *Harper's New Monthly Magazine*, LXXVII, 799-800 (October, 1888). (Howells was an early friend and close literary adviser; his comments are informed by intimate acquaintanceship and sound judgment.)

HOWELLS, WILLIAM DEAN. "Henry James, Jr.," *Century*, N.S. III, 25-29 (November, 1882).

HOWELLS, WILLIAM DEAN. "Mr. Henry James's Later Work," *North American Review*, CLXXVI, 125-37 (January, 1903); CCIII, 572-84 (April, 1916).

HOWELLS, WILLIAM DEAN. "Mr. James's Masterpiece," *Harper's Bazaar*, XXXVI, 9-14 (January, 1902). (Treats of *Daisy Miller*.)

HOWELLS, WILLIAM DEAN. "James's *Passionate Pilgrim and Other Tales*," *Atlantic Monthly*, XXXV, 490-95 (April, 1875).

HUEFFER, FORD MADOX.—See also FORD, FORD MADOX.

HUEFFER, FORD MADOX. *Henry James: A Critical Study*. New York: 1916. (Hueffer was well acquainted with James in England.)

HUEFFER, FORD MADOX. "Two Americans—Henry James and Stephen Crane," *Literary Review*, I, 1-2 (March 19, 1921), 1-2 (March 26, 1921).

HUGHES, HERBERT L. *Theory and Practice in Henry James*. Ann Arbor: 1926.

HUNEKER, JAMES GIBBONS. "The Lesson of the Master," *Bookman* (New York), LI, 364-68 (May, 1920).

HUNEKER, JAMES GIBBONS. "A Note on Henry James," in *Unicorns*. New York: 1917, pp. 53-66. Also in *Modern English Essays*, Ernest Rhys, ed. New York: 1922, V, 64-76.

JAMES, HENRY. "*The Ambassadors*: Project of Novel" (Edna Kenton,

Bibliography

ed.), *Hound & Horn,* VII, 541-62 (April-May, 1934). (Throws light on James's creative procedure; a partial printing of the unpublished MS. James sent Harper & Brothers in September, 1900.)

JAMES, HENRY. "A Letter to Mr. Howells," *North American Review,* CXCV, 558-62 (April, 1912).

JAMES, HENRY. "Two Unpublished Letters," *Hound & Horn,* VII, 414-16 (April-May, 1934).

JOHNSON, ARTHUR. "A Comparison of Manners," *New Republic,* XX, 113-15 (August 27, 1919).

JONES, DORA M. "Henry James," *London Quarterly Review,* CXXVI, 117-20 (July, 1916).

KELLEY, CORNELIA PULSIFER. "The Early Development of Henry James," in *University of Illinois Studies in Language and Literature,* XV, nos. 1-2. Urbana: 1930. (Indispensable, careful, elaborate, sound, authoritative.)

KENTON, EDNA. "Henry James and Mr. Van Wyck Brooks," *Bookman* (New York), LXII, 153-57 (October, 1925).

KENTON, EDNA. "Henry James in the World," "Some Bibliographical Notes on Henry James," "*The Ambassadors:* Project of Novel," *Hound & Horn,* VII, 506-13, 535-40, 541-62 (April-May, 1934).

KENTON, EDNA. "Henry James to the Ruminant Reader: *The Turn of the Screw,*" *Arts,* VI, 245-55 (November, 1924).

KENTON, EDNA. "The 'Plays' of Henry James," *Theatre Arts Monthly,* XII, 347-52 (May, 1928).

KNIGHT, GRANT COCHRAN. "The Triumph of Realism: Henry James," in *The Novel in English.* New York: 1931, pp. 276-87.

KNIGHTS, L. C. "Henry James and the Trapped Spectator," *Southern Review,* IV, 600-15 (Winter, 1938).

LARRABEE, HAROLD A. "The Jameses: Financier, Heretic, Philosopher," *American Scholar,* I, 401-13 (October, 1932).

LEACH, ANNA. "Henry James: An Appreciation," *Forum,* LV, 551-64 (May, 1916).

LEE, VERNON.—See PAGET, VIOLET.

LEIGHTON, LAWRENCE. "Armor against Time," *Hound & Horn,* VII, 373-84 (April-May, 1934).

LEWIS, J. H. "The Difficulties of Henry James," *Poet Lore,* XXXIX, 117-19 (Spring, 1928).

LEWIS, WYNDHAM. "Henry James: The Arch-Enemy of 'Low Company,'" in *Men Without Art.* London: 1934, pp. 138-57.

LITTELL, PHILIP. "Books and Things," *New Republic,* III, 234 (July

Bibliography

3, 1915), VI, 191 (March 18, 1916), XIII, 254 (December 29, 1917).

LITTELL, PHILIP. "Henry James as Critic," *New Republic*, I, 26-28 (November 21, 1914).

LITTELL, PHILIP. "Henry James's Quality," and " 'Middle Years,' " in *Books and Things*. New York: 1919, pp. 215-23, 224-29. "Henry James's Quality" appeared previously, *New Republic*, VI, 152-54 (March 11, 1916).

LOGAN, M. "Henry James," *Nation*, LVII, 416-17 (November 30, 1893).

LOOMIS, CHARLES BATTELL. "An Attempt to Translate Henry James," *Bookman* (New York), XXI, 464-66 (July, 1905).

LUBBOCK, PERCY. *The Craft of Fiction*. New York: 1921, see index; also London: 1921. (An outstanding critical study of fiction.)

LUBBOCK, PERCY. "Henry James," *Quarterly Review* (London), CCXXVI, 60-74 (July, 1916); *Living Age*, CCXC, 733-42 (September 16, 1916).

LYND, ROBERT. "Henry James," in *Old and New Masters*. New York: 1919, pp. 70-85.

MACCARTHY, DESMOND. "Henry James," in *Portraits*. New York: 1932, pp. 149-69.

MACCARTHY, DESMOND. "Money, Birth and Henry James," *New Statesman*, IX, 375-76 (July 21, 1917).

MACCARTHY, DESMOND. "Mr. Henry James and His Public," *Independent Review* (London), VI, 105-10 (May, 1905).

MACCARTHY, DESMOND. "The World of Henry James," *Life and Letters*, V, 352-65 (November, 1930); *Living Age*, CCCXXXIX, 491-98 (January, 1931); *Saturday Review of Literature*, VIII, 81-83 (August 29, 1931).

MACDONELL, ANNIE. "Henry James," *Bookman* (New York), IV, 20-22 (September, 1896); reprinted as "Henry James as a Critic," XLIII, 219-22 (April, 1916).

McGILL, ANNA BLANCHE. "Henry James, Artist," *Poet Lore*, XVI, 90-96 (Winter, 1905).

McGILL, V. J. "Henry James: Master Detective," *Bookman* (New York), LXXII, 251-56 (November, 1930).

McLANE, JAMES. "A Henry James Letter," *Yale Review*, N.S. XIV, 205-08 (October, 1924).

MACY, JOHN ALBERT. "Henry James," in *The Spirit of American Literature*. New York: 1913, pp. 324-39.

Bibliography

MARSH, EDWARD CLARK. "James: Auto-Critic," *Bookman* (New York), XXX, 138-43 (October, 1909).

MATTHEWS, BRANDER. "Henry James and the Theatre," in *Playwrights on Playmaking, and Other Studies of the Stage*. New York and London: 1923, pp. 187-204; *Bookman* (New York), LI, 389-95 (June, 1920). (Discusses eight plays by James.)

MICHAUD, RÉGIS. "Henry James . . . ," in *The American Novel Today: A Social and Psychological Study*. Boston: 1928, pp. 47-54. (Offers the man-without-a-country psychological interpretation of James's characteristics.)

MICHAUD, RÉGIS. "William et Henry James d'après leur correspondance," *Revue de France*, 141-59 (September, 1922).

MOORE, MARIANNE. "Henry James as a Characteristic American," *Hound & Horn*, VII, 363-72 (April-May, 1934).

MORGAN, LOUISE. "The Weakness of Henry James," *Outlook* (London), LVII, 89 (February 6, 1926).

MOSES, MONTROSE J. "Henry James as a Letter Writer," *Outlook*, CXXV, 167-68 (May 26, 1920).

MOULT, THOMAS. "Dedicated to Art," *English Review*, XXXI, 183-86 (August, 1920).

NADAL, ELIRMAN SYME. "Personal Recollections of Henry James," *Scribner's Magazine*, LXVIII, 89-97 (July, 1920).

NEWBURGH, M. L. H. "Mr. Henry James, Jr., and His Critics," *Literary World*, XIII, 10-11 (January 14, 1882).

NOBLE, JAMES ASHCROFT. "Partial Portraits," *Academy*, XXXIII, 406-07 (June 16, 1888).

ORAGE, ALFRED RICHARD. "Henry James," in *Readers and Writers (1917-1921)*. New York: 1922, pp. 9-13.

ORCUTT, WILLIAM DANA. "Celebrities Off Parade: Henry James," *Christian Science Monitor*, XXVI, 12 (August 24, 1934).

ORCUTT, WILLIAM DANA. "Friends Through Type," in *In Quest of the Perfect Book: Reminiscences and Reflections of a Bookman*. Boston: 1926, pp. 73-107.

PAGET, VIOLET. "The Handling of Words: Meredith, Henry James," *English Review*, V, 427-41 (June, 1910).

PARRINGTON, VERNON LOUIS. "Henry James and the Nostalgia of Culture," in *Main Currents in American Thought*. New York: 1930, III, 239-41. (One of the best among the short, critically disparaging articles.)

PATTEE, FRED L. "Following the Civil War," in *The Development of the American Short Story*. New York: 1923, pp. 191-208.

Bibliography

PENNELL, JOSEPH. "In London with Henry James," *Century*, CIII, 543-48 (February, 1922).

PERRY, BLISS. *Commemorative Tribute to Henry James*. Academy Notes and Monographs. New York: 1922. (Prepared for the American Academy of Arts and Letters.)

PERRY, RALPH BARTON. "Henry James in Italy," *Harvard Graduate Magazine*, XLI, 189-200 (June, 1933).

PERRY, RALPH BARTON. *The Thought and Character of Henry James*. 2 vols. Boston: 1935; see index, II, 778.

PHELPS, WILLIAM LYON. "Henry James," *Yale Review*, N.S. V, 783-97 (July, 1916).

PHELPS, WILLIAM LYON. "Henry James: America's Analytical Novelist," *Ladies' Home Journal*, XL, 23, 174-75 (November, 1923).

PHELPS, WILLIAM LYON. "Henry James, Reviewer," *Literary Review*, I, 4 (June 4, 1921).

PHELPS, WILLIAM LYON. "James," in *Howells, James, Bryant and Other Essays*. New York: 1924, pp. 123-55.

PHILLIPS, LeROY, ed. *Views and Reviews by Henry James*. Boston: 1908. (A most serviceable collection.)

POUND, EZRA. "Henry James," in *Instigations*. New York: 1920, pp. 106-67; also in *Make It New: Essays by Ezra Pound*. New Haven: 1935, pp. 251-307. (Valuable. Elaborate outline of ideas and technique used by James in developing *The Ivory Tower;* see especially *Instigations*, pp. 159-67.)

POWYS, JOHN COWPER. "Henry James," in *Suspended Judgments: Essays on Books and Sensations*. New York: 1916, pp. 367-98.

PRATT, CORNELIA ATWOOD. "Evolution of Henry James," *Critic*, N.S. XXXI, 338-42 (April, 1899).

PRESTON, HARRIET WATERS. "*The Europeans*," *Atlantic Monthly*, XLIII, 106-08 (January, 1879).

PRESTON, HARRIET WATERS. "The Latest Novels of Howells and James," *Atlantic Monthly*, XCI, 77-82 (January, 1903).

PRESTON, HARRIET WATERS. "Mr. James's *American* on the London Stage," *Atlantic Monthly*, LXVIII, 846-48 (December, 1891).

QUINN, ARTHUR HOBSON. "Henry James and the Fiction of International Relations," in *American Fiction: An Historical and Critical Survey*. New York and London: c.1936, pp. 279-304.

RANDELL, WILFRID L. "The Art of Mr. Henry James," *Fortnightly Review*, N.S. XCIX, 620-32 (April, 1916).

RANDELL, WILFRID L. "Henry James as Humanist," *Fortnightly Review*, N.S. CX, 458-69 (September, 1921).

Bibliography

RAYMOND, E. T., pseud. See THOMPSON, E. R.

READ, HERBERT. "Henry James," in *The Sense of Glory: Essays in Criticism*. New York: 1930, pp. 206-08.

ROBERTS, MORLEY. "Meetings with Some Men of Letters," *Queen's Quarterly*, XXXIX, 65-70 (February, 1932).

ROBERTS, MORRIS. *Henry James's Criticism*. Cambridge, Mass.: 1929; also London: 1929. (Indispensable study of James's critical essays.)

ROSCOE, E. S. "Henry James at the Reform Club," *Bookman* (New York), LX, 584-85 (January, 1925).

ROURKE, CONSTANCE. "The American," in *American Humor: A Study of the National Character*. New York: c.1931, pp. 235-65.

SAMPSON, GEORGE. "Letters in Criticism," *Bookman* (London), LVIII, 76-77 (May, 1920).

SCHELLING, FELIX EMMANUEL. "Some Forgotten Tales of Henry James," in *Appraisements and Asperities as to Some Contemporary Writers*. New York: 1922, pp. 169-74.

SCHUYLER, MONTGOMERY. "Henry James's Short Stories," *Lamp*, XXVI, 231-35 (April, 1903).

SCOTT, DIXON. "Henry James," *Bookman* (London), XLIII, 299-306 (March, 1913).

SCOTT, DIXON. "Henry James," in *Men of Letters*. London: 1916, pp. 78-110.

SCUDDER, HORACE E. "A Few Story-Tellers, Old and New," *Atlantic Monthly*, LXXII, 693-99 (November, 1893).

SCUDDER, HORACE E. "James, Crawford, and Howells," *Atlantic Monthly*, LVII, 850-57 (June, 1886).

SCUDDER, HORACE E. "*The Portrait of a Lady* and Dr. Breen's Practice," *Atlantic Monthly*, XLIX, 126-30 (January, 1882).

SCUDDER, HORACE E. "Review of *The Tragic Muse*," *Atlantic Monthly*, LXVI, 419-22 (September, 1890).

SHERMAN, STUART PRATT. "The Aesthetic Idealism of Henry James," in *On Contemporary Literature*. New York: 1917, pp. 226-55; also *Nation*, CIV, 393-99 (April 5, 1917). (An able, acute study.)

SHERMAN, STUART PRATT. "Henry James," in *The Columbia University Course in Literature*. New York: 1929, XVIII, 218-33.

SHERMAN, STUART PRATT. "The Special Case of Henry James," in *The Emotional Discovery of America*. New York: c.1932, pp. 35-47.

SMITH, JANET ADAM. "Henry James and R. L. Stevenson," *London Mercury*, XXXIV, 412-20 (September, 1936).

SNELL, EDWIN MARION. *The Modern Fables of Henry James*. Cambridge, Mass.: 1935.

Bibliography

SPENDER, STEPHEN. "Henry James," and "Henry James and the Contemporary Subject," in *The Destructive Element: A Study of Modern Writers and Beliefs*. London: 1935, pp. 11-110, 189-200.

SPENDER, STEPHEN. "A Modern Writer in Search of a Moral Subject," *London Mercury*, XXXI, 128-33 (December, 1934).

SPENDER, STEPHEN. "The School of Experience in the Early Novels," *Hound & Horn*, VII, 417-33 (April-May, 1934).

SQUIRE, SIR JOHN COLLINGS. "Henry James's Obscurity," in *Books in General*. London: 1919, pp. 179-84.

SWINNERTON, FRANK. "Artful Virtuosity: Henry James," in *The Georgian Scene: A Literary Panorama*. New York: c.1934, pp. 19-39.

TAYLOR, WALTER FULLER. "Fiction as Fine Art: Henry James (1843-1916)," in *A History of American Letters*. New York: c.1936, pp. 289-94.

THOMPSON, E. R. "Henry James and Max Beerbohm," in *Portraits of the New Century (The First Ten Years)*. New York: 1928, pp. 282-99.

TICKNOR, CAROLINE. "Henry James's 'Bostonians,' " in *Glimpses of Authors*. Boston: 1922, pp. 243-56.

TILLEY, ARTHUR. "The New School of Fiction," *National Review*, I, 257-68 (April, 1883).

TOOKER, L. FRANK. "The Fiction of the Magazine," *Century*, N.S. LXXXVI, 260-71 (June, 1924).

TROY, WILLIAM. "Henry James and Young Writers," *Bookman* (New York), LXXIII, 351-58 (June, 1931).

UNDERWOOD, JOHN CURTIS. "Henry James: Expatriate," in *Literature and Insurgency: Ten Studies in Racial Evolution. . . .* New York: 1914, pp. 41-86.

VAN DOREN, CARL. "Henry James," in *The American Novel*. New York: 1921, pp. 188-220.

VEDDER, HENRY C. "Henry James," in *American Writers of Today*. Boston: 1894, pp. 69-86.

WALBROOK, H. M. "Henry James and the English Theater," *Nineteenth Century*, LXXX, 141-45 (July, 1916); *Living Age*, CCXC, 505-09 (August 19, 1916).

WALBROOK, H. M. "Henry James and the Theater," *London Mercury*, XX, 612-16 (October, 1929).

WALBROOK, H. M. "The Novels of Henry James," *Fortnightly Review*, N.S. CXXVII, 680-91 (May, 1930).

Bibliography

WALKLEY, ARTHUR BINGHAM. "Henry James and His Letters," *Fortnightly Review,* N.S. CVII, 864-73 (June, 1920).

WALKLEY, ARTHUR BINGHAM. "Henry James and the Theater," and "Talk at the Martello Tower," in *Pastiche and Prejudice.* London: 1921, pp. 155-59, 206-10; also New York: 1921.

WARREN, AUSTIN. *The Elder Henry James.* New York: 1934. (Includes valuable sketch of the son's early life.)

WARREN, AUSTIN. "James and His Secret," *Saturday Review of Literature,* VIII, 759 (May 28, 1932).

WATERLOW, S. P. "Memories of Henry James," *New Statesman,* XXVI, 514-15 (February 6, 1932).

WATERLOW, S. P. "The Work of Mr. Henry James," *Independent Review,* IV, 236-43 (November, 1904).

WAUGH, ARTHUR. "The Art of Henry James," in *Tradition and Change: Studies in Contemporary Literature.* New York: 1919, pp. 246-52; also London: 1919.

WEST, REBECCA. *Henry James.* New York: 1916. (Short, well-phrased study with clever thrusts.)

WEST, REBECCA. "Reading Henry James in War Time," *New Republic,* II, 98-100 (February 27, 1915).

WESTCOTT, GLENWAY. "A Sentimental Contribution," *Hound & Horn,* VII, 523-34 (April-May, 1934).

WHARTON, EDITH. "A Backward Glance," *Ladies' Home Journal,* LI, 19, 73, 78, 80 (February, 1934). Also in *A Backward Glance.* New York: 1934, pp. 169-96. (Valuable comments and reminiscences by a novelist who knew James well.)

WHARTON, EDITH. "Henry James in His Letters," *Quarterly Review* (London), CCXXXIV, 188-202 (July, 1920).

WHEELWRIGHT, JOHN. "Henry James and Stanford White," *Hound & Horn,* VII, 480-93 (April-May, 1934).

WHITE, J. WILLIAM. "Professor White's Interpretation of Henry James's Action," *Spectator,* CXV, 204-05 (August 14, 1915).

WHITE, RICHARD GRANT. "Recent Fiction," *North American Review,* CXXVIII, 101-06 (January, 1879).

WHITFORD, ROBERT CALVIN. "The Letters of Henry James," *South Atlantic Quarterly,* XIX, 371-72 (October, 1920).

WILLIAMS, ORLO. "The Ambassadors," *Criterion,* VIII, 47-64 (September, 1928).

WILSON, EDMUND. "The Ambiguity of Henry James," *Hound & Horn,* VII, 385-406 (April-May, 1934). Elaborated in *The Triple Thinkers: Ten Essays on Literature.* New York: c.1938, pp. 122-64.

Bibliography

(Develops thesis that "The Turn of the Screw" is a figment of the imagination of the narrator by reason of sex repression.)

WILSON, EDMUND. "The Exploration of James," *New Republic*, L, 112-13 (March 16, 1927).

WINTERS, YVOR. "Henry James and the Relation of Morals to Manners," *American Review*, IX, 482-503 (October, 1937).

WOLFF, ROBERT LEE. "The Genesis of *The Turn of the Screw*," *American Literature*, XIII, 1-8 (March, 1941).

WYATT, EDITH FRANKLIN. "Henry James: An Impression," in *Great Companions*. New York: 1917, pp. 83-99; *North American Review*, CCIII, 592-99 (April, 1916).

YOUNG, FILSON. "Bunch of Violets," *English Review*, XXII, 317-20 (April, 1916).

ZABEL, M. D. "The Poetics of Henry James," *Poetry: A Magazine of Verse*, XLV, 270-76 (February, 1935).

Index of James Characters and Titles

Index

Croy, Kate (*The Wings of the Dove*), 11, 13, 24, 35, 102, 103, 144, 153, 179, 182, 193, 257

Daisy Miller, 5, 7, 8, 9, 32, 51, 70, 87, 101, 110, 117, 120, 131, 143, 152, 160, 175-176, 187, 220, 260
Dallow, Julia (*The Tragic Muse*), 101, 177, 179
Day, Pandora (*Pandora*), 143
Deane, Drayton (*The Figure in the Carpet*), 203
Death of the Lion, The, 70, 82, 126, 205-207
Densher, Merton (*The Wings of the Dove*), 11, 88, 126, 144, 153, 182, 193
Doane, George (*The Great Good Place*), 208
Dodd, Herbert (*The Bench of Desolation*), 194
Dormer, Nick (*The Tragic Muse*), 96, 101, 177, 179, 223
Dosson, Francie (*The Reverberator*), 167
Doubleday, Paul (*The Reprobate*), 262
Duchess, the (*The American*), 146-147
Duchess, the (*The Awkward Age*), 15

Erme, Gwendolyn (*The Figure in the Carpet*), 203
Essays: on Balzac, 2; on Flaubert, 2-3, 174; on Hawthorne, 114-115; on the new novel, 74; on George Sand, 2, 20, 21; on the Théâtre Français, 2; on Turgenev, 2, 114
Europeans, The, 3-4, 84, 87, 110, 117, 118, 141, 143, 144, 145, 168, 183

Fancourt, Marian (*The Lesson of the Master*), 208-210
Fane, Greville (*Greville Fane*), 259
Farange, Maisie (*What Maisie Knew*), 183
Figure in the Carpet, The, 75, 82, 92, 93, 94, 99, 123, 124, 126, 203, 204
Finer Grain, The, 192
Flaubert, Gustave, essay on, 2-3, 174
Flickerbridge, 168
Forbes, Dora (*The Death of the Lion*), 207
Fordham Castle, 187
Four Meetings, 144
French Poets and Novelists, 114, 216

Garland, Mary (*Roderick Hudson*), 104, 117, 142, 143

Gaw, Abner (*The Ivory Tower*), 188, 189
George Sand: The New Life, 2, 20, 21
Gereth, Mrs. (*The Spoils of Poynton*), 101, 102-103
Gereth, Owen (*The Spoils of Poynton*), 103
Gloriani (*The Ambassadors*), 223, 232, 270
Golden Bowl, The, 80, 84, 88, 89, 90, 103-104, 125, 144, 154, 182, 185, 192, 194, 216, 233, 236-245, 257, 262, 268, 275, 277
Goodwood, Caspar (*The Portrait of a Lady*), 265, 268
Gostrey, Maria (*The Ambassadors*), 219, 220, 232, 233
Governess, the (*The Turn of the Screw*), 160-165, 269
Great Good Place, The, 208
Greville Fane, 259
Grose, Mrs. (*The Turn of the Screw*), 161-163
Guy Domville, 106, 180

Harland, Henry (*The Story-teller at Large: Mr. Henry Harland*), 132-133
Hatch, C. P. (*The American*), 109
Hawthorne, 131, 133-134, 135
Hawthorne, Nathaniel, essay on, 114-115
Headway, Mrs. (*Roderick Hudson*), 141
Hudson, Roderick (*Roderick Hudson*), 32, 104, 117, 141-142, 223

In the Cage, 79, 180, 258
International Episode, An, 5, 122, 137, 142, 143, 144, 187
Ivory Tower, The, 118, 126, 183, 187, 188, 189, 192

Jessel, Miss (*The Turn of the Screw*), 164
Jolly Corner, The, 186, 188

Lady Barberina, 144
Lambeth, Lord (*An International Episode*), 142
La Rochefidèle, Madame de (*The American*), 150
Leavenworth, Mr. (*Roderick Hudson*), 141-142
Lesson of the Master, The, 33, 82, 199, 208-210
Letters of Henry James, The, 54, 55, 58, 66, 67, 134, 211

Index

Index